presenting ACTIVEX™

Warren Ernst

201 West 103rd Street
Indianapolis, IN 46290

Copyright © 1996 by Sams.net Publishing

FIRST EDITION

All rights reserved. No part of this book shall be reproduced, stored in a retrieval system, or transmitted by any means, electronic, mechanical, photocopying, recording, or otherwise, without written permission from the publisher. No patent liability is assumed with respect to the use of the information contained herein. Although every precaution has been taken in the preparation of this book, the publisher and author assume no responsibility for errors or omissions. Neither is any liability assumed for damages resulting from the use of the information contained herein. For information, address Sams.net Publishing, 201 W. 103rd St., Indianapolis, IN 46290.

International Standard Book Number: 1-57521-156-4

Library of Congress Catalog Card Number: 96-68942

99 98 97 96   4 3 2

Interpretation of the printing code: the rightmost double-digit number is the year of the book's printing; the rightmost single-digit, the number of the book's printing. For example, a printing code of 96-1 shows that the first printing of the book occurred in 1996.

Composed in AGaramond and MCPdigital by Macmillan Computer Publishing

Printed in the United States of America

Trademarks

All terms mentioned in this book that are known to be trademarks or service marks have been appropriately capitalized. Sams.net Publishing cannot attest to the accuracy of this information. Use of a term in this book should not be regarded as affecting the validity of any trademark or service mark. ActiveX is a trademark of Microsoft Corporation, Inc.

President, Sams Publishing   *Richard K. Swadley*

Publishing Manager   *Mark Taber*

Managing Editor   *Cindy Morrow*

Marketing Manager   *John Pierce*

Assistant Marketing Manager   *Kristina Perry*

Acquisitions Editor
Beverly M. Eppink

Software Development Specialist
Bob Correll

Production Editor
Lisa M. Lord

Indexer
Tom Dinse

Technical Reviewer
Dena Fleet

Editorial Coordinator
Bill Whitmer

Technical Edit Coordinator
Lynette Quinn

Resource Coordinator
Deborah Frisby

Formatter
Frank Sinclair

Editorial Assistants
Andi Richter
Carol Ackerman
Rhonda Tinch-Mize

Cover Designer
Tim Amrhein

Book Designer
Gary Adair

Copy Writer
Peter Fuller

Production Team Supervisor
Brad Chinn

Production
Mary Ann Abramson
Carol Bowers
Sonja Hart
Mike Henry
Paula Lowell

Overview

Contents

Note: This book is based on a stable beta version of Internet Explorer 3.0 and Microsoft Visual Basic, Scripting Edition (also called VBScript). We've expended a lot of effort to ensure that it's as accurate as possible. However, if any discrepancies between the material covered here and the official product release of Internet Explorer 3.0 and VBScript come to light, they will be fully documented and available online. You can get the latest updates, if any, from Macmillan Publishing's Sams.net site (`http://www.mcp.com/samsnet`).

Disclaimer from the Publisher

The information in this book is subject to the following disclaimers:

- The information in this book is based on a beta version that's subject to change.
- Microsoft will not provide support for the beta product.
- Visit Microsoft's Web site at `http://www.microsoft.com/intdev` for additional information and updates.

Dedication

To my mom—thanks for all your love and encouragement. We'll make it through life with a laugh and a smile.

—Warren Ernst

Acknowledgments

Even though there's just one name on the spine of this book, there were a lot of people who had a hand in creating it. Therefore, I'd like to take this space to give a hearty thanks to some of those people who helped in intangible ways.

First and foremost, the authors would like to thank Lisa Lord and Fran Hatton for their help in coordinating the many aspects of this book. Their expertise in putting together a book and keeping me on my deadlines made this book possible.

I would also like to thank Lisa Rivera for her continuing love and support while I spent the time writing this book instead of heading to the beach for a picnic.

—Warren Ernst

Lead Author

Warren Ernst (wernst@cris.com, http://www.deltanet.com/users/ wernst/) is a technical writer, computer trainer, Webmaster, graphic artist, and "general computing guru." Warren became involved with the computer industry in 1988, performing technical support and testing for Beagle Bros. Software, Smith Micro Software, Toshiba of America, Advanced Technology Center, and NASA's Jet Propulsion Labs, going on to write and design user manuals, online hypertext help systems, and Web pages for these companies and their products. He was a contributor to Sams.net's *Netscape 2 Unleashed* and is the author of Que's best-selling *Using Netscape* and *Using Netscape in Windows 95*. He is also the owner of a small computer-consulting firm, which specializes in training, hardware and software consultation, writing, and "keeping computers from ruining your life." He spends what remains of his spare time on collecting llama trinkets and full-sized arcade games and wasting time on his computers at home.

Contributing Authors

John J. Kottler has been programming for 14 years and has spent the past 6 years developing applications for the Windows platform; he has also been programming multimedia applications for over 2 years and has spent this past year developing for the Web. His knowledge includes C/C++, Visual Basic, Lotus Notes, PowerBuilder, messaging-enabled applications, multimedia and digital video production, and Internet Web page development. In the past, he has published numerous articles in a computer magazine, writing original programs and instructing developers on programming techniques. John has also been recently published in Sams.net's *Web Page Wizardry, Web Publishing Unleashed,* and *Netscape 2 Unleashed* and Sams Publishing's *Programming Windows 95 Unleashed.* He was also a co-developer of the shareware application Virtual Monitors. A graduate of Rutgers University with a degree in computer science, he enjoys inline skating, cycling, or playing digital music in his spare time. John may currently be reached at the following e-mail addresses: 73157.335@compuserve.com, jkottler@aol.com, or jay_kottler@msn.com.

Michael Morrison is the author of *Teach Yourself Internet Game Programming with Java in 21 Days*, a contributing author of *Tricks of the Java Programming Gurus* and *Java Unleashed*, and the co-author of *Windows 95 Game Developer's Guide Using the Game SDK*. He currently lives in Scottsdale, Arizona with his much better half, Mahsheed. When not killing time on the Web, Michael enjoys adding to his vast collection of cuts and bruises by skateboarding and mountain biking. You can contact Michael on CompuServe at 74037,3444 (74037.3444@compuserve.com).

Kevin Walsh is a development manager for workgroup document management software at Intergraph Corporation in Huntsville, Alabama. Kevin has been knocking around on computers since he started as a keypunch operator and control panel wirer for EAM equipment in 1976, while in the service of the U.S. Navy. He has worked in a variety of capacities, including journeyman programmer, custom development consultant, software product marketing, and project lead architect.

Daniel Wygant (dfwygant@ingr.com) is a Senior Software Analyst with Intergraph Corporation in Huntsville, Alabama, where he has been employed for nearly 12 years. He received his B.S. in Pure Mathematics from Florida State University. His development experience includes UNIX, Windows NT, and Windows 95. Daniel is currently involved with the OLE Data Server for CAD formats. His interests include OLE and Internet programming, such as ActiveX DocObjects, ActiveX controls, ISAPI extensions, and ISAPI filters. His publications include articles in *Windows NT* magazine.

Keith Brophy and **Timothy Koets** wrote the VBScript appendix. Keith is currently Software Release Coordinator for X-Rite, Incorporated, a leading worldwide provider of color and appearance quality control software and instrumentation in Grandville, Michigan. Timothy is a software engineer at X-Rite.

Tell Us What You Think!

As a reader, you are the most important critic and commentator of our books. We value your opinion and want to know what we're doing right, what we could do better, what areas you'd like to see us publish in, and any other words of wisdom you're willing to pass our way. You can help us make strong books that meet your needs and give you the computer guidance you require.

Do you have access to CompuServe or the World Wide Web? Then check out our CompuServe forum by typing **GO SAMS** at any prompt. If you prefer the World Wide Web, check out our site at http://www.mcp.com.

Note: If you have a technical question about this book, call the technical support line at (800) 571-5840, ext. 3668.

As the team leader of the group that created this book, I welcome your comments. You can fax, e-mail, or write me directly to let me know what you did or didn't like about this book—as well as what we can do to make our books stronger. Here's the information:

FAX: 317/581-4669

E-mail: newtech_mgr@sams.mcp.com

Mail: Mark Taber
Comments Department
Sams Publishing
201 W. 103rd Street
Indianapolis, IN 46290

Introduction

by Warren Ernst

The Internet, as it exists today, is a great tool for searching for existing information, regardless of where in the world it's actually located. Business applications currently excel at giving users tools for creating new information from scratch. Very rarely will you find "hybrid" programs that are capable of both generating new information and communicating via the Internet, mostly because the tools that make creating such programs weren't widely available or powerful enough to make a "no-holds barred" program truly useful. Microsoft has plans to change this division of programs, and it's called ActiveX.

ActiveX is the name of a group of software technologies and methods that promise to make it easy to create "traditional business applications" with powerful Internet connectivity and "traditional Internet communications programs" with true computational power. Building on the OLE (Object Linking and Embedding) technology that has been available for some time, ActiveX essentially expands the realm of "object sharing" from merely the desktop to the whole Internet, making this new class of program possible. Since ActiveX technology is modular in design, programs can be written in such a way that they can work as standalone applications, embedded "smart" objects within Visual Basic programs or Web pages, or as traditional OLE objects within business documents, all with the potential to communicate with the Internet, should you choose.

As ActiveX gains wider acceptance, the Internet will find itself changing from merely a wellspring of static information "pages" to a source of working programs that manipulate, display, change, and create new information or data. Communication with others through the Internet will occur within our word processors, spreadsheets, drawing progams, and so forth, without having to switch to dedicated browsers or Internet programs.

Or at least, that's the theory.

Being a very new technology, ActiveX has yet to take the Internet world by storm and change it overnight. But from the ActiveX technologies that have been exploited, it looks like Microsoft's vision of tomorrow's Internet might not be too far off. That's what this book, *Presenting ActiveX*, hopes to help you accomplish: to explore the possibilities ActiveX makes available to software developers.

As an introduction to ActiveX, this book will benefit the following people:

- Managers and planners interested in seeing what ActiveX technology will do for their products or organization.
- Web page developers looking to increase the appeal and functionality of their Web pages.
- Programmers who want to get an idea of how ActiveX works.
- Hobbyists who want to stay abreast of the latest Internet technologies.

How to Use This Book

This book is an introduction to the basics of ActiveX: how it's similar to and different from Java technologies, how to "run" ActiveX programs and modules, how ActiveX works with and without the Internet, and what the basics are of constructing ActiveX technologies. This book is organized so that users with a wide range of technical backgrounds leave with a better understanding of what ActiveX really is.

The Scope of This Book

This book discusses the significance of ActiveX and the impact it will have on the Internet and programming in general. It gives you an overview of the Microsoft Internet Explorer 3.0 Web browser, including where to get it from the Internet and how to install it to begin using ActiveX technologies. It then surveys the main features of the different aspects of ActiveX in "plain English," with plenty of examples, screen shots, diagrams, and a minimum of actual code and technical jargon. Next, the book reviews the procedures and methods for creating your own ActiveX modules with Visual Basic and Visual C++. Finally, it covers some of the existing future issues of using ActiveX.

Presenting ActiveX is not meant to be a comprehensive programming guide or complete reference of ActiveX—in fact, Microsoft makes that sort of material publicly available in the ActiveX Software Development Kit CD-ROM. Instead, this book provides a quick start for project planners, software developers, and Webmasters, complete with introductory material plus basic programming examples and code samples. Pointers to current material on the Internet about these subjects are also supplied where appropriate.

Finally, this book is based on the ActiveX Software Development Kit as it was available during the early summer of 1996, so if some time has passed since then, some aspects might be out of date or somewhat changed to reflect actual usage. The Microsoft home page at `http://www.microsoft.com/` should be consulted occasionally to review new developments with ActiveX and to download new portions of the ActiveX SDK.

How This Book Is Organized

This book is divided into five parts (the fifth includes four appendixes), each of which contains three to five chapters. Each part is intended to approach ActiveX from different perspectives, so although some material might overlap from part to part, each will have a different "slant."

Part I, "Fundamentals of the Internet and ActiveX," is an overview of the Internet and the role ActiveX can play within it. These chapters explore the current deficiencies of the Internet in transmitting information that isn't static and unchanging, how the Internet can support new technology, and how to use Internet Explorer 3.0 to start using ActiveX today.

Part II, "Components of ActiveX," defines and explains the available portions of the family of ActiveX technologies. Each chapter takes a single ActiveX technology, explains how it's similar to or different from existing technology, reviews how it's used and created, and presents examples you can experience.

Part III, "Developing ActiveX Controls," takes you a step further than Part II by actively taking you through the process of creating different ActiveX modules, including scripting, precompiled modules, and Web server enhancements.

Part IV, "Issues and the Future of ActiveX," reviews some of the potential pitfalls and working solutions to using ActiveX, compares these issues to those associated with Java-based technologies, and explores how ActiveX will be incorporated into the next version of Windows NT.

The appendixes review ActiveX resources available on the Internet, present a glossary of terms, offer a quick reference to VBScript syntax, and detail what is on the book's CD-ROM.

Fundamentals of the Internet and ActiveX

CHAPTER 1

Computing and the Internet Today

by Warren Ernst

The Internet is on the verge of a minor revolution, of sorts, even though you as an Internet user might not be aware of it. It will transform not how the Internet is designed or constructed, but how you *use* it.

There's a good chance you've already been exposed to this potential future in the form of Java applets and JavaScript in the Web pages you encounter with your browser. These Web pages temporarily give your Web browser something it's never had before: smarts—at least in a limited, temporary way. And by "smarts," I mean that your browser can do more than just display static, unmoving, unchanging Web pages; it can display information in a new, "intelligent" way.

Microsoft hopes to drive this Internet revolution, a revolution that will not only give Web browsers smarts, but also give "conventional business applications"—such as word processors, spreadsheets, and database programs—Web-browser–like connectivity. Microsoft plans to accomplish this with wide use of a technology collectively called ActiveX, a convention of coding and API (Application Programming Interface, or the method that programs use to communicate with each other), and an evolution of existing Microsoft technologies that should simplify modifying existing programs and generate results that truly are revolutionary.

To understand the potential benefits of joining current "Internet" and "conventional business" applications, you need to understand the Internet (and the programs used to interact with it) and the business programs currently in use and the similarities and differences between them.

Connectivity Versus Computing

On the surface, a spreadsheet program and a Web browser are operated similarly. In Windows 95, for example, both Excel and Netscape are started from their icons in the Start menu; both use pull-down menus, dialog buttons, and the mouse for interaction, and each is minimized, resized, and closed in the same way. They might even have similar purposes to many users: Excel can be used to merely view spreadsheet files, and Netscape can be used to view Web page files.

Even though they might look and feel similar, however, these applications are clearly different; each can do something remarkable that the other can't. Excel can compute new data from known information (at least in the hands of someone who knows how), for example, and Netscape can retrieve remote information from the Internet.

Still, you don't think the distinction is big enough to get worked up about? You're not convinced that there really is that much of a difference between connectivity and computing, and that there's no revolution in combining the distinct elements of the two with ActiveX? You wouldn't be alone, but perhaps reviewing the differences as they exist between connectivity programs and computing programs will put the power of mixing the two into perspective.

Connectivity: Retrieving Internet-Based Information

The modern Web browser, such as Netscape or the Internet Explorer, represents the pinnacle, to date, of connectivity software. It manages to manipulate half a dozen Internet protocols and twice as many file formats, all through a connection that can range in speeds from 1 kilobyte per second all the way to 10 megabits per second, and seems to do all this with deceptive ease. Even a novice computer or Internet user can use one of these programs to retrieve Internet-based data with almost no previous instruction—it's almost entirely a point-and-click affair.

Yet this simple interface belies an exceptionally complex latticework of programming that is the ultimate *communications* program—that's what a Web browser is really all about. All a Web browser does is communicate to various Internet servers, first requesting servers to communicate back to establish a basic link, then asking the server to transmit information that, in and of itself, requires little computing power to display to the Web browser's user. Of course, this is a brief summary of the process of displaying a Web page, but by breaking it down, you'll see that a Web browser is little more than a communications-based, graphically oriented, Internet walkie-talkie.

Here are all the steps a Web browser takes to display a simple Web page once you give it a URL. Don't worry—this will be in plain English. Trust me, it's interesting:

1. The browser looks at the URL and breaks it down into its component parts. It determines that if you gave it a URL of http://
   www.cris.com/~wernst/index.html, you want to use the HyperText Transfer Protocol (*http*) to try to get a Web page named *index.html* from an Internet host (or server) named *www.cris.com* in a subdirectory called *~wernst*. You see, there's very little computing involved in breaking down the URL—the browser merely performs the equivalent of diagramming a sentence, as you used to do in grammar school.

2. The browser looks at your network configuration settings to find the Internet address of the nearest predefined Domain Name Server

(DNS), a computer that has a big database or table of all the Internet servers out there. It communicates to the DNS the name of the server you want (in this case, www.cris.com), and the DNS tells the browser what the numeric Internet address (called an IP address) is (which in this case is 199.3.12.172) through the TCP protocol. At this point, only two lookup tables have been accessed, and there's been some communication between the DNS and the browser—but not much real computing.

3. Next, the browser takes the addressing information from the DNS and communicates to www.cris.com through its IP address of 199.3.12.172 with HTTP because it was specified in the URL. This initial communiqué basically breaks down into "Hello www.cris.com. I am a Web browser named (Netscape, Internet Explorer, or something similar) and would like some Web pages (or other information) from your directories. Is this OK? Are you alive?" Usually, the server replies with the equivalent of "Sure. What do you want?" At this point, you've now had two more lines of communication from start to finish and very little computation.

4. The browser, now knowing the server is serving, requests the file: "I would like the file index.html from your subdirectory ~wernst, please." The server looks through its directories for the file, finds it, checks to make sure it's a valid file type with its own set of lookup tables, sends the message "I found it. Here it comes," and sends the file. If it can't find the requested file, it sends the message "Huh? I don't have the file you've asked for," (or some other error message, depending on the type of problem) and the communication stops. At this point, you just have more communication and table lookups—but not much computation.

5. Assuming the file exists, the browser receives the Web page in the form of an HTML file and starts to decode it. HTML files are human-readable text files, essentially, requiring almost no real computation to decode and display. When the browser finds an embedded image, for example, it sends another communiqué to the server: "Just a minute. I also need the file image1.gif for this page. Can you send it now?" The server, upon receiving this new message, checks its directories and file

type tables to make sure the requested file can be sent, says "OK," and sends the inline image file. This process repeats for every inline image in the HTML file and ends the communiqué once the browser says it has all the inline images. As the files are sent (with lots more communication), the browser builds the page onscreen with the codes in the HTML file as a guide and the inline images as they're received, using a fraction of your CPU's computing power to generate onscreen fonts, colors, and images.

Figure 1.1 graphically represents all these steps.

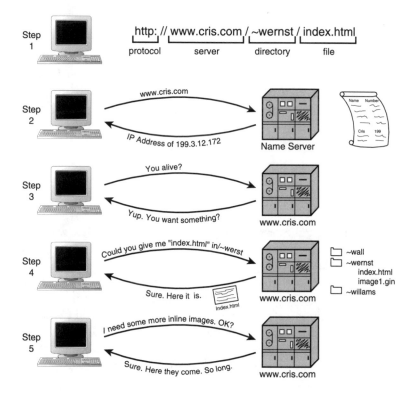

Figure 1.1.
Steps involved in getting a regular Web page.

There are some important points to draw from this scenario. First, transmitting a Web page requires a lot of communication, and with more than just the

Web server specified in the URL—the specified Web server's address had to be requested from the Domain Name Server, with a communication protocol distinctly different from the HyperText Transfer Protocol used to talk with the Web server.

Second, the process of retrieving a Web page is broken down into several smaller messages between the browser and the Web server, each with a different purpose; it isn't just one big burst transmission between the browser and server that gets the HTML file sent, even though it might look like it while you're Web surfing.

Third, there's very little computing power used to get all this information moved around and displayed. The DNS uses a lookup table to find the IP address of the requested Web server, the Web server uses a lookup table to check file types and directory locations, and the browser itself uses a lookup table to determine what fonts and colors to use for displaying the Web page. The browser has no leeway or decision-making capability when it comes to figuring out what parts of the page to display—it simply goes through the HTML file line-by-line and follows the instructions within the file, without deviation. The browser has no need for, and hence doesn't have, much computing power or "smarts" (as I like to call it).

Note: I've been using the term "lookup table" for quite some time without explaining how little computing power is required to use it or even describing it conceptually. Suffice it to say, then, that a lookup table can be thought of as consulting a two-column table, finding an entry in the first column and seeing what it corresponds to in the second column, then doing something with the second column's entry. This might remind you of using a Captain Video decoder ring when you were a kid to transform a bunch of numbers into letters to write a message in code. Lookup tables work exactly the same way, but on a larger scale; to a computer, this is a simple task to execute.

Finally, and perhaps most important, *no new information is created in this process.* All the communication is being used to transmit existing information from one location (the Web server) to another location (the Web browser) just to be viewed. That's not to say that the information isn't new to the user of the Web browser, but the information in the Web pages existed before it was retrieved by the browser, and it will remain untouched once the browser is through with it. As with anything, there are exceptions to this, but these points hold true for the vast majority of static, unchanging Web pages.

What About Forms and CGI Scripts?

The previous section's discussion described the process of viewing a "regular" Web page within a Web browser, one that didn't include forms to fill out or dynamically changing information. Would a Web page form increase the computation going on within a Web page, you ask? For the Web server, yes, it would; for the Web browser, absolutely not.

When the information entered into a Web page form is sent to the server by clicking the Submit Form button on most Web pages, all the browser does is send a message like "I have some information that someone typed into the form fields in that Web page you just sent me. If you can take them, here they are." After receiving an "OK" message from the server, it sends out the form information exactly as it was typed and waits for a response.

The server then takes this information, breaks it down, and probably runs an actual program that computes something, looks something up in another table, or executes a script (or performs any one of many other methods of computing new information). Whatever it actually does, the server computes the results and generates an HTML file on the fly with the newly computed information. Next, it responds with: "I have an HTML file for you to display. If you can take it, here it comes." The browser displays the new HTML file, whose contents are probably the results of the server's computation.

Therefore, as with a conventional Web page, the browser merely communicated with the server and displayed Web pages; it didn't actually do much of its own computing. The server does all the computing (and perhaps generates new information in the process) itself, independently of the browser's capabilities.

Computing: Generating New Information Locally

Although the title of this section sounds rather lofty, the fact is you generate new information with your computer practically every day without thinking about it that way. You might use Microsoft Excel to calculate data and draw graphs, Microsoft Word to type new data sheets, term papers, or entire books, or Microsoft Access to enter, keep track of, and search through volumes of data—in short, you create data.

Even if you use these programs only to *view* data created by others, you have the potential to create information either from scratch or from other data on your hard drive, which is something no Web browser has the potential to do (browsers with HTML editors built in, such as Netscape Gold, notwithstanding). Furthermore, these programs work with files available through your immediate file system—in most cases, your set of hard and floppy disk drives—though a local area network (LAN) such as Novell might be included as well. They aren't set up to work beyond the boundaries of your immediate surroundings.

In fact, for a software- or service-oriented business, the information output of desktop applications might well be the only "product" resulting from work and effort, as opposed to widgets from an assembly line or software from a compiler. To these people, the fact that these programs generate new information where there was none before is obvious.

"Connectivity" and "Computing" Are Separate Animals

Whether by accident or design, most people are aware of the fundamental differences between connectivity software and computing software, so they use them differently. No big surprise, this observation; however, it illustrates how inefficiently you're working when you use separate classes of programs for a larger task requiring both connectivity and computation.

Suppose you want to write a proposal with Microsoft Word, send it to an FTP site so someone can collaborate with you, retrieve it again to finish the file, then send it by e-mail to a third party. Naturally, you'd start the task by opening Word, using it to create your document, then saving it to your hard disk when it's finished.

Next, you'd launch your separate FTP program (dialing your modem to make an Internet connection, if necessary), log into the FTP site, pick the Word DOC file from its directory on the hard drive, ensure that the FTP binary mode was enabled, and upload the file. Once your collaborator was finished, you'd start your FTP program, log into the site, change directories, set the binary mode, retrieve the file, and save it to a local directory. Then you'd quit the FTP program, launch Word, open the file, make any further changes, and save the document.

Finally, you'd start your separate e-mail program, create a message and address it, go through the e-mail program's attachment process, then send off the file to its final destination. When the process is finished, you will have used three completely different programs, each consuming time and memory and creating the potential to introduce errors. Why is software used this way?

Why Computing and Connectivity Haven't Mixed

Computing and connectivity software don't really mix right now because "that's the way it's always been," but this remark creates a sort of "the chicken or the egg" issue. Until the past year or two, business applications with true computational power (such as Excel or Word) had no need for connectivity because there wasn't really any place to connect to or much of a need to do so. Computing and creating information were, therefore, rather local affairs; if a file needed collaboration, chances are you worked in the same office as the other person, so you could exchange a floppy, or, more recently, use the LAN.

With the explosion of the Internet, people realized that even though they were separated by vast distances, two (or more) people could work together to some degree, as long as each had Internet access; people could use connectivity programs to communicate with each other. Because of the way these two sets of programs are written, however, you are forced to use specific connectivity programs to connect and computing programs to get work done.

Why Computation and Connectivity Will Be Mixed Soon

Times and computer users have been changing, however. It seems that a critical mass of users needing to both create and connect has been reached, and hybrid programs with computing and connectivity powers are being envisioned. In fact, a tool currently exists—Sun's Java programming language and

JavaScript—to begin giving connectivity programs like Web browsers a *little bit* of smarts. Unfortunately, even with Java applets, your browser can have only so much intelligence and computational power. That's why Java programs are *applets* instead of *applications;* there's only so much a Java applet can do.

To make it reasonably easy to give connectivity programs real computational ability, and computational programs real connectivity, Microsoft has introduced and refined technology it calls *ActiveX.* With ActiveX tools and methods (explained in Part II, "Components of ActiveX"), creating programs with both computational and connectivity capabilities, from existing programs or from scratch, is not only possible but has a remarkably short development timetable.

Chapter 2, "Microsoft's Vision of the Internet's Future," will explore these programs' possibilities and potential.

Microsoft's Vision of the Internet's Future

by Warren Ernst

For the most part, when people want to make use of information on the Internet, they use Internet-connectivity software specifically designed to be an excellent communicator, such as a Web browser. When people want to create new information, they use business applications with computational abilities, such as a spreadsheet or word processor. Because most connectivity programs don't have much computational ability (which I like to call "smarts"), when people use them to surf the Internet, they generally don't create new information—they simply view existing information stored remotely. Presently, most business applications don't have any serious Internet connectivity built in, so when new information is created using these applications, real work occurs only locally, without remote Internet access or work-sharing between remote users.

The Internet, however, has grown enough in sophistication, reliability, and speed to support a new class of programs, one that blends the smarts of business applications and the communications abilities of Internet programs. All that's needed to take advantage of the Internet for real computing is the software tools to make it happen, and Microsoft is creating the tool to do it: ActiveX.

This chapter suggests what sort of applications can be created by using ActiveX, hypothesizes how the Internet can be used in the near future, and looks at how the Internet is currently being used with the first ActiveX-enabled applications.

Combining Connectivity with Computing

ActiveX combines two traditionally separate types of applications into one, with an emphasis on one type of application or another. For example, ActiveX can give an Internet application, such as a Web browser, true computing power and give a business application, such as a spreadsheet, true Internet connectivity—ready to use existing Internet protocols to communicate with the outside world with the single click of a mouse button.

In other words, ActiveX makes an entire range of Internet-enabled programs possible. On one side of the scale, a Web browser might perform simple computations itself, easing the burden on a traditional Web server; on the other side, a word processor might use its built-in Internet connectivity to allow remote filesaving through FTP sites. Somewhere in the middle, a spreadsheet might have a "chat window" in it to allow two people connected through the Internet to work on the same spreadsheet file at the same time, without a separate Internet communications program and even without dedicated Web or FTP servers. (See Figure 2.1.)

This example of the spreadsheet application is possibly the most exciting, since it breaks completely new ground by combining elements of traditional computing and connectivity programs, allowing people separated by vast distances to get real work done through the Internet. With this sort of spreadsheet program, not only can the two collaborators "chat" by typing messages to each other in real-time, but they can work on the same worksheet file at the same time—as one person enters values, the other sees them instantly and can further modify them.

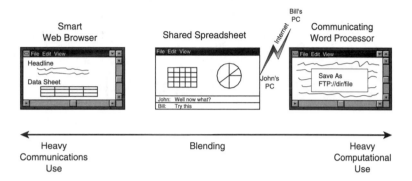

Figure 2.1.
What ActiveX can accomplish—different classes of programs.

With ActiveX, business applications can indeed communicate effectively over the Internet, and Internet communications programs can compute information for themselves, reducing Internet bandwidth and increasing speed.

How Is ActiveX Different from Java?

Without getting into ActiveX specifics yet, it's important to point out that some of what's been described seems similar to what can be done by using Sun Microsystems's Java programming language—but not all of it, and certainly not in the same way.

Java, an object-oriented language that looks and feels like C++, excels at bringing some computational power to Java-enabled Internet communications programs, mostly Web browsers for now. Although it has communications abilities, these abilities are used with the existing communications abilities of Web browsers and aren't expected to be communicators on their own. Java can be written to perform all communications itself—and even to create entire applications from scratch—but it seems that only Sun itself can write an entire application with Java from scratch (such as the HotJava Web browser).

ActiveX, on the other hand, is designed to be easy to use for not only adding smarts to existing communications programs such as Web browsers, but also for adding Internet communications ability to existing business applications and for creating entirely new hybrid applications from scratch, using familiar methods and a range of programming languages.

How Does ActiveX Fit into the Big Internet Picture?

For the most part, ActiveX works with a minimum amount of standards re-writing for the Internet, which is important if ActiveX is to gain popularity. In fact, it embraces a great deal of existing technology, so even programmers and clever Web page authors who have already dived headfirst into learning Java and JavaScript find that what they know is enhanced by using ActiveX. Here's how ActiveX Technology can be combined with existing technology to create active, innovative Web pages:

- ActiveX makes use of existing standards, such as URLs and Internet communications protocols already familiar to Internet users. New, dedicated servers aren't required for ActiveX-enabled Web pages or applications.

- You can use ActiveX modules, called *controls*, alongside existing Java applets in your Web pages, so using old and new computing features in a Web page is possible.

- With ActiveScripting, you can still use JavaScript to "glue together" new ActiveX controls on a Web page, allowing complete flexibility and providing a bridge to ease the transition from old to new technology.

- When new features and protocols are needed for new types of commu-nication, ActiveX can encapsulate its new commands and protocols within existing ones, eliminating the need for new types of Internet servers as new technology and software is introduced.

How the Internet and the Web Changes with ActiveX

It's not quite accurate to say that ActiveX will change the Internet; instead, it will change the way people use it and think about it. After all, the Web and hypertext didn't change the Internet either—they, too, merely changed the way people used it and thought about it. In fact, when you review the current state of both the Internet and the Web, you can see how ActiveX will change how you use the Internet.

The Internet Today

This section's discussion on the Internet outlines not necessarily the cabling and hardware that connect networks, but rather how the Internet is used by people who aren't necessarily using a Web browser.

Without Web browsers, Web pages, and index sites like Yahoo, the Internet is basically location-centric, and information is tied intimately to its location. If you want to get information about a specific topic, since there aren't any links to follow, you would have to almost intrinsically know a gopher or FTP site, telnet IP address, or a specific newsgroup. Existing indexing programs must not only keep track of information and the sites the information is in, but also present these details on your screen in a useful way.

However, once you do locate a site with information you're interested in, have figured out how to interact with it (since any one of several communications protocols might be used), and sorted through file-type issues by using converters and such, the Internet is exceptionally useful. However, you must keep track of many things yourself: locations, formats, protocols, and different access programs. This was the scope of the Internet before the World Wide Web; without Web browsers, it continues to be.

The World Wide Web Today

If nothing else, the World Wide Web transformed the way the Internet is used—from being location-centric and program/protocol-centric to being information-centric. In effect (fancy graphics and special effects notwithstanding), the Web lets users concern themselves only with finding some information about the subject they're interested in; thanks to hypertext links, they can find similar information without worrying about locations or protocols. The Web browser acts somewhat like a common information viewer and retriever.

Once the Web browser finds existing information on the Internet, it's generally expected to just browse it—hence its name. It interacts only superficially with this information, unable to truly make changes. Also, Web browsers aren't universal file viewers. Their focus is to navigate the different protocols and networks that form the Internet and make it all look simple; therefore, not every bit of information can be viewed unless it's first converted into a browser-friendly format.

The Internet and Web with ActiveX

With the introduction of ActiveX, all of the above will remain true for those Internet users and Web surfers who aren't using ActiveX functionality. Since ActiveX doesn't force the online world to bend a certain way to work, existing Web pages with "conventional" functionality can continue to function as they always have. However, for those people using ActiveX-enabled programs and sites, three big changes are in store:

■ Documents no longer need to remain static—that is, true interaction with either information or applications will be possible. This dynamic will permit "living documents" and sources of interactivity.

■ Web sites don't have to be simply pretty stores of information—they can be interactive "Web applications." A site can perform a particular task, rather than just provide existing information.

■ There will be interactive information sources online that are far more than simply "Web sites." Since ActiveX will enable business applications to use the Internet for communication, collaboration between people working on a common task won't need a central site to act as a "common ground" between them and their conventional "communications programs." Instead, they can use their Internet-enabled applications to work directly with other people's Internet-enabled applications, thus creating and calculating new information directly.

What's Next

The next section, beginning with Chapter 4, "The Components of ActiveX," begins exploring the specifics of ActiveX and shows you how to start using it today. Before you can, however, you need to use an ActiveX-enabled program in the form of Microsoft's Internet Explorer, version 3.0. The final chapter in this introductory section, "Internet Explorer 3.0: Microsoft's Gateway to the Internet's Future," shows you how to get and install version 3.0 of the Internet Explorer and highlights some of its newer features.

CHAPTER 3

Internet Explorer 3.0: Microsoft's Gateway to the Internet's Future

by Warren Ernst

So far, ActiveX components and general computing ideas have been presented in the abstract, but there's already much to see and do with ActiveX, and you'll get a world-class Web browser to boot! That Web browser is Microsoft's Internet Explorer version 3.0; it's already the second most popular Web browser available (behind Netscape), surpassing NCSA's Mosaic in use last year. The Internet Explorer 3.0 could even give Netscape a run for its money in the Web browser race, simply because of its wide array of features, attractive interface, speed, and of course, the ability to use ActiveX controls and documents. It's literally the springboard of ActiveX technology, because with it, you can begin to explore the power of ActiveX and the Internet at the same time.

This chapter reviews the steps needed to retrieve and install the Internet Explorer 3.0, goes over some of its new features and interface, and tests its ability to use ActiveX controls. Once you do this, you'll have both an excellent Web browser and the best tool available for seeing the examples presented later in this book.

Getting Started with Internet Explorer 3.0

I know what you're thinking: "*Another* Web browser? What's wrong with Netscape?"

Nothing's wrong with Netscape; it's a capable and robust Web browser that opened up the Internet to more people than any other program. But that's not to say there's no room for improvement. In fact, you might say that Microsoft first adopted an "if you can't beat 'em, join 'em," approach to making version 3.0 of the Internet Explorer, by adding ActiveX compatibility to sweeten the deal, *then* offering it free to boot! This section walks you though Explorer's features and shows you how to get and install it.

Explorer's Winning Features

First and foremost, Internet Explorer is the first, and most capable, browser available for making use of ActiveX controls, ActiveX documents, and ActiveX scripting with Visual Basic Script. However, since you've not yet seen any of these things (or even have a good idea what they really are, unless you've skipped ahead), this alone might not mean much to you, so take a look first at its Web-browsing abilities.

Microsoft recognized that Netscape creates standards of its own, whether they are special, "Netscape only" HTML tags or a format to write plug-in modules to enhance Web browser functionality, so they embraced it part and parcel. In other words, the Internet Explorer can do pretty much anything Netscape can, including use of the `<Blink>` HTML tag, the VDO (or any) Netscape plug-in module, and HTML level 3 Web pages with frames and tables. Additionally, version 3 can use Java applets and JavaScript-enabled Web pages.

On top of all this, Microsoft brings additional features into its browser. Microsoft has had its own "Microsoft only" HTML tags for some time, and they are finally starting to catch on. This means that, while using the Explorer, you can take advantage of the `<Marquee>` tag for inline scrolling text, background sound effects and video, special table effects, and many others.

Did I mention that the Explorer loads pages faster than any other Web browser, too? And that it's completely free, regardless of where you work or what you use it for (as specified in the license agreement, but there's nothing unusual about the agreement)? Clearly, Microsoft did its homework when it came to creating a Web browser, and you get to reap the benefits.

Retrieving Internet Explorer 3.0

Internet Explorer 3.0 is freely available on the Internet, and the easiest way to retrieve it is to use a Web browser and jump to the Microsoft World Wide Web site and follow the prompts. The topmost page for Internet Explorer 3.0 can be found at `http://www.microsoft.com/ie/`, so jump directly to this ever-changing page and follow the links that let you download the latest version of Explorer.

As of early summer 1996, once you jump to this page with your browser, click the "Internet Explorer: Get It" link and follow the prompts on the resulting pages to download the version of Explorer that matches your operating system (either Windows 95 or Windows NT). Once the file transfers, you can proceed to the next section of this book.

If you don't have access to a Web browser or prefer to use FTP to retrieve Internet Explorer 3.0, you can get the file from the Microsoft FTP site at `ftp.microsoft.com`. Once you FTP to the server, change directories to /msdownload, then to either /ie3 or /ie3b (depending on whether the browser is either fully released or in beta). Once in this final directory, download the file that's suitable for either Windows 95 or Windows NT. The Windows 95 version of Explorer follows the scheme of msie3*xxx*.exe, where *xxx* represents a minor change in version number. The NT version's filename follows the scheme of ntie3*xxx*.exe, where *xxx* represents a minor change in version number.

> Tip: Don't forget to set your FTP transfer mode to BINARY, or the file won't install correctly.

Installing Explorer

Once you have Explorer's compressed installation file on your local hard drive, installing it is easy. The installation file is a self-extracting and setup-running program, so double-clicking the file msie*xxx*.exe (or ntie3*xxx*.exe, if you are running Windows NT) from either the Disk Explorer or Drive Window starts the process (remember that *xxx* represents a minor change in version number). When the installation process starts, it will confirm that you want to install Internet Explorer and ask you to confirm a location on your hard drive. Once it has this information from you, it copies Explorer to its destination directory, plus the default set of ActiveX controls and some new Dynamic Link Libraries (DLLs) to your system directory, and prompts you to restart your system.

> Note: If you haven't closed your Internet connection, be sure to do it before restarting your system, or else you won't be "cleanly" logged out from your network.

Starting Internet Explorer for the First Time

Once your system has restarted, Internet Explorer is ready to go! To start it, click the Start button, open the Programs folder, and choose Internet Explorer (the icon isn't in a subfolder), or if there's an icon on your desktop labeled "The Internet," double-click it.

Once it finishes loading the program and the default Web page, you should see something similar to Figure 3.1.

Version 3.0 of Internet Explorer has changed its appearance quite a bit from the earlier versions, and of course, die-hard Netscape users are in for a little shock, but the new interface works very well. The biggest change is the Toolbar/ Location Bar/Quick Links combination toolbar, which can be dragged, resized, and switched around in several ways. Each one of these "toolbars" roughly corresponds to the following toolbar in Netscape:

Explorer Toolbar = Netscape Toolbar

Explorer Address Field = Netscape Location Field

Explorer Links = Netscape Directory Buttons

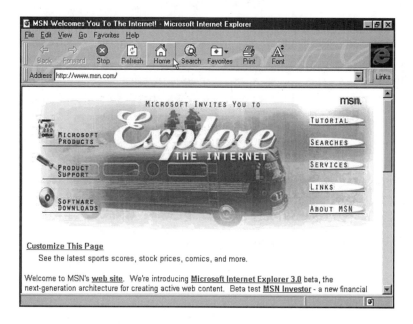

Figure 3.1.
Internet Explorer 3.0 automatically displays Microsoft Network's home page.

Unlike Netscape, where the size of the toolbar is controlled by a Preferences dialog box, the toolbars are sized and controlled interactively by dragging the mouse within Internet Explorer. For example, you can position the cursor over the Links box and drag it to the left, exposing the Links icons and reducing the size of the Address field. You can drag the divider between the toolbar and content area up or down to increase or decrease the size or number of toolbars visible at once.

Naturally, clicking on a colored, underlined word activates the hypertext hotlink it represents and displays the new Web page in the content area. As the page loads, the status indicator in the upper-right corner moves to indicate activity and stops when the page is completely transferred. The Stop button in the toolbar stops a page's transfer; the Back and Forward buttons move you through the pages you have seen. Some of Explorer's other features are reviewed in the following section.

Configuring Internet Explorer

Most of the configuring options for Explorer are self-explanatory, especially if you've been surfing the Internet for a while with another Web browser. There are, however, some settings that could use more explanation. First, to configure Explorer, you need to access its Options dialog box, so choose Options from the View menu. Once it opens, you'll see that it's a tabbed dialog box—clicking a tab along the top of the dialog box changes the box's contents.

The File Types tab simply calls the Windows 95/NT File Types Registry dialog box, where various file types are associated with different programs. Since most installation programs automatically modify the registry themselves, there's almost never any need to manually associate a file type with a "Helper Application" yourself, but you can if you want.

The Places tab lets you specify the home page that loads by default when Explorer starts, the search page that appears when you click the Search button in the toolbar, and the links that appear in the Links toolbar. Note that you even though you can manually type a URL to change these settings, you can also simply display the page you want in Explorer's content area, *then* use this dialog box to change the Home Page or Search Page settings by clicking the Use Current button. (See Figure 3.2.) You can also change the number of sites that appear in the History list with this dialog box.

Use the Connection tab to alter your connection to the Internet while using Explorer. The upper portion controls aspects of a dial-up connection through a modem, letting you specify a default connection (if you have different dial-up accounts) and an automatic disconnect time, which will hang up your modem after a certain period of inactivity. The lower portion lets you configure Explorer to work through a proxy server on a LAN, though you will need to get the correct settings from your System Administrator.

The Advanced tab controls Explorer's cache directory, letting you specify where and how much space should be dedicated to temporarily storing previously viewed Web pages. The more space you set aside, the more likely it is that the page will reload quickly next time you jump to it. Clicking the View folder displays the contents of the cache; the Empty folder clears it.

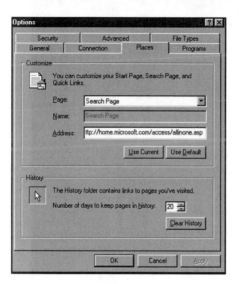

Figure 3.2.
The tabbed Options dialog box looks different for every tab selected, but you can use it to easily make several changes at once.

The Security tab lets you change how rigorously Explorer alerts you to potential security problems, such as while using a Netscape Secure Sockets–enabled site, transmitting information with a form, or downloading a program or ActiveX control. The Active Content section of the dialog box allows you to specify how rigorously Explorer will check a control for potentially damaging code.

The General tab lets you set the default link colors, enables or disables automatic loading of inline images, sounds, or video clips for faster or more colorful Web surfing, and the default background color for Web pages that don't specify one. The International tab simply determines which character set and font to use for displaying pages written in languages other than English.

Using Explorer

Now that you've got Internet Explorer installed and running on your system, you'll find that using it is a snap if you're used to other Web browsers. There are some differences and unique qualities to Explorer that you might not have seen before, and these features are covered in the following sections.

The Explorer Commands

The new toolbar has already been mentioned, but there are many new commands hiding within its folding structure. Most of the commands are, in fact, duplicated within the menu structure, so you could probably work just fine without the toolbar, but it does offer quick access to most of the commands you would use.

Among the new commands is the Search button, which jumps to a "Metasearch" page on Microsoft's server. (See Figure 3.3.) With it, you can easily perform a Web-wide search through Lycos, Yahoo, Excite, InfoSeek, or Magellan search engines—just type the search term in the field next to the search engine you want to use and click the Search button.

> Note: Strangely, Alta Vista isn't available from this page, but Microsoft is said to be adding it in the near future.

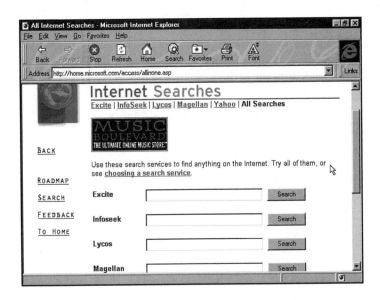

Figure 3.3.
The toolbar's Search button offers a quick way to access many Web searching programs at once.

The toolbar also includes the following buttons:

Button	Function
Font	Cycles through a set of five different font sizes
Refresh	Reloads the current page
Home	Displays your home page
Print	Prints the entire page or just a portion

The Address field has a new feature unique to any Web browser: a persistent History List. In other words, clicking the down-arrow button next to the Address field pulls down a list of the most recent sites you've visited, even if you visited them during earlier online sessions. It doesn't clear itself when Explorer is shut down, which means there's no need to clutter up your Favorite Places list just because you have to interrupt your browsing for another reason.

Finally, the Links buttons quickly brings you to specially created Microsoft pages that focus on the button's topics. For example, the Today's Links button brings you to a new page that highlights different Web sites every day. The Services button displays the various services and programs Microsoft offers to its customers, the Web Tutorial button displays a short set of instructions for using the Web, Product Updates shows you the most current versions of Internet Explorer you can download, and the Microsoft button jumps to the top-level Microsoft Home Page.

Favorite Places

Netscape calls them Bookmarks, and Mosaic calls them HotList entries, but whatever you call your list of frequently visited Web sites, Internet Explorer has them too and calls them Favorite Places. You can work with and manage your list of Favorite Places in a couple of ways, depending on what you're used to, but first, some background.

Netscape and Mosaic store their lists of Web pages in a single file, and add more lines to this single file every time you tell them to add a site to your list. Explorer, on the other hand, stores every Favorite site in its own file in a special directory in your Windows folder called "Favorites." Therefore, if you have ten Favorite sites in your list, you have 10 small files in the Favorites subdirectory, and there will be 10 entries in the Favorites menu. To group similar Favorite Places together in a submenu within the Favorites menu, these files are stored in a subdirectory within the Favorites subdirectory. The name of the Favorite Place or submenu is the filename, and the URL is stored as a single line within the file.

Once you know all this about Favorite Places, you'll find that using them with the Explorer makes a lot more sense. When you find a site you want to add to your Favorite Places list, choose Add to Favorites from the Favorites menu, then use the resulting Add to Favorites dialog box to save the site to your list. The dialog box works just like the Windows 95 disk drive Explorer when you click the Create In button, allowing you to save new sites directly within your heirarchy of Favorite Places folders, which means clicking the plus symbol expands a folder and clicking the minus symbol reduces it. Since Windows 95 doesn't have rigid file-naming rules, you can have descriptive names for your Favorite Places, but the name defaults to the Web page's title. (See Figure 3.4.)

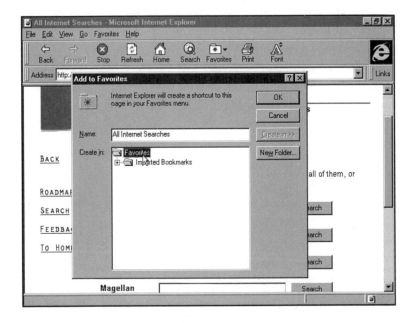

Figure 3.4.
In the Add to Favorites dialog box, you can change the name of a Favorite Places entry by typing the changes in the Name field.

> Tip: If you already have a Netscape Bookmark file, Internet Explorer automatically imports it into a folder called Imported Bookmarks. It leaves the original file untouched.

Once you've added entries to your Favorite Places list, you'll undoubtedly want to access them. For quick access, just pull down the Favorites menu and select the site you want from the list. For more detail and drag-and-drop Favorite Site management, click the Favorites tool in the toolbar and double-click the desired site, or drag and drop it into or out of folders.

Using ActiveX Controls and Java Applets

The whole point to using Java applets and ActiveX controls embedded in Web pages is that their use is seamless. Even though ActiveX controls are so new that some details are still being worked out, this is generally true.

Internet Explorer comes with the `Chart`, `Intrinsic`, `Label`, `Preload`, `New Item`, and `Timer` controls, with new ones added with each release of Explorer (check out `http://www.microsoft.com/ie/appdev/controls/default.htm` to see all of them in action in one place) and installs them during Explorer's installation process. When you encounter a Web page that uses one of these controls, it's used automatically without any action on your part.

New controls may or may not be used automatically, depending on the type of control and how far the Microsoft Control Downloading Specification has been accepted in the Internet community. In some cases, you might need to manually download the new control with Explorer and run its installation process before viewing a page that takes advantage of it. In others, the control can automatically download and install itself with your permission. As the specification gains wider acceptance, more and more controls will automatically transfer and install themselves on-the-fly.

Java applets, by their nature, automatically download and run themselves within Internet Explorer without any intervention. Instructions for their use are normally displayed in the Web page the Java applet came with.

What's Next

In this chapter, you have learned how to install and use Microsoft Internet Explorer 3.0, which is the first browser capable of taking advantage of ActiveX technologies. The next chapter, "The Components of ActiveX," explains the different parts that combine to make ActiveX a reality and shows you some of it with Internet Explorer 3.0.

Components of ActiveX

CHAPTER 4

The Components of ActiveX

by Warren Ernst

Up to this point, the term "ActiveX" has been thrown around somewhat ambiguously (both by the media and myself), sometimes being spoken of as if it were a single program you must buy from Microsoft, sometimes as a non-specific set of concepts and ideas that make Web pages more visually interesting and interactive, and sometimes as a way to make the Internet work with all the business programs you already use to create documents, spreadsheets, and presentations. With all these different descriptions floating around, each with a certain degree of truth behind it, it's sometimes hard to figure out just what Microsoft (and everyone else) is talking about when referring to ActiveX.

Therefore, to try to nail down a description, ActiveX is a *computing technology* composed of several different components, each performing a specialized task with common elements that are programmed similarly. Some components add computing power to Web pages, others allow document-objects to call viewing programs from across the Internet, and others add new capabilities to Web servers. All the components use methods that are, if not capable of being shared among each other, at least similar to each other. All use Object Linking and Embedding (OLE) technology to some degree to perform their tasks and are usually programmed in a language fine-tuned to Windows and OLE, such as Microsoft's Visual C++. With ActiveX technologies, Windows programmers will have a much easier time combining traditional Internet connectivity programs with powerful desktop software packages, and Internet users will find it easier to use the Internet to create business documents and use Web browsers to perform computing tasks.

These technologies exist today and are being put into use for innovative programs and Web programs that you can explore with Internet Explorer and other programs available from Microsoft. This chapter breaks down the technology that comprises ActiveX into its fundamental components. Subsequent chapters delve deeper into each component on an individual basis.

ActiveX Controls: The Building Blocks of ActiveX

The fundamental element of ActiveX technology is the ActiveX control, formerly called an OLE control. An ActiveX control is a modular piece of software that performs tasks and computes information, communicates to other programs, modules, and the Internet by using OLE, and can be easily used and reused by any program or programming environment that can "contain" ActiveX controls, such as Web browsers like Internet Explorer 3.0, or programming environments like Visual Basic, Visual C++ 4.0, or FoxPro. Controls have computational power, communications power, and their own small graphical interface (though its GUI can be disabled for truly custom applications); they can be used like Java applets within Web pages or as any other control in a program created with an ActiveX-compatible programming language. It's for this reason that the term "control" should mean something to Windows programmers, but it might not mean much to an Internet or business application user who has no need to write programs that use controls.

There are many different types of ActiveX controls, each with different capabilities, but all with the potential to do many things. Some are especially adept at Web page special effects, so some of these are included with Internet Explorer 3.0. Others are adept at numeric calculation or image manipulation and are included with programming languages. Some are good at manipulating databases and are included with Microsoft Access and FoxPro. And, of course, if a pre-existing ActiveX control doesn't have the capabilities you need, you can create new ones yourself.

Since ActiveX controls can be as different from each other as the different programs on the shelf at a software store, it's somewhat difficult to say what all ActiveX controls share, can do, or have the potential for. And since new ones are being written all the time, it's hard to predict what the majority of new ones will do. However, it is exactly this unknown application of ActiveX that makes the technology so exciting; it truly is an open technology! Despite the inability to predict where ActiveX will take you, it's certainly worthwhile to at least consider the capabilities provided by ActiveX controls:

- Compute and manipulate data
- Communicate
- Save programming effort

ActiveX Controls Can Compute and Manipulate Data

In case you haven't noticed, Web pages display only predetermined information in a Web browser and are incapable of generating new information from existing data. For that matter, the HTML environment is limited because it can't manipulate existing data in any way. Web pages are static, unchanging lines of human-readable text that perform no computing task whatsoever. ActiveX controls, on the other hand, are capable of computation and data manipulation.

Since ActiveX controls can easily be embedded within Web pages or entire programs, they provide a simple way to add either computing ability to Web pages or a specialized computing task to a larger program. (See Figure 4.1.)

To work in a Web page, the Web page browser must be able to "contain" ActiveX controls—to work in a custom-built application, the programming language must be able to "contain" them, too. Currently, Microsoft Internet Explorer 3.0 and Netscape Navigator (with the NCompass ActiveX plug-in module) are ActiveX containers, so controls will be able to run in most people's browsing programs.

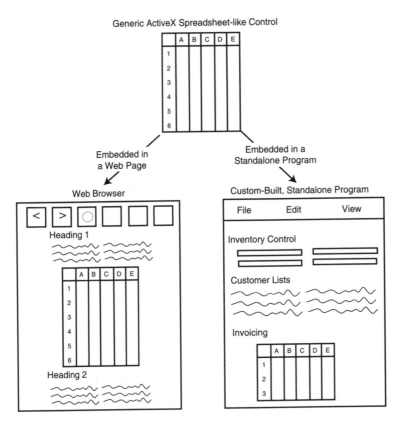

Figure 4.1.
Once an ActiveX control is built, it can be used for a wide variety of purposes.

It's hard to discuss computing and manipulating data without considering performance at some point. It turns out that performance is a particularly significant benefit of using ActiveX controls, especially for manipulating data. Since ActiveX controls hide the details of how the data computations are being performed, you're free to create a highly optimized data-processing control that yields speedy results for the calling application. Additionally, since ActiveX controls can be written in any language, you gain the benefit of using a quicker language, like C++ over Visual Basic (or Java), if you so choose.

ActiveX Controls Can Communicate

Computing information without being able to share it through a wide array of methods can be a problem and can limit a control's usefulness (which is a common Java applet problem), so ActiveX controls have many communications options available to them. First, since their lineage can be traced to OLE controls, ActiveX controls are completely conversant in the language of OLE. This means that ActiveX controls can share data with or give instructions to any other OLE-capable object, including other ActiveX controls (even those in the same Web page), desktop applications like Word or Excel, the Web browser, or even the operating system itself. This includes, but is not limited to, the host computer's file system, giving ActiveX controls the ability to read and write files.

Second, ActiveX controls can be fully TCP/IP enabled, already aware of the popular conventions and protocols that make Internet-wide communication possible. This means that, with a few simple functions on the programmer's part, a control can send a request for a Web page at a URL with the HTTP protocol or retrieve a remote file through FTP. When embedded in a "traditional business application," this means Internet connectivity might be only a pull-down menu away.

When these two powers of ActiveX controls are combined, OLE links could be introduced over the Internet itself. This would allow programs or modules of Web pages, desktop applications, and ActiveX-enabled Web servers to share data and computational power like never before. Microsoft is currently working with the Internet community to make this new form of distributed computing a widely accepted standard, and it's already working at some locations.

The ability of ActiveX controls to communicate widens the concept of workgroup computing to include the whole of the Internet. With OLE, it's possible to work with dynamically linked data in local workgroups. In other words, one person could have a Word document containing an embedded Excel spreadsheet that's being modified by another person. The Word document is kept up-to-date with the spreadsheet through an OLE link, therefore allowing both people to jointly work on the task at hand. ActiveX controls extend this capability beyond the local workgroup by providing a means to have linked information across the Internet, thereby making the physical location of each workgroup member less of an issue. This is a major step forward, especially for those of us who like to work at home!

ActiveX Controls Save Programming Effort

Finally, ActiveX controls are reasonably easy to create from scratch; if no control exists to perform the task you need, you can create one. Currently, you need Microsoft's Visual C++ programming environment and must follow the ActiveX programming guidelines (available electronically or on CD-ROM), but support for other languages will be available at some point, including Java and Visual Basic. This is an important aspect of ActiveX controls: They can be implemented in any programming language. So if you already have significant programming experience, you can go the C++ route; if you want to keep things a little more simple, you can use Visual Basic. Also, if you've jumped on the Java bandwagon, Microsoft has mentioned a future ability to build ActiveX controls using Java.

Since ActiveX controls are modular objects, you can introduce a certain degree of functionality to both your Web pages and all your programs by just creating one ActiveX control. You can then initialize it slightly differently, depending on whether it's in a Visual Basic program or a Web page. The whole idea of developing modular controls is that they can be reused in many different ways. If you don't care to program an ActiveX control yourself, since they are so easy to build and use, you might find one either in the public domain or a commercial market that suits your needs. You can then simply embed it within your work—the ultimate time saver!

ActiveX Scripting with Visual Basic Script

For Internet users and Webmasters, the thought of custom-creating ActiveX controls using Visual C++ just to add some functionality to a Web page might (and should) create some anxiety. Fortunately, there's another option for enabling OLE communications within Web pages that is fast, powerful, and easy to learn: ActiveX's scripting component—Visual Basic Script (or VBScript, or just VBS).

Similar in concept to JavaScript, VBScript is a Web page scripting language that has all the power (and more) of JavaScript, the gentle learning curve of Visual Basic, and the OLE communications power of ActiveX controls, all rolled into one. It is written in plain English directly into Web pages, alongside the HTML coding in an HTML file, and is interpreted on-the-fly by the VBScript-enabled Web browser displaying the page, such as Internet Explorer 3.0. It may be the perfect scripting language for the Internet because it has real computing power, can easily initialize ActiveX controls, and is relatively simple to learn.

VBScript Is Easy to Learn

Visual Basic Script is a subset of Windows' most popular programming language, Visual Basic 4.0, so people already familiar with VB will feel right at home with VBScript. It's also a subset of Visual Basic for Applications (VBA), so if you write scripts and macros for Word or Excel, VBScript will also feel familiar. On the other hand, if you have never programmed in Visual Basic, you'll find that it isn't that hard to begin writing useful scripts with VBScript and that these new skills will carry over beautifully for Visual Basic, which is a skill worth having if you work with Windows.

Visual Basic is a strain of BASIC (with lots of extras), which means it's among the easiest programming languages to learn if you have no programming experience. If you know another language already, your programming skills will carry over quickly. This is very different from learning JavaScript, which requires in-depth knowledge of C++ and the basics of object-oriented programming to be used effectively. All you really need to start writing powerful scripts is general programming knowledge, not specialized C++ knowledge.

VBScript Is a Powerful Communicator

As a member of the ActiveX family of components, VBScript can communicate through OLE to any other OLE-compliant piece of software, which, as has been mentioned, includes ActiveX controls, desktop applications like Word and Excel, Internet Explorer 3.0, and the operating system. Since it's so easy to write a VBScript that can easily communicate with such a wide variety of objects, a great number of Web page possibilities open up to someone with just a little Visual Basic experience.

Since VBScripts can communicate with ActiveX controls, they can initialize controls within Web pages to work with Internet data. In fact, since VBScripts can interact with Web page users through forms, fairly generic controls can be custom-configured to specific purposes on-the-fly. VBScripts can also modify Web page forms based on user input from other Web page forms or controls, or from other OLE-equipped applications or operating system calls. In short, VBScript can act like the "glue" that binds Web page users, generic ActiveX controls, and information from business applications into new and active Web pages, the likes of which have never been seen before.

Writing the "Universal Program and File" as ActiveX Documents

Part of the problem (well, "problem" is too strong a word) with the Web today is that it's at the mercy of the HTML file format. I say "problem" is too strong a word because, were it not for the acceptance of HTML a couple years ago, the Web would not have become the popular communications medium it is today. However, now that the Internet has matured and users want more and different forms of information that just aren't suited to HTML, there's a problem both for users and software developers.

To the software developer, the problem arises when you have a program that's well suited to Internet access, but creates or uses files that aren't HTML and aren't suitable for being converted into HTML or embedded within HTML, such as three-dimensional models and real-time data feeds. What to do to ensure that anyone who comes across your Web page can see the data or information generated from your program? Your options weren't all that great until ActiveX documents became a reality. In fact, programmers have been forced to divide their efforts and expertise between two entirely different types of programming: programming for local use and programming for the Internet. One of the primary goals of ActiveX is to unify software development so that applications can be developed without regard for the differences between local access and Internet access.

One solution to moving applications to the Web is to make your program a "Helper Application," where it's called as a secondary window outside the browser. However, this increases window clutter and might confuse users with a totally different interface. You might consider making your program a Netscape plug-in module, but doing so eliminates your interface entirely and reduces the nature of your product to something that just works within another company's Web browser. You'd also have to compile a separate version just for Web browser use.

The new and alternate method is to write your program and the program's data structure as ActiveX documents, so that they both enjoy the benefits of OLE over the Internet.

OLE Editing, Anytime, Anywhere

Imagine using a file format able to automatically launch the program that can use it from directly within a Web browser. ActiveX documents can. When Internet Explorer 3.0, an ActiveX document "container," comes across a file format it can't read that is an ActiveX document, the file's native program can launch *within* Explorer's window, combining Explorer's toolbar and menus with those of the viewing program. The result is a file that opens without conversion in the same, single window used to view Web pages, but with the functionality required to manipulate the new file.

Additionally, virtual reality and PowerPoint presentations can be seen on the Internet as ActiveX documents. When these files are encountered, they are considered OLE objects by Internet Explorer and launch their respective programs within Explorer's window, combining commands and interfaces in a way that most users find much simpler than Helper Applications or plug-in modules. For the future, Microsoft is working with the Internet community so that OLE links will extend not only to the user's local hard drive or network, but across the Internet. Soon, when an ActiveX document file format requiring another program located on the Internet transfers to Explorer, it will transfer along with the file and appear within the browser automatically. For the Internet user, nothing could be simpler.

One Program, Many Uses

To the programmer, the results from a little more work to enable ActiveX documents are well worth the effort. The program component of an ActiveX document is really just a Windows program with OLE edit-in-place capability and a few additional OLE extensions. Although these modifications to existing programs aren't trivial, you get many extra features by embracing them.

First, your standalone program will automatically work within an ActiveX document "containing" Web browsers, like Internet Explorer, whenever your data file format is opened and will be available for in-place editing through the Internet. It will also work within the Microsoft Office Binder and the operating system shell of future versions of Windows 95 and Windows NT. It will work as you always thought it would, as a standalone application if you like, and it all comes from one executable and one set of source code, without the need to maintain multiple versions. For the programmer, nothing could be more flexible!

ISAPI Filters: ActiveX Technology for Web Servers

Who says only Web browsers can benefit from Internet-wide OLE-based technology? When you consider that much of the information retrieved from the Internet is being created by Windows-based "business applications," why not have Web servers send out the information from the platform on which it was created? And then use OLE-based ActiveX technology to use existing Windows resources to add new Web serving features? This is what ActiveX-enabled Web servers are all about, and the key to it is the ISAPI, or Internet Server Application Programming Interface, and the ISAPI filters that use it.

The ISAPI filter can be thought of as the next generation of CGI scripts, but written for any brand of Windows-based Web server that follows the ISAPI specification. An ISAPI filter, unlike a CGI script, can analyze and respond to the information stream before it enters or after it leaves the traditional control of a Web server, then send it on its path as if it had never been touched. In a sense, it tells the Web server: "If something like this happens, let me take care of it and get back to you." Contrast this to CGI scripts, which only indirectly handle data from the connection, with the Web server acting as the middleman.

ISAPI filters are simply Dynamic Linked Libraries (DLLs) with an OLE link to the Web server, which allows them to communicate with the server and manipulate the data stream in an unprecedented way. This OLE capability can also be used to call desktop applications and borrow some of their computing power to generate information, convert formats, and so on, to augment the filter's own computational ability. This technology will also play a role in enabling the ActiveX document OLE link across the Internet.

What's Next

Now that you have some idea of what ActiveX is made of, component by component, the next few chapters will discuss these components in detail and in plain English, starting with ActiveX documents. Part III, "Developing ActiveX Controls," dives deeper into these topics, discussing programming methods and tips.

CHAPTER 5

ActiveX Documents

by Warren Ernst

When it comes to using a file format for creating information to be distributed and viewed on the Internet, nothing is as popular as HTML (Hypertext Markup Language). Combining both information formatting and linking in the same file, HTML transformed the way most people use and think about the Internet. Before HTML, searching for information required in-depth knowledge of different file formats, communication protocols, and the programs that used them— and keeping track of them all could easily be a full-time job (and was). Today, after the rise of HTML, Internet users no longer need to worry about the formats, protocols, and dozen programs previously needed to work effectively online; instead, Web browsers such as Netscape and Internet Explorer combine retrieving information stored in different Internet servers with file viewing. As long as the information you need on the Net is converted into HTML, Web browsers are all you need to get online information.

Although the near-universal acceptance of HTML as *the* online information format has opened many doors and broadened the nature of the Internet, it really isn't a perfect solution for all types of information. For example, sounds, graphic images (both two- and three-dimensional), and animation sequences, obviously, can't be represented with HTML. "Live" information—such as video feeds, real-time statistical data, running stock quotes—is tricky too, requiring modules embedded within HTML files (such as ActiveX controls or Java applets) and new Web browsers with new capabilities that enable it to accept and run these modules, or "Helper Applications" that run outside the Web browser itself. If you use several Helper Applications for these new file formats, you're right back where you were before the Web—lots of different programs and formats.

Desktop applications that aren't "wired to the Internet" have also had this historical problem of dealing with different file formats for different jobs; they've handled the problem with varying degrees of success. File format converters, importers and exporters, and copying and pasting have all resulted as viable methods for combining information best suited for different file formats into one "document." However, the most flexible and innovative method by far is Object Linking and Embedding, or *OLE*. With OLE, you can easily transfer information from one file format to another and edit it in the master file by using the original format's properties and tools within a single window. It works, however, only if you have OLE-enabled programs and they are all installed on your computer.

ActiveX documents combine the best elements of OLE information sharing and the connectivity of Web browsers, allowing non-HTML formats to zip around the Internet and be viewed and manipulated with Web browsers, because these files transfer their properties and tools along "for the ride," so to speak. This chapter discusses how non-HTML files can call tools from across the Internet to let you work with them within Web browsers, shows how you can write applications that work within Web browsers and other programs, and illustrates how ActiveX documents are doing this today.

The Problems of New Information and New File Formats

Much of the information on the Internet is now stored in HTML, even if that information isn't especially well suited for the HTML format. Of course, video and audio information can't be stored in HTML. Although this wasn't much cause for concern two years ago when text and still-graphics images were almost all that was available on the Internet, it's a problem now. With the availability of 28.8 modems, personal video cameras and microphones, and live information feeds from scientific equipment or the stock market, HTML has shown its limitations. Despite these new types of information, however, developers and information sources still cling to the HTML format for a simple reason—it's practically guaranteed that the widest Internet audience possible can view the information.

This means that if you are a software developer and you want the information your program generates to be usable for the widest segment of the current Internet-using public, your program must do one of the following:

- Import or export HTML files
- Be capable of being linked to Web browsers in the form of Helper Applications
- Be rewritten as a Netscape or Explorer plug-in
- Be rewritten as a Java applet

This, of course, would be the ideal solution:

- Use a new method to automatically integrate with Web browsers, transferring the information and the code to use it across the Internet automatically

The positives and negatives of the first four common options are discussed in the following section, but the fifth option, where ActiveX documents come in, is explained in the "ActiveX Documents: The Best of All Worlds" section, later in this chapter. By reviewing the positive and negative qualities of the more conventional options first, you can more clearly see the advantages of using ActiveX documents over the Internet for your programs.

HTML for Everything

If your new program generates data you want available widely online, you could make sure your program can import and export HTML files in addition to your preferred, native format. This isn't a terrible solution if your program generates static, text-based data or generates data easily saved in a commonly embedded file format for Web pages, but there are some obvious drawbacks. The biggest one is that there must always be two files containing the same information at any given time—one for the local users of your program, and one for the online users. Since there are two files with the same data, the information might get "out of sync" because of a filenaming or other simple error, with the result that online users get one set of information and native users get another. Clearly, this is an unacceptable prospect.

Of course, if your information is completely text-based and static, you can probably minimize the potential for lack of synchronization to a comfortable level, but not all information is well suited for HTML. Complex, multipage documents don't necessarily translate well to HTML, especially if they were precisely typeset or required exact coloring.

Real-time data streams from instruments don't translate well into HTML, either. NASA's Jet Propulsion Labs (JPL) recently distributed real-time data of the Galileo space probe's Jupiter orbit insertion on the Internet by using HTML, but Web server problems prevented many people from getting the information. JPL had their programs generate a GIF file embedded in an HTML file every 60 seconds, and online users had to click their browser's Reload button every minute to get updated spacecraft readings. Unfortunately, with several thousand people clicking their Reload buttons every minute, the Web server overloaded—preventing *anyone* from getting data for a while.

Clearly, in some situations the wide acceptance of HTML can't offset the inherent limitations of the format. In these cases, another option is needed.

Make Your Program a Helper Application

If you've concluded that your information just can't survive a translation into HTML, then the simplest way to ensure that online users can read your data is to make sure your program can accept a call from a Web browser to display data retrieved online. This requires nothing more from a program's developer than a command-line parameter that automatically launches the program as a

Helper Application and loads the specified file, something along the lines of a Web browser launching a program stored on the local hard drive with the command c:\programs\abcviewer.exe file.abc.

For example, Adobe Acrobat files can't be read directly by Web browsers, so one option for using them online is to install the Acrobat Reader standalone application, then tell your Web browser where the application is located on the local hard drive. Once the Web browser knows about this "Helper Application," it will automatically launch it and load the file into it once the data transfer finishes. The online user can then read the data with this external program and quit the program when finished. In the case of Adobe Acrobat PDF files, a Web browser downloads the PDF file (which might contain an electronic "newspaper"), determines what file type it is, and launches the corresponding Helper Application: Adobe Acrobat Reader. Once the file transfer is through, it's sent to the Helper Application for use. This process is illustrated in Figure 5.1.

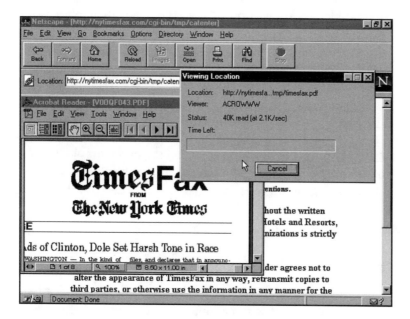

Figure 5.1.
Once started, a Helper Application runs completely independently of the Web browser and might sport an entirely different user interface as well.

This is certainly simple for the programmer, but it puts an extra burden on users, who must first separately download your program and then install it themselves. If it needs to be configured, users must do this, as well. Once the program is set up, users must then tell their browser where the application is located on the hard drive and what file types it can actually use. Only then will the non-HTML file load automatically, but users must still deal with additional program windows and perhaps a different user interface.

Also, there is never any way for the programmer or Web page writer to be certain that the online user actually has the Helper Application installed. Of course, he or she can supply a link to the Helper Application and directions for installing it, but "users can be users" and might skip past it, going directly for the information they want even though they can't view it yet.

Make Your Program a Plug-In Module

One way around the problem of forcing users to download, install, configure, and link an external Helper Application to a Web browser themselves is to rewrite your program to turn it into a Web browser plug-in module. *Plug-in modules* are programs specifically written to run "embedded" within a particular Web browser. Currently, Netscape plug-ins are the most popular format. Since other browsers are becoming "Netscape plug-in compatible," this format might be considered an emerging standard.

Plug-ins solve many problems for Internet users but increase the burden on programmers tremendously. For users, plug-ins end the problems of separate program downloads, installations, and configuring, since they handle all this themselves and automatically integrate into the Web browser, too. Plug-ins eliminate the need to worry about receiving a file type that can't be read because they check files before they transfer, as shown in Figure 5.2. Since they work within the Web browser, there's no separate window for users to get confused by or separate interface to learn.

Unfortunately, creating a plug-in from a conventional, standalone application isn't a trivial task. The end result is something that works only within (and looks like part of) another company's Web browsing program, which isn't the result anyone would want after working for months on a new program. Additionally, all toolbar items and pull-down menus must be removed, since they aren't supported in plug-ins, and replaced with a single pop-up menu for command access, a method many new users aren't accustomed to. You also need to change all memory allocation calls to Netscape's memory allocator, and the plug-ins aren't cross-platform—they are compiled into native code. Finally, you'll probably need to maintain different versions of essentially the same program: one for the plug-in module for online users and one for the standalone application for non-online users. All in all, there are many serious drawbacks to making your non-HTML data files readable by plug-in modules alone.

Figure 5.2.
Before transferring a live video/audio format called VDO, the system performs a plug-in check to see whether the file is usable.

Making Your Program a Java Applet

Java applets—like Helper Applications—are great for users but can be quite a burden on programmers. For the user, Java applets load into a Web browser just like a Web page, then execute on-the-fly to handle the non-HTML file only as needed. When it's no longer needed, the Java applet removes itself from the system and frees up space. The applet should work on any system the user might be surfing with, as long as it's running a browser with a Java Virtual Machine: Macs, PCs, and UNIX boxes with Netscape or Internet Explorer can all use the same information in the same file with the same Java applet.

Unfortunately, if you have an existing application written in a language other than Java, converting it into an applet is definitely a chore. First, you need an entirely new development platform, the Java Development Kit (JDK); however, it's available free of charge. Even though Java code might look and feel like C++ code, it isn't a direct port, so you have to get familiar with new standard classes. Once you've created your applet, you'll notice that Java is a very slow language, and your program will suffer a tremendous performance hit. However, the emergence of just-in-time Java compilers will probably remedy this drawback somewhat. Also, Java has no way to communicate with programs outside the Java Virtual Machine or write files to the client computer, so it won't be an effective information-transfer conduit for all situations. Therefore, you'll be forced to maintain two sets of source code: one for the Java applet and one for the standalone application.

ActiveX Documents: The Best of All Worlds

The entire ActiveX documents metaphor combines the best elements of all the preceding options, making it easy for developers to write software that works well both inside and outside Web browsers, for Webmasters to distribute information stored in non-HTML files, and for users to access it all. In a way, you can think of ActiveX documents as a logical extension of OLE because they can draw from not only the programs on a local hard drive, but across the Internet as well.

How ActiveX Documents Work

If you've ever used the OLE features of your existing programs, then you already have a glimpse of how ActiveX documents work. For example, when you use WordArt within Microsoft Word, there is a separate, small program that runs within Word's regular window whenever the WordArt object is edited. In fact, the WordArt program is a standalone program that also has the OLE in-place activation interface, which means it can run inside any OLE server–enabled program, such as Word. With OLE in-place editing, you can double-click the WordArt object in the Word file to make WordArt appear within Word automatically. (See Figure 5.3.) Clicking anywhere in the Word document closes WordArt, and Word resumes as normal.

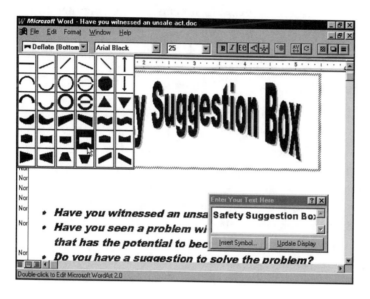

Figure 5.3.
Editing an object created by an OLE-enabled program launches it within the "containing program."

ActiveX documents work similarly—except that the OLE link isn't limited to programs already installed on a user's hard drive (although they can certainly be used)—the OLE in-place editing can occur with programs stored remotely on the Internet. This means that Webmasters can distribute non-HTML files filled with information, and the Web browser could automatically load the module (with the user's permission) to access it through a remote ActiveX document OLE link, much like the way Word loads WordArt to access WordArt objects on your hard drive.

ActiveX documents go a step further, however; they encompass the entire document metaphor in a logical piece of information. To better understand this, consider the impact of OLE on documents: The in-place editing provided by OLE applies only to parts of a document, such as an image. OLE components are limited to being document parts; they can't know anything about the document at large. What this means is that the frame application is entirely responsible for managing the viewing and printing of the document in the standard OLE environment. ActiveX documents, on the other hand, encompass the entire concept of a document, including the means by which it is viewed and printed, as well as how it is stored. Applications still supply the view frame where the document is displayed and edited, but the document manages itself, for the most part.

To convert an existing application into an ActiveX document, you must support several additional OLE interfaces (described fully in the ActiveX SDK) beyond the "conventional" ones. Although this task isn't trivial, it isn't terribly hard either, and the resulting benefits of the extra work are tremendous: You get an application that can run as a standalone program and will integrate directly with any ActiveX document container, such as Internet Explorer 3.0, Microsoft Office Binder, or the next version of Windows's shell (Nashville), in addition to existing OLE-enabled applications. In short, you get a versatile program with full OLE and Internet abilities for a reasonable amount of extra effort.

All this is done with the programming language you are probably already using, without having to maintain two separate code bases.

ActiveX Documents in Action

If you've had enough of the theories behind ActiveX documents and want to actually see an Internet-based object call a module, look no further than the ActiveX SDK CD-ROM, where you'll find the Traveler Three-Dimensional Chat beta program. Once you install and run it, it connects you to a three-dimensional world where you can chat (with a microphone and sound card) with other users. The "world" is stored in a SDS file and is, in fact, an ActiveX document.

Figure 5.4 shows the Traveler program running as a standalone application, which happens when you double-click its icon in the Start menu. Be sure to notice how it has its own set of menus and a toolbar and how it communicates to the Internet through a conventional http:// URL, just like a Web browser.

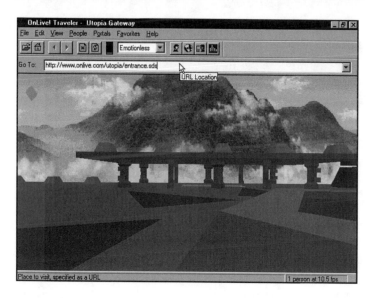

Figure 5.4.
The Traveler Chat application running as a standalone application.

This URL also works with Internet Explorer 3.0 once Traveler is installed, since the URL of `http://www.onlive.com/utopia/entrance.sds` points to an ActiveX document. Jumping to it with Explorer causes Traveler to load within Explorer, adding a new toolbar and menus to the menu bar. In fact, you can interact with the Traveler "world" accessed with Explorer exactly as though you had accessed it by using Traveler as a standalone application. That's because it's the same program running within Explorer as an OLE in-place editor, just as WordArt was to Word.

The Benefits of ActiveX Documents

To the user of this ActiveX document, the transition from Web browser to Traveler is virtually seamless because the new program loads into the container program automatically. In this case, the new program was already on the local hard drive, but it might just as well have been on a remote server. Microsoft is finalizing the specifications for this remote OLE link with the Internet community. This program has its own toolbar and required menu, yet remains in the browser's window, combining the ease of a plug-in module with the flexibility of a Helper Application. Since the non-HTML stored data is an object, it can load or retrieve, by using an OLE link, software that can view and interact with it, so users can always use information stored in any format.

Software developers can continue to use their familiar programming tools and languages, yet maintain only one code base for a program that's so versatile. Even more important, software developers can leverage the code they've already written with OLE technology and apply it to the Internet by using ActiveX. This is a crucial point, influencing how ActiveX succeeds as a technology compared to Java, for example. Unlike Java, ActiveX has the benefit of a massive code base from the outset, thanks to its being based on OLE. More specifically, when it comes to ActiveX documents, it's not hard to imagine that Microsoft is busy integrating ActiveX into all its major productivity products.

In other words, ActiveX will give you early support for such mainstream document types as Word documents, Excel spreadsheets, and PowerPoint presentations. This means you can seamlessly integrate any of these document types into the traditional Web page environment. This might not seem quite as important for the Internet at large, but consider its consequences in the emerging push for *intranets*, local Web-based networks within companies. The focus of internal networks has long been aimed at sharing information (documents) among workgroups of people; ActiveX delivers on this goal on a large scale.

When examining the benefits of ActiveX documents, consider, too, the inherent improvements being made to the way you interact with software. Microsoft has been gradually pushing toward a *document-centric* approach to computing, in which documents take center stage over applications. In other words, the goal is to let the user focus on a document, rather than the application used to work with the document. OLE itself is a significant step toward this end, but it's still lacking in some ways, not the least of which is its nonexistent support for Web-based computing. Of course, this is only logical, since the Web has gained acceptance only recently. ActiveX documents take document-centric computing to its next level, building on and surpassing OLE to accommodate the Web.

What's Next

Now that you've seen how to combine your programs with a Web browser client program, the next chapter, "ActiveX Controls," shows how your programs can interface with Web server programs in a whole new way.

ActiveX Controls

by Warren Ernst

The key to giving Web pages computing ability is giving them direct access to precompiled modules with the *smarts* mentioned in the first chapter of this book, then letting these modules run within the Web browser viewing the enabled Web pages. Of course, there are different strategies you can take to create, embed, and run these modules, with the earliest and most popular being Java applets embedded and enabled within HTML files and JavaScript acting as a sort of glue to bind it all together.

Although the ActiveX strategy of enabling Web pages doesn't take away your ability to use Java applets and JavaScript, it does give you another option, one with benefits beyond those of Java and JavaScript, with the benefit of allowing them to be reused for your other software projects. It's also an option that gives Web pages the ability to use OLE for communicating with the rest of the browser's system. This option is to use ActiveX controls as embedded smart modules for your Web pages (and other programs to boot). This chapter reviews the benefits of using ActiveX controls (formerly called OLE controls) within Web pages, how they are created, how they are used within Web pages, and some imaginative uses for them.

What Are ActiveX Controls and Their Advantages?

Simply put, ActiveX controls are modular programs designed to give a specific piece of functionality to a parent application. These parent applications, called ActiveX control "containers," are just programs that supply the environment for an ActiveX control to run. Right now, Microsoft's Internet Explorer 3.0 is such a container, but there are others. Ultimately, popular Microsoft applications like Word and Excel will be ActiveX containers. The control-container relationship is not that much different from the relationship between Java applets and Web browsers.

How Java Applets Work

Java applets are "compiled" into "bytecode," a state sort of halfway between a full executable and source code, that will run wherever there is a Java Virtual Machine, which in this case are the Netscape, HotJava, and Internet Explorer Web browsers. Since they aren't compiled into full executables, and are instead interpreted as soon as they are received, this means they're quite slow. However, just-in-time Java compilers are in the works that will compile the bytecode Java programs into native executables that run much faster.

The Java Virtual Machine completely shelters the Java applet from the rest of the computer system, which has both benefits and drawbacks. Since the Virtual Machine assigns memory and interprets bytecode on the fly, Java applets are platform independent and unable to perform actions that might have the potential to damage things, such as directly access portions of memory or write to a disk—it's supposedly impossible to create a virus in a Java applet, and I haven't seen any evidence to the contrary. Unfortunately, this same Virtual Machine limits what Java applets can do: They can't read or write files on the user's local machine, they have no standard way to communicate between themselves, and they can't really interact with the Web page they are based in. Java applets are truly self-contained nuggets of computational ability.

How ActiveX Controls Work Differently

ActiveX controls are, in fact, completely compiled executables that rely on another system for basic input and output, namely the ActiveX *container*. Microsoft's Internet Explorer 3.0 is the containing program you're most familiar with right now—and the NCompass ActiveX Netscape plug-in module is also popular—but containers aren't limited merely to Web browsers. Current environments with ActiveX control containers include Visual Basic, Visual C++, Visual FoxPro, and Microsoft Access, which means that controls (either custom-created controls or pre-existing ones) used to add smarts to Web pages can also be reused to add smarts to the other programs you create. This is a big advantage of ActiveX controls over Java applets; sure, technically you can create standalone Java applications, but the ability of ActiveX controls to seamlessly integrate into existing products is currently a significant step beyond Java.

Controls are precompiled into native code, so although they won't work across platforms like Java applets, they will run much faster, opening up more possibilities for control-based Web applications than Java could. Of course, this adds the difficulty of contending with different development efforts to support multiple platforms. Controls can communicate much better with both the Web page they're based in and the rest of your system than Java can. By using Visual Basic scripting in a Web page, controls can communicate through the methods, properties, and events you're probably already familiar with from other Windows programs, meaning controls can immediately alter a Web page currently in view or manipulate desktop applications with OLE.

ActiveX controls also use a different security scheme than Java applets, so there is no need to impose a "no local file input/output" limitation on them, which allows even more sophistication. Java applets are "secure" because there's essentially no way they can do anything meaningful to your system, since they run within a sheltered Java Virtual Machine. ActiveX controls' security comes from "code-signing," which allows you (or your programs) to determine the source of the control and whether the code has been modified since it was signed by its creator. In other words, once the validity of a control is confirmed, it is given more system access, permitting more functionality than a Java applet could ever have. You can think of code signing as the logical equivalent of signing your name on a legal document; your signature guarantees that the agreement is indeed based on your commitment. Likewise, your code signature guarantees that you created the ActiveX control. This might not seem important on an individual level, but think about code signing in terms of major commercial ActiveX controls; you need to know that a control has come directly from Microsoft and not from the hands of a virus developer.

Figure 6.1 graphically summarizes the different abilities of ActiveX controls versus Java applets.

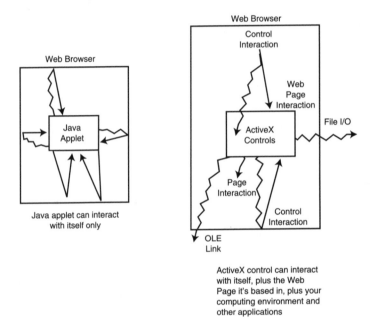

Figure 6.1.
The abilities of ActiveX controls compared to those of Java applets.

Creating ActiveX Controls from Scratch

It's possible to create ActiveX controls from scratch with different methods and languages, but the foundation for creating them is OLE, which means that

Microsoft programming tools are usually the best tools to use. In fact, you can think of ActiveX controls as OLE controls extended with Internet communications abilities. The specifications of these abilities are available from Microsoft in the ActiveX Development Kit, available both as a CD-ROM set available from the Microsoft Developer Network or as a download directly from the Internet. To download the kit, try `http://www.microsoft.com/intdev/sdk/` and follow the download links.

Currently, the only programming environment for writing ActiveX controls from scratch is Microsoft's Visual C++, but this should soon change to include the Java language and possibly Visual Basic or Borland's Delphi and Borland C++. If you are already using Microsoft's Visual C++ to create OLE-enabled programs, then you are practically creating ActiveX controls already. Just use Visual C++'s own OLE control development facilities and the Microsoft Foundation Class Library (MFC), and the result will be fairly small control executables that are ready to run, as long as the user has the correct MFC dynamic link library (DLL) installed. At this point, the MFC DLL is almost a megabyte in size, which translates into a single 5-minute download at 28.8 modem speeds, but it has to be transferred and installed only once. This required download is like needing the Visual Basic runtime library DLL before you can run Visual Basic Applications. Microsoft plans on releasing a streamlined—that is, smaller—compatible MFC DLL in the future, so controls created with the current MFC will still work.

From a programming perspective, using MFC to create ActiveX controls has many benefits, particularly inheriting your control from a pre-existing set of MFC classes that handle much of the overhead involved in managing an ActiveX control. I've heard enough horror stories from the early days of OLE programming to know that any standard code you can reuse is well worth the effort involved in learning how to use it. Beyond that, writing the control in C++ instead of C makes the process more logical and ultimately fits the tools to the problem better, since ActiveX controls are indeed objects.

You can also use the ActiveX Template Library (ATL) with Visual C++ to take some of the "down and dirty" OLE coding out of creating controls, but you would need a thorough understanding of Microsoft's Component Object Model (COM) and the ActiveX control architecture. However, if you have this experience or are willing to roll up your sleeves and learn it, you can create very small, fast controls that won't require the MFC DLL. The ActiveX Template Library is available at `http://www.microsoft.com/visualc/v42/atl/default.htm`, as is its license agreement.

If it seems like there's more work involved in creating ActiveX controls, that's because there is, but the results from this extra work are program modules/objects you can reuse across a wide range of applications, whether it's Web pages, Visual Basic programs, FoxPro/Access database programs, or almost anything else.

Using ActiveX Controls Within Web Pages

ActiveX controls, whether custom-created for a particular task or taken "off the shelf," are placed in a Web page the same way—by using the <OBJECT> HTML tag. This tag is organized to specify first the control's identification, then which data the control should use, then settings for the control's appearance and behavior, and finally some of the control's initial parameters. Listing 6.1 demonstrates the use of the <OBJECT> tag.

Listing 6.1. The ActiveX control, embedded with the <OBJECT> tag, can be placed in either the <BODY> or <HEAD> section.

```
<HTML>
<HEAD>
<TITLE> Page Title </TITLE>
</HEAD>
<BODY BACKGROUND="sjy.jpg" BGCOLOR="#ffffff" TEXT="#000000">
<H1>First Heading</H1>
<HR>
<OBJECT CLASSID="clsid:{7142BA01-8BDF-11cf-9E23-0000E8A7440}"
      ID=View_control HEIGHT=190 WIDTH=300 BORDER=4 ALIGN="left"
➡HSPACE="10" VSPACE=0>
      <PARAM NAME="Image" VALUE="http://www.bdiamond.com/surround/
➡demo/images/marin.svh">
</OBJECT>
…Page Continues
```

Chapter 12, "Controlling the Internet Information Server Through ActiveX ISAPI Filters," explains the <OBJECT> tag in detail, but there are a couple points worth noting here. First, the CLASSID is a number custom-generated for the control at the time of the control's creation and is a unique identification number for the control. This number is guaranteed to be unique among all controls; this is imperative because thousands of controls will eventually be co-existing on the Internet. If you were to use this same control in different areas of the page, it would continue to use the same ID number. This is the identification number used by your operating system's program registry, which contains other control settings (such as hard drive location, among other things). A similar identification name is given to the control as its ID, which is the English (as opposed to numeric) name used by scripts for manipulating and controlling the object interactively from the page. Once the object is specified and its location set, parameters used by the control for its operation are specified by the settings in the <PARAM> tag. Generally, when using off-the-shelf controls, sample <OBJECT> tags are listed to make inserting them into HTML files easier.

When an ActiveX-enabled Web browser encounters an ActiveX control in an <OBJECT> tag, it either downloads the control from its specified location in the <OBJECT> tag or refers to its internal list of saved controls in the operating system registry and executes it within its content area. Currently, only controls that are downloaded separately and registered manually, or controls that ship and install automatically with Internet Explorer 3.0, can be used in Web pages, but Microsoft has proposed several ActiveX control-downloading mechanisms to the Internet community. A discussion of the proposals for on-the-fly downloading of new ActiveX controls can be found at `http://www.microsoft.com/intdev/signcode/codedwld.htm`.

What ActiveX Controls Enable

ActiveX controls make Web pages possible that haven't been seen before because they enable a completely new, almost "live" interaction. They can permit interactive data manipulation within Web pages when combined with VBScripting, as shown in the Web page at `http://nihal02.cdc.deakin.edu.au/cdcsoft/emadWeb/xlabel.htm`, pictured in Figure 6.2.

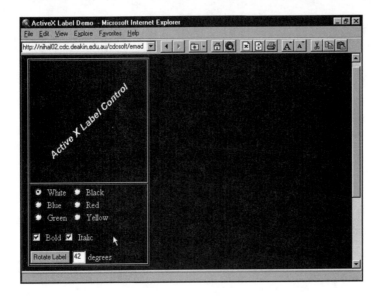

Figure 6.2.
This Web page combines a VBScript and the ActiveX Label *control.*

With this page, manipulating the form's radio buttons and fields sends parameter data directly to the ActiveX control handling the text in the box through OLE. In this simple test page, only a text string is being manipulated, but other ActiveX controls could manage three-dimensional images, live information from a remote source on the Internet, or a business application.

ActiveX controls can also permit new multimedia file formats that you can interact with directly in Web pages or any other ActiveX container program. For example, Black Diamond Consulting has created the Surround Video SVH format, an image format that can be rotated 360 degrees (as if you were turning around and viewing the surrounding landscape) by using embedded hypertext links and an interactive ActiveX control. By downloading and installing these controls, jumping to the sample page lets you view all of San Francisco Bay (from any direction from a single vantage point) directly from the Explorer Web Browser. (See Figure 6.3.) To try it yourself, jump to Black Diamond's home page at `http://www.bdiamond.com/`, follow the Surround Video links, download the Surround Video ActiveX controls for yourself, and follow the installation instructions. Once you do, jump to `http://www.bdiamond.com/surround/demo/demo2.htm` and drag the mouse around the image of San Francisco Bay. You'll soon see the bay like you never have before!

Figure 6.3.
Dragging the mouse within the view of San Francisco lets you get a complete 360-degree image.

However, should you want to add this 360-degree viewing function within your own programs (even those that don't necessarily use the Internet), you could do so easily if you're using Visual Basic or another Microsoft programming language that incorporates the ActiveX control-containing ability.

Moving On

This chapter has reviewed the building blocks of ActiveX features: the ActiveX control. In the next chapter, "ActiveX Scripting," you learn how controls and scripts can be combined into living documents that aren't bound to a particular format or file viewer.

CHAPTER 7

ActiveX Scripting

by Warren Ernst

Somewhere between the full-blown intelligence programmed into ActiveX controls and the static text-display capabilities of HTML lies the useful, simple, and flexible world of Web page scripting. With Web page scripting, you can "program" Web pages to perform actions without compiling dozens (or hundreds) of lines of complicated code—instead, the script transfers within the text of the HTML file, then "runs" as the page is displayed. The beauty of scripting in Web pages is that it's relatively fast and easy, requiring no special modifications to the Web page server; you need to add only enough lines of scripting code to get a job done, without a lot of extra overhead. You can have a Web page script perform useful tasks with as little as three lines of code. Web page scripts can also act as a sort of "glue" for adding larger, preprogrammed objects, such as Java applets or ActiveX controls, into your Web pages, without having to create custom controls or applets yourself.

The suite of ActiveX methods includes a new scripting language for the Internet: Visual Basic Script (or VBScript, for short). Although the more established scripting language JavaScript can be used to glue ActiveX controls together, VBScript brings to the table many advantages over JavaScript, including increased speed, a more shallow learning curve, and a tight coupling to the rest of the ActiveX environment through the use of OLE. In fact, with OLE you can even use VBScript to work with desktop applications that aren't conventionally used over the Internet.

What Is Web Page Scripting?

Much of the new functionality you're starting to see in Web pages is actually Web page scripting, rather than full-blown Java applets or ActiveX controls, since it's easier to include scripted code in a Web page than write an entire applet or control. For example, to perform a simple calculation, someone familiar with writing scripts can create a useful script in a couple of minutes instead of the many hours (or more) it would take for an applet. Unfortunately, JavaScript, the Web page scripting language built from the Java language, might not be the most suitable language for scripting because of its object-oriented heritage. This section covers why Web page scripting is useful, outlines general scripting uses, and explains why JavaScript might not be the best scripting solution in many cases.

Why Scripting Is Useful

There are many properties inherent in all Web page scripts (regardless of the language they are written in) that make them an exceptionally useful tool in the Web page writer's toolbox. First and foremost, scripts enable client-side computing within Web browsers; in other words, scripts make it possible for Web browsers to do some computing themselves instead of relying on the Web page server. Either by performing computations and generating output themselves, or by initializing and running applets or controls, scripts normally start off the computing process within the Web page.

Using scripts in combination with controls or applets is especially useful because it allows you to write fairly generic controls that can be reused, as opposed to writing and compiling a new and unique control for each Web page that performs a similar function. For example, you could write a control or applet that displays scrolling text in a box, but not hardcode the message, font, or size (for example) directly into it. Instead, you could write the control to expect these (and other) generic parameters from the Web pages they're used in, and these parameters can be delivered to the control by a script, as shown in Listing 7.1.

Listing 7.1. In this JavaScript example, the script is setting the size, text, spacing, borders, and font of the LEDSign applet. ActiveX controls work similarly.

```
<applet codebase="./LEDSign/LED" code="LED.class" width=500
➥height=48 align=center>
   <param name="script" value="rumor.led">
   <param name="border" value="2">
   <param name="bordercolor" value="0,200,0">
   <param name="spacewidth" value="3">
   <param name="wth" value="122">
   <param name="font" value="./LEDSign/fonts/default.font">
   <param name="ledsize" value="3">
```

Scripts are also simpler to implement in a Web page than writing a full-blown control or applet, so using them to create some smarts in a Web page can take far less time for a developer. The reasons for this are twofold: You typically need just several lines of scripting code to perform an action, and there's no need to generate bytecode or executables with a separate compiling program. Scripts are interpreted by the Web browser to perform a computation or action, much the way HTML tags are interpreted by the browser to display text in the content area. Additionally, since scripts aren't compiled, there aren't any extra overhead library functions that might add unnecessary size to the programming module; this keeps the file transmission simple and fast.

Web page scripts are normally written into the HTML file itself, which means that your program, when written as a script, will never be separated from the Web page you designed it for, regardless of the quality or speed of the Web browser's network connection. Only one file is being transferred to create a page, not several different ones. Occasionally, applets and controls get sent incompletely through slow or unstable Internet connections to viewers. As a result, the page's functionality gets lost and won't work—which is something that will never happen with a script. The drawback to linking script code to Web pages is that you must include multiple copies of a script when you want to use it again on another page. This requirement means maintaining multiple copies of the same script, which can be troublesome.

What About JavaScript?

So far, this discussion has centered on the capabilities of Web page scripts in general—capabilities that should be available to programmers regardless of the actual scripting language selected. Unfortunately, some of these "natural" scripting properties are less evident when using the popular Web page scripting language JavaScript, mostly because of its Java-based heritage. Certainly, you can use JavaScript in combination with ActiveX controls and other VBScript-based ActiveX scripts in the same page, so if you're already well-versed in JavaScript, you can use it to initialize ActiveX controls, create engines for Web page forms, or generate special effects.

On the other hand, if you aren't already skilled in JavaScript, learning it so you can make use of applets or controls is not without pitfalls. For starters, detailed JavaScript scripts require some sort of knowledge of C++ and object-oriented programming skills because JavaScript's syntax and organization carry over directly from Java, which is mostly derived from C++. Listing 7.2, a JavaScript script that scrolls text along the bottom of the Web browser window, is 36 lines and reads very much like C++ code.

Listing 7.2. Unless you know C++, this JavaScript code is complicated. VBScript is far simpler to understand.

```
/* Copyright (C)1996 Q&D Software Development
   All Rights Reserved.

*/
function scroll_status (seed)
{
        var msg = "This is the scrolling message text";
        var out = " ";
        var c   = 1;

        if (150 < seed) {
```

```
            seed--;
            var cmd="scroll_status(" + seed + ")";
            timerTwo=window.setTimeout(cmd,100);
    }
    else if (seed <= 150 && 0 < seed) {
            for (c=0 ; c < seed ; c++) {
                    out+=" ";
            }
            out+=msg;
            seed--;
            var cmd="scroll_status(" + seed + ")";
            window.status=out;
            timerTwo=window.setTimeout(cmd,100);
    }
    else if (seed <= 0) {
            if (-seed < msg.length) {
                    out+=msg.substring(-seed,msg.length);
                    seed--;
                    var cmd="scroll_status(" + seed + ")";
                    window.status=out;
                    timerTwo=window.setTimeout(cmd,100);
            }
            else {
                    window.status=" ";
                    timerTwo=window.setTimeout("scroll_status
                    (150)",100);
            }
    }
}
// -- End of JavaScript code ------------- -->
```

The flip side of JavaScript's similarity to C++ is that object-oriented languages tend to be very structured, which is a good thing. As languages, Java and JavaScript are very structured and give you clean approaches to common problems associated with other procedural languages, like Pascal and Basic. However, structured object-oriented programming makes more sense in a full-blown development environment, such as a Java applet or application. For quick solutions in the context of a Web page, the object-oriented nature of JavaScript is of little added benefit, unless you're already an object-oriented programming whiz.

What Is ActiveX's VBScript?

ActiveX is intended to make it easier to create real computing power within Web pages, and the suggested scripting language of ActiveX, Visual Basic Script (or VBScript), follows this same philosophy. VBScript combines the simplicity of Visual Basic with all the power of JavaScript and then some. Therefore, you can continue using JavaScript in ActiveX-equipped pages but take advantage of all the benefits VBScript has to offer.

The Benefits of VBScript

Perhaps the best thing about using VBScript is that it's based on Visual Basic, a popular and simple programming language with a large following. VBScript is actually a subset of Visual Basic for Applications (VBA), the scripting language built into most Microsoft business applications, which is itself a subset of Visual Basic 4 for Windows. A complete list of functions and features that are and aren't in VBScript, VBA, and Visual Basic 4 can be found at http://www.microsoft.com/INTDEV/vbs/vbscript.htm#lang.

Therefore, because of its heritage, if you already have some experience with either creating applications with Visual Basic or creating application scripts, you will find VBScript easy to use immediately. On the other hand, if you don't have any Visual Basic experience, you'll find that learning VBScript is a great first step to getting acquainted with the full Visual Basic 4 programming language to easily create full-blown applications or controls later.

Of course, as with any scripting language, you will need some sort of programming experience to use VBScript effectively, but VBScript is simple enough that it shouldn't hinder the learning process. VBScript uses real English, for the most part, and never requires you to learn object-oriented methods or obscure notations like >> or %=, as you would with JavaScript. Again, this may be a benefit to non-programmers or an annoyance to anyone with experience in programming languages beyond Visual Basic. The assumption is that hard-core programmers will opt to write ActiveX controls with a more structured object-oriented language like C++, but non-programmers will stick with VBScript. Incidentally, this situation directly parallels the relationship between the users of Java and JavaScript.

How VBScript Works

VBScript scripts work similarly to scripts created with other Web page scripting languages. Scripts are written in plain text and embedded within Web page HTML files; they are interpreted and "run" by the VBScript language engine built into the Web browser as the HTML file is transferred.

> Note: Currently, Microsoft's Internet Explorer is the only Web browser that already has the VBScript language engine built into it. However, Microsoft plans to make free licenses available to Web browser vendors and developers, so there will probably be a VBScript language engine soon in the form of a Netscape plug-in module, as well as support in browsers from Oracle, Spyglass, Netmanage, and other companies.

VBScripts are embedded within an HTML file by using the `<SCRIPT>` HTML tag, which includes the following parameter: `<Language=VBS>`. This parameter tells the browser that everything between the `<SCRIPT>` and `</SCRIPT>` tags in the HTML file is handled by the VBScript language engine, which then interprets the script and generates results immediately.

For example, here's a small (but complete) HTML file with a complete, though small, VBScript script written between the `<SCRIPT>` tags. It executes upon clicking the On-Page button, which is generated with conventional `<FORMS>` commands.

Listing 7.3. A script tied to a Web page button.

```
<HTML>
<HEAD>
<TITLE>A Web Page with VBScript Code</TITLE>
<SCRIPT LANGUAGE="VBS">
<!--
Sub BtnHello_OnClick
     MsgBox "Hello, world!"
End Sub
-->
</SCRIPT>
</HEAD>
<BODY>
Here is some body text<p>
<FORM><INPUT NAME="BtnHello" TYPE="BUTTON" VALUE="Click Here">
➥</FORM>
</Body>
</HTML>
```

When this page is transmitted to a browser with a VBScript language engine, the script written between the `<SCRIPT>` tags is interpreted by the VBS language engine and tied to the click event on a button named BtnHello. There-fore, the message `Hello, world!` appears in a text box when the button is clicked. (See Figure 7.1.)

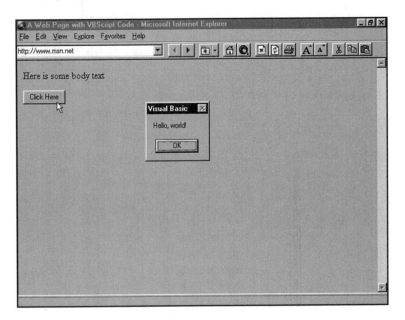

Figure 7.1.
The HTML file from Listing 7.3, in a VBScript-enabled browser once the button has been clicked.

Larger, more detailed scripts work the same way, with the scripting occurring either in the Head or Body sections of the HTML file, depending on when the script is supposed to "run."

What VBScripts Can Control

Visual Basic scripts can do far more than the simple example above and can even do more than JavaScript scripts.

First, VBScript can validate Web page form data, performing calculations, checking lookup tables, or simply verifying the existence of information in a particular form field. Since it can do all this without intervention from the Web page server, it can reduce the server's workload, making the rest of your pages transmit faster. This is an important capability of VBScript because anything that can be easily relegated to the client end of a Web connection will greatly improve performance. Not only does it help minimize server workload, but it also decreases the amount of information being sent back and forth to the server.

VBScript can also interact directly with the browser and make it perform actions. For example, it can look at how a form is filled out, then automatically fill out other parts of the same form on the same page, depending on what is selected. (See Figure 7.2.) In this case, selecting an option in the left column automatically selects or deselects items in the right column, generates a name for the combination in the bottom field, and calculates a cost based on the selected items in the right column. It all occurs interactively with VBScripts.

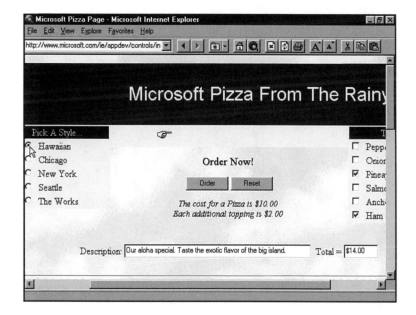

Figure 7.2.
In this demonstration Web page, VBScripts calculate amounts and select checkboxes as soon as they detect a change in the form, without page-reloading delays.

Finally, VBScripts have the muscle of OLE behind them, so they can communicate with your OLE-enabled desktop applications through a soon-to-be-available OLE Scripting Manager. This tool will manage the technical details of getting and calling OLE entry points and managing the namespace available.

But the true power of all these features is that they are accessible to programmers with a language much easier to learn and use than JavaScript: Visual Basic Script.

What's Next

This chapter has discussed the benefits of using VBScript to script simple computing tasks and to act as a "glue" for ActiveX controls. The next chapter, "ActiveX Internet Information Servers," explains what an ActiveX-enabled Web server is and discusses the Internet Information Server and ISAPI filters.

CHAPTER 8

ActiveX Internet Information Servers

by Warren Ernst

Isn't it strange that the most popular computer platform for
Web *browsers* is not the most popular computer platform for
Web *servers*? In fact, it isn't even close—UNIX and the
Macintosh operating systems outnumber Windows-based
Web servers by something like 5 to 1, even though there could
be eight times as many Windows-based Web browsers than
both Mac and UNIX versions combined at any given time.
To be sure, UNIX computers are what the Internet was based
on, but now that practically any computer type can be hooked
up permanently to the Internet to act as a Web server, you'd
think there would be a lot more Windows-based Web servers than there are today.

Given the right tools, there *should* be, since there are more Windows programmers than ever right now, and it only makes sense that informational files made on one computer platform be served by the same platform. Well, it might not make too much sense now, since the majority of the files you get from Web pages are platform-independent HTML and GIF files. But with more and more Windows-based desktop programs generating new file formats, and with users simply wanting information created with desktop applications in their native formats, it's beginning to make sense to just leave them where they are and let a Windows-based Web server serve them.

This is the philosophy behind ActiveX-based Internet Information Servers using ActiveX technology and ISAPI filters. ISAPI, which stands for Internet Server Application Programming Interface, is a new way to add functionality to Web servers in separate modules. ISAPI can be thought of as the successor to CGI (the Common Gateway Interface), as a means for outside programs on the serving computer to communicate with Web servers to affect input and output; ISAPI filters can be thought of as the equivalent to CGI scripts. With an ActiveX Web server, however, you can use both, depending on what you're comfortable with and what you hope to accomplish.

This chapter explains why using Windows ActiveX-based Web servers has advantages over other platforms and servers, how ISAPI filters are different from CGI scripts, what the general guidelines are for writing ISAPI filters, and how existing desktop applications can be used to serve Web pages.

The Power and Ease of ActiveX-Enabled Web Servers

It's hard to imagine a new Internet technology making life easier for the Webmaster and the Web surfer, but that is Microsoft's goal in designing the ISAPI for Windows-based Web servers. With ISAPI, Webmasters and surfers will find increased computing power and simplicity when getting "wired up."

Increased Power and Potential

The increased potential and power of an ActiveX Web server comes from a couple of trends. First, the Web is being used more and more by business people to transmit business information, in addition to the traditional "computer hobbyist." Since most business information is created with desktop computer applications, like Microsoft Word, PowerPoint, and Excel with Windows-based PCs, Webmasters are beginning to ask "Why are we always converting this stuff?"

Of course, this is a rhetorical question, because most Web servers are set up to deal only with sending out HTML files, and most browsers are capable of only displaying HTML files. But ActiveX controls and documents are changing the types of files a Web browser can use, and viewing a PowerPoint presentation, Word document, or Excel spreadsheet is starting to be something an ActiveX-enabled browser can do.

But even for non-ActiveX–enabled browsers that can read these files, a person (such as the Webmaster) manually converting existing business documents introduces the possibility that files might not get updated properly; the resulting files for online users won't be the same as the files that local users see, which defeats the purpose of having them online anyway. The fact is that most Microsoft business applications can export their native files into HTML files themselves and are OLE-enabled just as ActiveX components are. As such, an ActiveX-enabled server could then call on one of these business applications to convert a requested file into HTML on-the-fly, then send it out as an online user requests it, guaranteeing that any HTML file derived from a business application file is always synchronized.

Increased Ease and Simplicity

On top of the obvious benefits of having a Web server communicating with business applications that produce the information Web surfers want, there are many side benefits. First, most Windows-based Web servers are far easier to install and configure than most UNIX servers. Most Windows servers use simple installation programs and dialog boxes that you can point and click your way through, but most UNIX servers still use the UNIX command line to set things up. Of course, if that's all you're used to, this isn't a great concern, but as more and more people become Webmasters who have never used a UNIX box, this becomes a consideration. Additionally, if you're like most Webmasters writing HTML files from scratch, chances are you use a Windows-based PC to write them. With a Windows-based server, there's no need to transfer files from computer to computer, because you can write them on the very same computer that serves them.

On top of this, the Windows 95 and NT operating systems run on computers that cost far less to buy and operate than most UNIX boxes and Macintoshes, so there's less initial investment selecting a Windows-based Web server with ActiveX technology.

Integration with Existing Technologies

ActiveX-enabled Web servers also benefit from existing technologies based on Microsoft's wide range of products and the OLE standard. Microsoft already has a very advanced, high-performance SQL server product, so it's only logical that the SQL services offered by the Internet Information Server are built on the expertise Microsoft gained while developing their standalone SQL server.

This ability to leverage a wide range of existing, stable technologies is a crucial piece of the Microsoft Web server puzzle. The bottom line is that the Internet Information Server can't be judged entirely on its own accord because tangential technologies can add significant value to it. This advantage is unique to Microsoft and has long been their hold card in grabbing wide support for new products and technologies. I wouldn't expect the Internet server market to be much different in this regard.

The Differences Between CGI and ISAPI

Up to this point, I've been discussing conventional server technology, such as CGI scripts, and ActiveX technology, such as ISAPI, as if they were mutually exclusive, and that's not the case. Nor is it the case that ISAPI works only with a particular Windows-based Web server written by Microsoft. In fact, ISAPI is a fairly generic *method* to increase the functionality of Web servers and will happily coexist with traditional CGI scripts. This section compares and contrasts the fundamentals of CGI and ISAPI environments and highlights the differences in the way CGI scripts and ISAPI filters work.

CGI Versus ISAPI

The Common Gateway Interface (CGI) and the Internet Server Application Programming Interface (ISAPI) both perform the same task—to extend the capabilities of a Web server. They just provide a different framework for the actual computing module to do the job.

CGI programs (normally called scripts) run in an environment created especially by a Web server program—the server creates special information for the CGI program in the form of environmental variables and expects special responses back from the CGI program upon its execution. The point here is that the programs, which can be written in any language and communicate with the server only through more variables, execute only when the Web server interprets the request from the browser client program, then returns the results back to the server. In other words, the CGI program exists solely to take information from the server and return it back to the server. It's up to the Web server program to send that information back to the browser client.

The ISAPI specification is not nearly so limited in its ability to communicate. The ISAPI program (normally called a filter) can interact with information coming directly from the browsing client before the server has even "seen" it or can take information coming from the server to the client, intercept it, alter it in some way, then redirect it back to the client browser. It can also perform actions at the request of a server, just as CGI can.

It might not seem like an important distinction between the two, but it allows Web servers to serve out very different information, for example. Currently, Web servers send conventional HTTP response headers to browsing clients, but with ISAPI, the programs created to help the server could do it themselves, leaving the server to process other requests, or could modify the response headers to support a different kind of information.

Additionally, ISAPI programs are loaded in the same address space of the Web server. Contrast this with CGI, which creates a separate process on the server for every individual request. The end result is that the ISAPI approach gives you a higher level of performance than CGI and consumes far less RAM.

CGI Scripts Versus ISAPI Filters

I've always been a little uncomfortable with the CGI "script" moniker for the bona fide programs that operate in the CGI environment, but perhaps the term "script" has stuck because it's relatively easy to write short programs that perform small, repetitive tasks for Web servers. At any rate, CGI scripts can be written in almost any language, as long as that language supports the reading and writing of an operating system's environment variables. This means that for a UNIX box, scripts can easily be written in Perl, C, Forth, or almost any of the major languages. For a Windows-based PC, you could use DOS batch files, Visual Basic, Visual C++, Delphi, or even NT Perl (with some limitations).

The scope of the computational task will probably dictate what language is selected (I wouldn't want to perform complex calculations in Perl), but when all the computing is done, the results would have to be sent back to the server through more variables, and the server would have to construct the response and send it on its way.

ISAPI filters are normally written with Visual C++, both because filters are stored and executed as Dynamic Link Libraries (DLLs) and are fluent in OLE. A filter can take its cues directly from the stream of information heading into or out of the Web server, decide whether it's programmed to act on it, and then perform the action. It can also tell the server to do some processing of the information stream, then pass it along by using OLE or other means. "When something like this happens, let me handle it," the filter tells the server, and the server lets the filter handle it.

As it starts performing its task, the filter can make OLE calls to other business applications installed on the system or make use of existing ActiveX controls, when required. It can then send the information back to the server for further processing and even filter it further before it finally goes out. (Or better still, let another filter handle the post-processing, and keep the tasks separate.) The qualities that differentiate ISAPI filters from CGI scripts allow you to do the following:

- Provide Web page or site security by inserting an authentication "layer" requiring an ID and a password outside that of the Web browser's own security methods.

- Log incoming and outgoing activity by tracking more information than the Web sever does, and store it in a format not limited to those available with the Web server.

- Serve data out to browsing clients in a different way than the Web server would (or even could) by itself.

How ISAPI Filters Are Made

Chapter 12 discusses the nitty-gritty details of writing ISAPI filters on a technical level, but this section describes the requirements and processes from a slightly less technical point of view. Even more details are available on the ActiveX SDK CD-ROM available from Microsoft, along with sample filters.

Filters are generally custom-made for whatever application you have, unlike the plethora of ready-made ActiveX controls that are available. This is because, unlike the huge market for browser-side computing modules, the market for server-side computing modules is really very small, and filters are usually required to perform a *very* specialized task. As such, filters are probably the first ActiveX modules you will write.

ISAPI filters are generally created with Microsoft's Visual C++ and compiled into dynamic linked libraries. These DLLs export two functions to the ISAPI-compatible Web server: `GetFilterVersion()` and `HttpFilterProc()`, though for the purposes of discussion, the names aren't terribly important. The first function essentially registers the filter with the Web server when the server starts up. It first supplies version information to the server, next sets the filter's priority, then registers events that would activate the filter. The second function is actually called by the server and is used to send the filter the type of event occurring in the connection and the data associated with the event.

Once this information is passed between the filter and server, the filter can start doing its preprogrammed task and generate output.

Moving On

In this chapter, which concludes Part II, you've seen how ActiveX technology is available to a new generation of Windows-based Web servers and what it can accomplish. Part III, "Developing ActiveX Controls," contains chapters that deal with the more technical aspects of creating ActiveX controls yourself. Chapter 12, "Controlling the Internet Information Server Through ActiveX ISAPI Filters," builds extensively on the material found in this chapter.

Developing ActiveX Controls

CHAPTER 9

ActiveX Controls and VBScript

by John J. Kottler

Welcome to the interactive world of the Internet. In the past, Web pages were composed of static documents and pictures, then sites moved from static, non-changing documents to those generated dynamically by Common Gateway Interface (CGI) scripts on Internet servers. Current Web sites not only offer the ability to find information you're searching for, but also elegant ways to interact with the site. For instance, many sites feature searching capabilities that allow you to enter criteria to use when searching for information. The server takes this criteria, passes it to an appropriate program that performs the search, then returns the results to be displayed within your Web browser. Another good example is the use of Web sites that can be customized, where you can specify what information you're interested in just once; when you revisit that site, only relevant information is displayed, based on your initial choices of interest. A good example of a site that can be customized is MSN, the Microsoft Network, at www.msn.com.

Although much more interesting results can be generated dynamically by CGI scripts and forms, the Web still lacks an interactive edge. CGI scripts provide a mechanism for a Web client to communicate with a Web server; however, the connection is usually quite slow. This certainly doesn't allow for truly interactive applications. To create highly responsive Web pages, the interactive piece must be executed on the client's machine, where it will be most efficient.

Most Web sites today don't offer you true interaction. Rarely do you see something as interactive as a game on a Web site. However, this too is changing. The World Wide Web is rapidly evolving from static information to dynamic information to *interactive* information. Developments like Sun's Java (www.javasoft.com) and Macromedia's Shockwave (www.macromedia.com) have brought truly interactive applications to the pages of the Web. With these types of applications, it's possible to create multimedia presentations, Windows-type applications, and even games.

As you have already seen throughout this book, Microsoft's ActiveX technology (www.microsoft.com) also allows you to create truly interactive Web pages. By using ActiveX, you can insert rich data objects onto your Web pages to enhance interaction with the user, and Web page developers can create applications similar to those you find for the Windows operating system. For the developer, ActiveX simulates a development environment much like Visual Basic's. In fact, the OCX controls in Visual Basic's tool palette can be used equally as well on an Internet Web page as an ActiveX control can. To enhance the development abilities of Web pages further, Internet Explorer 3.0 even supports VBScript—a language based on Visual Basic's popular language.

Note: Although many development tools and languages allow you to use ActiveX controls, not all currently let you *create* ActiveX controls. The actual controls themselves are commonly developed by using tools such as Microsoft's Visual C++. In the future, you can expect to see other development tools begin to incorporate the ability to create ActiveX controls as well.

Why a Scripting Language?

So if ActiveX allows you to create interactive Web pages, why do you need a scripting language in the first place? If you're familiar with development tools such as Visual C++, Delphi, or especially Visual Basic, you can easily see the importance of a development language. When you create an application using any of these development tools, the application consists of two distinct pieces. The first piece is the set of controls available in the application's window. For instance, if you were creating an entry form for a database system, you would place a button to save the information entered on the form, text boxes that allow input for the database, and possibly additional controls, such as radio buttons or checkboxes. Figure 9.1 demonstrates a simple form generated with Visual Basic that could be used in a database application. However, if you merely created the window with these controls and ran the application, nothing would happen. The components are there, but they don't know what they should do.

Figure 9.1.
Developing Windows applications consists of two pieces: instructions for the computer and interactive components, such as those on this entry screen.

The second piece of the application is the *logic* that controls the application—the commands that tell each control what to do. For example, when a user clicks a Save button on a database form, the information on the form should be saved in the database. The actual *script* associated with clicking the button instructs the computer to perform some validations on the data entered, establish connectivity with a database, and translate and write the information from the form into the database. In a sense, the scripting language is the "glue" that keeps the Web page, and its controls, together.

In actuality, Web pages that you view on your computer are downloaded from a Web server to your computer. These pages are then interpreted by a Web browser on your computer to paint the screen appropriately. Since scripts written in a scripting language help define a Web page's characteristics, they are handled by the Web browser as well. This is often referred to as *client-side scripting*, since the instructions invoked by the scripts are processed locally on the client's computer.

Another advantage to scripting languages in a Web browser like Internet Explorer is that they allow specific tasks or calculations to be performed locally on the client machine, instead of constantly relying on the server. For instance, when creating an order form for products on a Web site, typically you would be required to submit the quantities of each product you would like to order to the server. The server, in turn, would make sure your entries were acceptable, calculate subtotals, tax, and grand totals, and return the results. With client-side scripting, the validation process and calculations could be performed locally on your computer, allowing error or calculation results to occur immediately instead of being routed first through the Internet. This is particularly useful when you're using Web pages with slow connections.

VBScript

VBScript is Microsoft's language that glues components together on a Web page. The language is based on Microsoft's popular development tool: Visual Basic. The language used for creating Visual Basic applications is based on BASIC (Beginners All-purpose Symbolic Instruction Code). This language is simple to use, which is partly the reason for its popularity, yet is powerful enough to produce complex applications. VBScript is a slightly modified version of the Visual Basic language, developed particularly for use in Internet Web pages.

VBScript enables developers to create Web pages with ActiveX controls that allow you to actually *do* something. The language allows instructions to be performed when certain actions are made by the user or performs other programming tasks, such as mathematical calculations. For instance, in the database example used previously, you could re-create this entry screen for the Web, as shown in Figure 9.2.

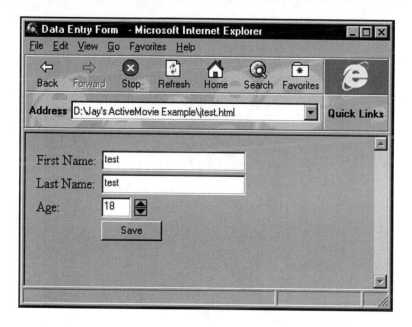

Figure 9.2.
A similar entry form as the one in Figure 9.1, but designed as a form for the Web. In this case, an ActiveX spin-button control was used for the Age field.

In this case, VBScript code is added to the Web page so that when a user clicks on the Save button, appropriate validations are made and errors are reported before posting the data to a database on the Internet Web server. With VBScript, it's possible to check all information entered locally on a client's computer before it's submitted to the server. Therefore, the results can be shown immediately, rather than sent first to the server for processing and then returned. This is a crucial step toward making Web pages interactive. You cannot have a truly interactive application if it requires 30 seconds just to process form data as it's routed through the Internet.

> Note: Although this chapter discusses using ActiveX and concentrates particularly on VBScript, it's important to realize there are additional languages available for scripting within a Web page. For instance, Netscape Navigator uses the JavaScript language, which is supported by Internet Explorer 3.0; however, Navigator doesn't currently support VBScript. Eventually these browsers, as well as others, will both support scripting languages and allow

developers to use them interchangeably within a Web page. This will prove beneficial for developers who want to reuse functions written in one language or another without having to translate the original function to another scripting language.

Embedding ActiveX Objects on a Web Page

Now that you have an understanding of what ActiveX controls are and how they can be used with scripting languages provided by the Internet Web browsers, you can examine the process of creating original Web pages by using ActiveX controls. If you're familiar with quick application development tools such as Visual Basic or Delphi, then you'll recall that adding controls to an application you develop is quite simple. With these tools, you simply choose the control from a tool palette and place it in your application's window. Unfortunately, embedding ActiveX controls requires a little more work if you're creating Web pages without the help of an authoring tool, such as Macromedia's Backstage (www.macromedia.com) or Microsoft's ActiveX Control Pad (www.microsoft.com).

ActiveX controls are used with Web pages and controlled by scripting languages found on the client side of the Internet. That is, ActiveX controls are maintained by the Web browser on your computer, not by a server. For these controls to be recognized by your computer system, they must be properly *registered* in the system registry. A system registry is available in both the NT and Windows 95 operating systems. This registry is actually a database filled with settings the operating system needs to function properly. The type of video hardware your computer uses or what applications are associated with data files are examples of information that may be stored in the registry. Many other applications may also register appropriate information for their functionality. Therefore, the registry contains information on all the ActiveX controls available to the system.

The <OBJECT> Tag

To embed an ActiveX control in a Web browser that will be displayed using the Internet Explorer browser, there are several steps required. First, you must use the <OBJECT> HTML tag. This tag indicates to the browser that an ActiveX object will be inserted at the point in the HTML where the tag appears. In addition to the <OBJECT> tag, there is a closing </OBJECT> tag. Between these tags, you can specify additional attributes for the object you're inserting onto a Web page.

The <OBJECT> tag can expect several attributes:

```
<OBJECT
    classid=ActiveX Class ID
    id=Object Name on Page
    width=Width of Object in Pixels
    height=Height of Object in Pixels
    data=URL for data for ActiveX object
    type=Internet MIME Type for the data
    standby=Text to display while object and data are loaded
    server=URL to Obtain Control

>
```

ClassID

Each ActiveX control is identified in the operating system by its unique identification number. This unique numbering scheme is also used to register OLE objects, such as Word documents or Excel spreadsheets. This unique number, referred to as a GUID (Globally Unique ID), is guaranteed to be different for every registered OLE/ActiveX control. Yet that ID is the same used to identify an ActiveX control on any other machine. For instance, the GUID for Microsoft's Internet Explorer is: {0002DF01-0000-0000-C000-000000000046}. This same number identifies Internet Explorer in either your computer's registry or another user's. Yet this number is entirely different from any other GUID in the registry for any other application.

So how do you find this obscure number? Unfortunately, this isn't a simple task when adding objects manually. Say you wanted to insert a Visual Basic control such as a spin-button control on your Web page. (See Figure 9.2.) The spin-button allows you to change the value of the Age field by clicking the up-arrow or down-arrow buttons. It's possible to use all of Visual Basic 4.0's controls because they are OLE (ActiveX) controls registered in the system registry.

Embedding a control requires the following steps:

1. Run the Registry Editor application.
2. Find the control you want to embed on a Web page.
3. Copy that control's GUID to the Clipboard.
4. Use the <OBJECT> tag with the appropriate GUID.

You can run the Registry Editor application by launching the regedit.exe application, often found in your Windows 95 or NT directory. This application, shown in Figure 9.3, lists registry entries in the window's left pane and displays appropriate settings for each entry in the right pane.

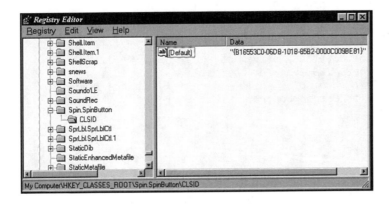

Figure 9.3.
An example of the Windows 95 System Registry.

OLE and ActiveX objects registered in the operating system appear in the My Computer\HKEY_CLASSES_ROOT\ directory of the registry. You can either browse through the registered components or search for a component by name. In either case, once you've found the item you want to embed on a Web page, double-click it to reveal details about the item. If the item is an OLE/ActiveX object, a CLSID (short for class ID) entry is available within the registry for that object. Clicking once on the CLSID entry reveals its default value in the right pane, which is the unique ID (GUID) for the ActiveX/OLE control.

> Tip: As you can see, GUIDs are quite long. You could write this number down and re-enter it in your HTML editor, but because of its cryptic nature, you are bound to make a mistake translating the number. Instead, copy the value into the Windows Clipboard. If you double-click the (Default) value found in the right pane, an Edit String dialog box will appear. This second window displays the name of the value you're editing as well as its data. In this case, the GUID is the value data. The data is automatically highlighted, so all you need to do is press Ctrl+Ins to copy the string to the Clipboard. When you're ready to insert the GUID elsewhere, simply paste the results from the Clipboard.
>
> Be careful *not* to change the GUID by accident. Changing or erasing the GUID will render the ActiveX/OLE control useless.

To complete the process, use the <OBJECT> tag for your Web page, specifying the class ID for the Web object with the GUID you copied to the Clipboard. Listing 9.1 shows the final result of the <OBJECT> tag to embed a Visual Basic spin-button control on a Web page.

Listing 9.1. The <OBJECT> tag can be used to insert ActiveX controls, such as a spin-button.

```
<OBJECT
    classid="clsid:B16553C0-06DB-101B-85B2-0000C009BE81"
    id=Spin_Button
    width=31
    height=35
    hspace=20
    vspace=0
>
</OBJECT>
```

What's in a Name?

The second attribute of the <OBJECT> tag is nearly as important as specifying the ID of the object to embed on a Web page. The id attribute is important for identifying an embedded Web page object using scripting languages, such as VBScript. Computers have no problem using the GUID to identify objects on a Web page, but chances are you might; you'd probably prefer using more easily distinguished IDs, such as names. The id attribute allows you to assign a name to the object. For instance, in the example of the spin-button shown in Listing 9.1, Spin_Button was the name given to the control.

It's possible to embed more than one control of the same type at a time on a Web page. Under such circumstances, it becomes even more necessary to name controls. As you'll recall, an ActiveX/OLE control always uses the same GUID to identify itself. Therefore, if you're placing more than one control of the same type on a Web page, both those controls will have the same GUID. To differentiate between multiple controls, each must be assigned a unique name so they can be identified later by program code.

Data and Types

ActiveX controls may expect explicit files for their data as part of the <OBJECT> tag; a control's filename can be specified by using the data attribute of the <OBJECT> tag. This attribute simply holds the URL, which can be used for retrieving a data file from the Internet.

If you are familiar with MIME (Multipurpose Internet Mail Extensions), then you will quickly recognize the value of the type attribute for the <OBJECT> tag. Each data file transferred from the Internet to a Web browser is registered as a particular type of data. Most often it is "text/html" data, which is readily displayed in the browser. However, you can expand these data types and supply ActiveX controls that can display the resulting data within the Web browser. For instance, video/x-msvideo is a valid data type for Microsoft Video for Windows files (.AVI), and audio/x-wav is suitable for digital audio files (.WAV).

These two attributes are used together to transfer data from the Internet and display it appropriately within the Web browser:

```
<OBJECT data=skiing.avi
        type="application/avi">
</OBJECT>
```

The Missing Link

As ActiveX controls are developed, people accessing a Web page can't be expected to have every type of control registered and installed on their computer system. Fortunately, Microsoft has considered this possibility, so the <OBJECT> tag provides an address specifying where ActiveX controls can be found on the Internet. Therefore, if an <OBJECT> tag specifies using an ActiveX control that isn't in the system registry, the server attribute tells the browser where it can retrieve that ActiveX control.

Specifying Object Parameters

You probably noticed that the <OBJECT> tag requires a closing </OBJECT>. Yet until now, there has been no additional HTML information between these tags. Any typical HTML information between these two tags is ignored by browsers that support the <OBJECT> tag. However, there is one type of HTML tag that's accepted between these two: the <PARAM> tag.

Most ActiveX controls you place on a Web page have attributes you can modify, often referred to as the control's *properties*. These properties may be set by VBScript, as you will see shortly, or by using the <PARAM> tag. An example of a property that can be set for the spin-button control covered in this chapter is its background color. For this example, make the background color white.

The <PARAM> tag accepts two parameters:

```
<PARAM NAME=Name of property to change
       VALUE=Value to set property to
>
```

Therefore, to set the background color of the spin-button control to white, you would use the <PARAM> tag in Listing 9.2 to set the backcolor of the spin-button:

Listing 9.2. The <PARAM> tag allows you to set properties of an object.

```
<OBJECT
    classid="clsid:B16553C0-06DB-101B-85B2-0000C009BE81"
    id=SpinButton
    width=15
    height=19
    hspace=0
    vspace=0
>
<PARAM NAME="backcolor"
       VALUE="16777215"
>

If you had ActiveX, you'd see a spin-button control.

</OBJECT>
```

Note: Determining the decimal value for colors can be an arduous process; this is the formula:

`color_value = red + (256 * green) + (65536 * blue)`, where the values for red, green, and blue range between 0 and 255.

You can also find these values using the RGB function in Visual Basic or, more simply, by using the Web Helper application included on the CD-ROM with this book.

Tip: To determine the properties, methods, or events for an ActiveX object, you must have adequate documentation for that object. If you use Visual Basic 4.0, you can test ActiveX controls and experiment with their properties, events, and methods in that environment. For instance, you can easily examine the properties available in an ActiveX control by viewing the Properties window for that control in Visual Basic.

Typical HTML text and graphics may be ignored between the <OBJECT> tags under ActiveX-aware Web browsers, but that same information will be displayed by browsers that don't support the <OBJECT> extension. Therefore, you can substitute standard text or graphics between the <OBJECT> tags that inform the user of a non-ActiveX Web browser that an ActiveX control exists on the page. Listing 9.2 contains text that's displayed only on browsers that aren't ActiveX enabled.

Control Pad

As you can see, the process of manually embedding ActiveX controls on a Web page is quite tedious. To make this easier for Web developers, many third-party companies are creating authoring tools that support embedding ActiveX controls. Microsoft also offers a utility called ActiveX Control Pad. With Control Pad, you can insert an ActiveX control into your HTML by selecting the control from a list, sizing the control graphically, then setting the properties in a dedicated window. The <OBJECT> tag and all related settings are then automatically generated and inserted into your HTML. This software is available for download at Microsoft's Web site (www.microsoft.com).

When you first start the ActiveX Control Pad, you are greeted with a skeletal HTML file in an editor interface. The essential tags for every HTML page are automatically generated in the editor's file. To insert an ActiveX control, simply choose Insert ActiveX Control... from the Edit menu. A list of all valid ActiveX controls registered on your system are then displayed. You can simply double-click on any control to embed that control within your Web page. For example, you might embed the Microsoft Forms 2.0 TextBox, which creates a standard input text field in a Web page.

Once you have selected the ActiveX control to embed, the ActiveX Control Pad displays two windows: one that allows you to graphically specify the size of the control you're embedding and a second that lists all the properties that may be set for that control. Figure 9.4 shows these windows as they appear for the Microsoft Forms 2.0 TextBox control.

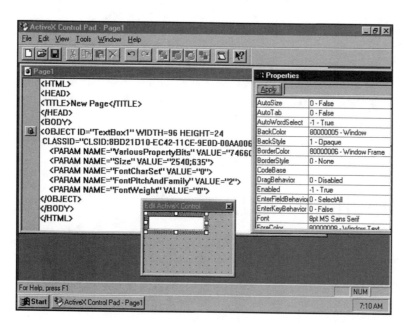

Figure 9.4.
The ActiveX Control Pad program allows you to easily specify the properties of ActiveX controls embedded on a Web page.

To see the results in HTML format, simply close these properties windows, and the HTML will be generated automatically and placed into the source code displayed in the ActiveX Control Pad.

> Tip: Make sure you have positioned your text cursor at the location in your HTML source where you want to embed an ActiveX control before actually inserting the control. The HTML <OBJECT> tag for the control is inserted in the source code at whatever position your text cursor was at last. You should make sure this cursor is waiting on a new line so that the <OBJECT> tag will not disrupt the rest of the HTML source.

Later, if you decide to change properties for an ActiveX control once it has been placed in your HTML code, you can simply click the button with a blue cube that appears next to the <OBJECT> tag for that control. The property window is then displayed for you to make changes.

The ActiveX Control Pad offers an easy solution for embedding ActiveX controls on a Web page. It also features a wizard for writing VBScript as well as a tool for creating HTML layouts. Chances are you'll use the ActiveX Control Pad to embed controls on your Web pages in the future because of its ease of use. However, it's also important to understand each of the tags used for embedding controls in an HTML document.

Introduction to VBScript

Now that you have a familiarity with ActiveX controls and embedding them within your Web pages, it's time to learn how to work with these controls through programming. This requires a scripting language—in this case, VBScript.

VBScript is a language for the Web browser based on the Visual Basic development language. Some of the fundamentals of VBScript development are covered in this chapter; however, a complete review of the language in detail is far beyond the scope of this book. Instead, if you're interested in detailed information about VBScript, visit Microsoft's VBScript site (www.microsoft.com/vbscript). You can also get additional information about the Visual Basic development language from several books, such as *Teach Yourself VBScript in*

21 Days, published by Sams.net Publishing, and *Teach Yourself Visual Basic 4 in 21 Days, Third Edition*, published by Sams Publishing.

Adding Script to HTML

Since VBScript functions on the client computer, the script commands must be transferred to the client computer. Therefore, VBScript, like other scripting languages for Web browsers, can be found embedded in the HTML documents that make a Web page.

To insert VBScript functionality in an HTML document, use the `<SCRIPT>` and `</SCRIPT>` tags. Like the `<OBJECT>` tags, anything between the `<SCRIPT>` tags is considered commands for a scripting language. This is the basic use of the `<SCRIPT>` tags:

```
<SCRIPT LANGUAGE="VBS">
    ...
    VBScript language commands
    ...
</SCRIPT>
```

You might have noticed that the `<SCRIPT>` tag accepts a `language` attribute. To allow multiple scripting languages within a single browser, you can specify what scripting language is found between the `<SCRIPT>` tags. This will allow developers to create programs using either JavaScript, VBScript, or both interchangeably within the same Web page.

> Note: Scripting language instructions should appear near the beginning of HTML files. ActiveX controls can trigger VBScript that exists anywhere within a Web page. HTML form controls that trigger VBScript must find the VBScript before the actual HTML form in the file.

VBScript Features

VBScript is a programming language, so it can accomplish almost any task. You can easily create complex formulas with conditional logic. You can also link controls on a form to perform particular actions when invoked. VBScript code consists of calculations performed in a logical order.

The power of a programming language lies in its ability to execute different tasks or functions depending on particular criteria. VBScript supports *conditional logic*, the ability to test criteria and perform actions based on whether a condition is true or false. VBScript also supports the concept of *loops*. Certain programming functions may require several iterations to build a result, so you can specify sections of VBScript code that should be executed several times (looped). These loops may be stopped after a set number of iterations, or conditionally when test criteria are met.

If, Then, Or Else

The If statement in VBScript is one method of testing whether criteria have been met in the application. When programming VBScript, it's important to realize that you must explicitly indicate which sections of the code are to be executed. For example, when using conditional logic, you must make clear which sections of VBScript code are executed when a condition is true or false.

Typical If...Then statements take on the following structure:

```
If condition then
    ... VBScript to execute when result is true
Else
    ... VBScript to execute when result is false
EndIf
```

Conditional tests could be as simple as if color="red", or if age>21, or they may be complex algorithms. In the structure of this If...Then statement, all VBScript that falls between the If line and the else line executes when the result of the condition is true. Likewise, all code between the Else and Endif lines executes when the result is false.

Loop-de-Loop

Programming tasks that execute more than once in a row can be done through looping statements. Like If statements, looping statements require definitive starting and ending points that indicate what sections of the VBScript code are executed more than once.

Loops are typically accomplished using either the For...Next statements:

```
For index = starting value to ending value
    ... VBScript to execute multiple times
Next
```

or with `While...Wend` statements:

```
While true condition
    ... VBScript to execute multiple times
Wend
```

In the `For...Next` scenario, you specify definite starting and ending values. The *index* of the `For` loop increments, starting from the *starting value* for the loop, and stops incrementing when it reaches the *ending value*. Each time the *index* advances, the VBScript code within the `For` and `Next` statements is executed.

`While...Wend` loops iterate continuously until a particular condition is met. In a sense, the `While` portion of the loop acts similarly to an `If` condition. Once the condition evaluates as being true, the looping process is stopped.

> **Note:** Be careful to avoid "infinite" loops, which are loops that never terminate. Infinite loops may cause your operating system to slow to a crawl or cause the Web browser to halt entirely. Make certain that any loops you create have realistic endpoints that can be met.

Same Old Routine

So far, you have seen how VBScript specifies blocks of code used within conditional logic statements as well as looping statements. Another method for grouping VBScript code together is using *subroutines*. Typically, subroutines have fragments of code that are reused routinely throughout an application. For instance, if you consistently use 10 lines of VBScript to format a text string, you could bundle those lines of code together in a subroutine. Then, at each instance in your application that requires this subroutine, you simply type one line of code that executes the subroutine, not the entire 10 lines.

This makes programming not only easier and faster, but also more accurate. By using subroutines for common tasks, an application is easier to maintain because changes need to be updated in only one subroutine instead of in the countless places duplicate code would appear otherwise.

Subroutines are even more productive because they accept *parameters* of their own. It's quite possible to pass a value to be processed to a subroutine, which makes subroutines more generic for use with different data in an application.

For example, in a subroutine that accepts two numbers, adds them together, and displays a message box with the result, the two numbers passed as parameters to the subroutine could be any two numbers.

VBScript defines functions by using the following syntax:

```
Sub name of subroutine(parameter1, parameter2, ...)
    ... VBScript within subroutine
End Sub
```

Like ActiveX controls, the name of the subroutine allows you to identify which one you would like to use elsewhere in your application.

What's Your Function?

Functions are very similar to subroutines; they group a series of VBScript commands together for easy reusability and also accept input parameters, as needed. The difference is that functions not only accept parameters, they also return a result.

The following defines a function:

```
Function name of function(parameter1, parameter2, ...)
    ... VBScript within subroutine
    name_of_function=result of VBScript
End Function
```

Since functions return values, they usually return the results after appropriate processing has finished to create that result. To return values from functions, you *must* set the name of the function to the end result value. For instance, Listing 9.3 demonstrates a function that subtracts a given number of years (passed as a parameter to the function) from the current year.

Listing 9.3. Functions written with VBScript can return results for other sections of an application.

```
function CalculateBirthYear(UsersAge)
    ThisYear=right(date,2)
    CalculateBirthYear=ThisYear-UsersAge
end function
```

VBScript and HTML Forms

Although ActiveX is a powerful mechanism for creating interactive Web pages, there was a time when an interactive Web page consisted merely of HTML forms. HTML forms, however, aren't in danger of extinction. Rather, client-side scripting languages, such as VBScript, will complement HTML forms to make them more useful.

This section introduces you briefly to key concepts involved in connecting HTML form objects with client-side scripting languages. Complete coverage of this topic would clearly extend beyond this book's original intent, so for additional reading on client-side scripting languages, consider reading *Teach Yourself JavaScript in a Week*, published by Sams.net Publishing.

The Main Event

VBScript, like other scripting languages such as JavaScript, allows you to attach program code to your objects on an HTML form. The code you write using VBScript is executed, depending on an *event* that a control on an HTML form triggers. Table 9.1 lists a sampling of common events found in scripting languages such as JavaScript and VBScript.

Table 9.1. Several events may be processed for an object in a scripting language like VBScript.

Events	Description	Applies To
`onFocus`	Code to be executed when an object is activated.	Text Fields
	Typically, activation is either through clicking on or tabbing to an object.	Text Areas Selections
`onBlur`	The opposite of `onFocus`, `onBlur` code will be executed when you click on an object other than the current object or tab off the current object.	Text Fields Text Areas Selections
`onSelect`	When you highlight text in a entry field, the `onSelect` code will be executed for that object.	Text Fields Text Areas

continues

Table 9.1. continued

Events	Description	Applies To
onChange	Code for onChange events is executed when the value of a field has been changed.	Text Fields Text Areas
onClick	When you click on an object, the scripting code for that object's onClick event is executed.	Buttons Radio Buttons Check Boxes Submit Buttons Reset Buttons
onSubmit	If you wish to execute scripting code when the Submit button has been clicked, you can use the onSubmit event.	Form Submission

Events are simply actions that can be triggered by an object on a form. For instance, button objects contain a "click" event, meaning that when a user clicks the mouse on a button object on a form, the action notifies VBScript. VBScript, in turn, can take that information and attach code to the event. In this way, program code can be executed when a button is clicked on a form.

Assigning Events in HTML

To properly use events in VBScript, you must assign the events to be used with each object on the HTML form, which also indicates what VBScript subroutine to execute when the event is triggered. Events can be associated to the input object created on a form by using HTML's <INPUT> tag.

As you will recall, the <INPUT> tag instructs Web browsers to create input controls for a form in HTML. It also specifies specific properties for the type of control being created. For instance, you can specify the width of an entry field to limit the length of input. Similarly, you can assign events to input objects and describe the actions to perform when the event is triggered.

The <INPUT> tag allows you to place text entry boxes, as well as checkboxes or radio buttons, on an HTML form. Each of these objects, when given a name on your HTML form, can then be referenced with VBScript. To specify what type of control to use on a form, the TYPE property of the <INPUT> tag can be set to text, checkbox, or radio. You can learn more about the <INPUT> tag by consulting other books, such as *Teach Yourself Web Publishing with HTML in 14 Days, Professional Reference Edition*, and *HTML and CGI Unleashed*, both published by Sams.net Publishing.

Listing 9.4 demonstrates the use of the onBlur event for an entry field.

Listing 9.4. Events can be triggered for input objects on HTML forms.

```
<INPUT   NAME=FName
         TYPE="text"
         SIZE=20
         onBlur="CheckFName()"
>
```

In this example, when a user presses the Tab key to move out of the First Name field while entering information, the onBlur event is triggered and the CheckFName subroutine is executed before the input cursor leaves the field.

Tip: Although you can write program code within the event assignments for the <INPUT> tag, you should call subroutines or functions to accomplish the task instead. Otherwise, maintaining the script's code and the object's attributes within the tags may become confusing.

Form Control Properties

Often, you want to be able to retrieve information from particular objects on an HTML form. For example, when a user clicks a Save button, that button's onClick event triggers a subroutine to be executed. The script in that subroutine could then read values from the entry fields the user keyed in and verify that they aren't empty and they follow correct formatting. To do this, the script in the subroutine must be able to retrieve information (and possibly update) in the entry fields.

Previously, in Listing 9.4, you learned how to attach events to input objects on HTML forms. In this example, the CheckFName subroutine is called when focus is removed from the First Name entry field. For CheckFName to verify that the First Name field is not empty, it must be able to retrieve the value for that field.

Listing 9.5 demonstrates how to retrieve information from a field and check whether it's blank. In this example, if the field is blank, a warning message is displayed. The form in this example was created by using a <FORM> tag named MyForm.

Listing 9.5. Simple field input verification can be done by using client-side scripting.

```
sub CheckFName()
    if document.MyForm.FName.value="" then
        Alert("You need to enter your first name.")
    endif
end sub
```

To access the value of a field, you must use its value property. However, to properly access this property, you must explicitly qualify the control, so you must include any relationships the control has with the Web page. In this case, the field FName is part of the MyForm form, which is part of the Web page document. MyForm and FName are components created by the HTML source code, but document is a reserved word in VBScript, indicating the current Web page document. It's important to specify that you are working with controls on a document, since you can also indicate controls in other objects, such as the browser's history list or ActiveX controls.

VBScript and ActiveX Controls

Just as you can assign and receive information about properties for form controls, you can perform the same task with ActiveX controls. In a sense, you could think of ActiveX controls as extensions to HTML input objects. ActiveX controls contain events, properties, and *methods* that you can invoke and use within a scripting environment, such as VBScript.

ActiveX Properties and Methods

Accessing ActiveX controls with VBScript is simple. When you originally embedded an ActiveX control on a page by using the <OBJECT> tag, you assigned that object a unique name to use within VBScript. Therefore, to reference an ActiveX control, you simply use that name in your VBScript code. You can use that name to reference any of that control's properties or methods.

> Note: Properties, methods, and events for ActiveX controls vary widely between controls. To effectively use an ActiveX control, you must have adequate documentation on its properties, methods, and events. You can also use other development tools, such as Visual Basic 4.0, to explore the capabilities of ActiveX controls.

Listing 9.6 demonstrates setting the foreground color of an ActiveX label control to a random color.

Listing 9.6. Properties of ActiveX controls can be easily set.

```
sub SetLabelColor
    MyLabel.forecolor = rnd() * 16777216
end sub
```

In addition to supporting properties that can be set and retrieved, ActiveX controls also support functions of their own that you can invoke. For instance, in the next chapter, "Using the `ActiveMovie` Control," you will learn more about `ActiveMovie`, an ActiveX control that enables you to control video playback on your computer. This control features several functions that control a video file; they are referred to as *methods* in ActiveX controls.

To invoke a method in an ActiveX control, use the same technique you would to access a property, but instead of using a property name, use an appropriate method. Notice however, that most methods, like functions in VBScript, accept parameters of their own; these input parameters are passed within parentheses after the name of the method. Additionally, since most methods are functions, be aware that they may return a value you can use elsewhere in your VBScript code.

Listing 9.7 demonstrates the use of an ActiveX control's method. The function `StartMovie` invokes the `run` method of the `ActiveMovie` ActiveX control. Since the `run` method is a function, it returns a value that's stored in VBScript as `result`.

Listing 9.7. Methods of ActiveX controls can be invoked by VBScript.

```
SUB StartMovie
    result = ActiveMovie.Run
END SUB
```

ActiveX and Events

So far, you've seen how VBScript code can affect ActiveX controls. However, ActiveX controls can just as easily affect VBScript. For instance, when using the spin-button mentioned earlier in this chapter, you can click the up and down arrows of the spin button. However, those actions are worthless if the VBScript cannot receive notification that you clicked the up or down arrows. The VBScript must be able to handle the event of a user clicking on the up or down arrows for the spin-button control and act appropriately.

Events that can be triggered for ActiveX controls vary, depending on the ActiveX control. Once you have found the event you want to capture from an ActiveX control, you must create a subroutine in your VBScript application that executes when the event is triggered. The name of the subroutine *must* be the ID that you assigned to the ActiveX control used in your VBScript code, followed by an underscore character, then the name of the event. For example, if a SpinButton control was placed on a Web page and given the ID "SpinButton," the following code lines would illustrate the SpinUp event used in VBScript for this control:

```
sub SpinButton_SpinUp()
...
end sub
```

Once the event's subroutine has been created in VBScript, you may include any code to be executed for that event within its subroutine.

Listing 9.8 demonstrates two events for a spin-button control. In this example, SpinButton is the name of the ActiveX control used on the Web page as it was defined with the <OBJECT> tag. SpinDown and SpinUp are two events triggered by the SpinButton ActiveX control.

Listing 9.8. Events from ActiveX controls can be trapped and processed in VBScript.

```
sub SpinButton_SpinDown()
    age=document.MyForm.AgeField.value-1
    if age<1 then age=1
document.MyForm.AgeField.value=age
end sub

sub SpinButton_SpinUp()
    age=document.MyForm.AgeField.value+1
    if age>100 then age=100
    document.MyForm.AgeField.value=age
end sub
```

What's Next

In this chapter, you have been introduced to ActiveX technology and how to use it within Web pages. You have also learned the fundamentals of VBScript and the benefits a client-side scripting language offers, particularly when interacting with ActiveX controls. In the next chapter, "Using the ActiveMovie Control," you will get the opportunity to investigate the possibilities of a robust ActiveX control: ActiveMovie, which allows you to control video content within a Web page. In the following chapter, you will also see the source code of a Web page designed with ActiveX controls.

CHAPTER 10

Using the ActiveMovie Control

by John J. Kottler

Throughout this book, you have learned about Microsoft's ActiveX technology and seen how it can be used to move Web pages from their current, static state to a new interactive plateau. However, creating Web pages with fancier interfaces is only part of making the Web interactive. Although users can now *do* something on ActiveX-enabled Web pages, they still want to see, hear, and feel results. To date, one of the most powerful media tools available is video. With video, you have the opportunity to see and hear things never before imaginable. Just as a picture paints a thousand words, sometimes audio and video animation paint a million.

Yet anyone who has browsed the Internet through a standard dial-up connection with a modem knows that such capabilities are beyond their reach. Current technology allows you to view video or audio information, but only after you have completely downloaded the source material to your personal computer. Depending on the content and your connection rate, this can take anywhere from a minute to 30 minutes or more.

In an attempt to make video and audio look instantaneous, and therefore become more of a reality for Web pages, Microsoft has introduced a new ActiveX component: ActiveMovie. Within Internet Explorer 2.x and 3.x, it's already possible to embed Video for Window files or MIDI (Musical Instrument Digital Interface) sound files on a page. When Internet Explorer views these pages, these files are immediately downloaded and displayed within the context of a Web page, like inline graphics. However, only simple video files can be embedded, ones that aren't very long and don't require a vast amount of time to download. The `ActiveMovie` control allows you to embed video within a Web page, yet offers a higher degree of control and supports many additional technologies. ActiveMovie can be found at Microsoft's Web site: `www.microsoft.com`.

Dynamic Programming

Video for Windows has been the long-established standard for playing video content on Windows-based machines. Although it's quite suitable to use Video for Windows and its underlying Media Control Interface (MCI) today, newer video technologies and user expectations are placing higher demands on the development environment. Although Video for Windows is included with newer operating systems, such as Windows 95, ActiveMovie will soon become its replacement for many reasons:

- ActiveMovie is just what its name implies: active. It is possible to control attributes of the video content dynamically while it is playing. For example, you can adjust the video's brightness or contrast while the video is playing.

- It is CODEC (COmpressor/DECompressor) independent. This means that `ActiveMovie` controls work with digital video of any format. With ActiveMovie, you can control MPEG, QuickTime, or Video for Windows video files.

- `ActiveMovie` is an ActiveX control, so it's object-oriented. In the past, controlling Video for Windows through the Media Control Interface required knowledge of the MCI commands. As an ActiveX control, it's much easier for developers to create applications that interact with video content because it shields you from the complexities of multimedia.

■ Instead of being required to transfer an entire video file, it's possible to transmit just the beginning and have the computer begin playing it. While that portion is playing, additional data is transferred in the background to be played. This "streaming" technology is supported by ActiveX and will make using and controlling video files over low-bandwidth connections, such as modem access to the Internet, feasible. In addition, streaming content uses the same control interface in ActiveMovie that's used for standard video.

As you can see, ActiveMovie gives great value to developers. A sample application created later in this chapter demonstrates how to use the ActiveMovie ActiveX control within a Web page to display both video content and streaming video content.

Streams and Plumbing

ActiveMovie makes use of streaming technology to make video content seem to download faster than it really does. The technique of streaming data is fairly simple. When a user chooses to view video content on a Web page, the video viewer is invoked. The data for the video file then starts to download from the Internet to the local PC. An important difference is that not all the data needs to be transferred for the streaming video viewer to start. Instead, only a few seconds' worth of video is downloaded to begin the playback of the video. While that video is playing, additional video data is passed from the Internet to the local PC in the background. The end result is a video that seems to begin playing almost instantly.

Another benefit of streaming video is that the video content can be much longer, or even infinite in length. For instance, with streaming video technology, it's possible to connect to a live video feed, such as a television or cable channel, at a site. Programming for that channel can be continuous, and the stream continues to read data from the Internet as long as it's instructed, since the data is constantly fed to the video viewer on a user's PC. However, as you know from browsing the Internet and experiencing delays, this continuous stream of data can lose its continuity. Most streaming technologies provide for this situation and either appropriately notify the user or simply "skip" until the actual data is transferred.

It's also important to notice that since data is streamed into a video viewer, less disk space is required locally on a user's computer for storing digital video. Because only a few seconds of video are necessary to start playback, a small buffer is created on a local hard disk. Old information in that buffer is cleared out, and new content is replaced as the video stream plays.

The quality of the video played back on a user's machine is directly related to the speed at which that person is connected to the Internet. You can think of the connection between a local PC and the Internet as a pipe. A pipe can handle only so much water passing through it at a time. If you try forcing more water through a pipe than what it can handle, water spills out over the ends of the pipe or the pipe bursts. In the case of the Internet, if more data is streamed to a local computer than what that computer's connection can handle, the data "spills," causing gaps and pauses in content, such as video.

Video requires a large amount of information, which in turn translates to a vast amount of water to push through a pipe. Typical video content will easily "spill" when a user is connected to the Internet by a traditional 28.8Kbps modem. The only solution to avoiding spills is to increase the size of a pipe. Technologies such as ISDN and cable modems offer larger pipes for denser data like video to flow more freely.

Until these larger pipes are laid through the Internet's plumbing, however, newer technologies can adjust their content based on the size of the "pipe" between a computer and the Internet. One example of this is Microsoft's ActiveMovie Streaming Format (.ASF) files. Using an editor like ActiveMovie Stream Editor, a developer can create content that can be streamed and displayed accurately by using restricted "pipes."

ActiveMovie Stream Editor

Creating content that can be viewed using low-bandwidth connections is certainly a challenge. It's difficult to determine how much information can be passed at once over such a connection. Determining how to display the content using the least amount of the bandwidth is where the problem lies. A

28.8Kbps connection to the Internet translates as a pipe that allows information to flow through at a rate of 3600 bytes per second. In a world where small and compressed pictures are easily twice that size, full-motion video through such a pipe is difficult.

However, Microsoft's ActiveMovie Stream Editor software helps you to develop content that uses audio and an animated slide show. The trade-off is a quick connection for media content, but low-quality audio and still pictures displayed in a sequence. Not exactly as compelling as full-motion video, but almost as useful.

Creating an ActiveMovie Stream

Once you have installed the ActiveMovie Stream Editor on your computer, you can begin to create streaming content for the `ActiveMovie` control. Figure 10.1 is an example of the ActiveMovie Stream Editor window with content already added to the workspace.

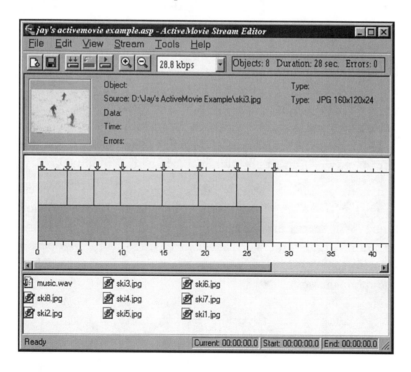

Figure 10.1.
The ActiveMovie Stream Editor makes creating streaming content for the Internet easier.

You will quickly notice that the workspace is divided into two regions: a timeline in the top half of the screen and a list of files for the project at the bottom of the screen. When you first start the ActiveMovie Stream Editor, you see a blank workspace. You must first choose the objects you want to present in the movie, then place them accordingly on the timeline.

Adding Content

Remember, an .ASF file is simply a series of still pictures presented in an orderly fashion. However, you can also add an underlying soundtrack or voice track. In either case, the audio and picture files must be added to the ActiveMovie Stream project you're creating. This ActiveMovie Stream project is then used to create an .ASF file, one of many file types supported by the `ActiveMovie` control.

To add a picture or audio file to the project, choose Add Files from the File menu or click the Add Files button on the Editor's toolbar; this opens a dialog box that prompts you to choose the audio (.WAV) or picture (.JPG/.BMP) files to add to the project. The objects you select are then added to the list at the bottom of the Editor window.

When adding digital audio content to your ActiveMovie Stream project, you must add files that are *compressed* using one of the digital audio compressors installed on your system. If you're using Windows 95 or Windows NT 4.0, these compression algorithms are included with the operating system. To convert a digital audio file (.WAV) to one of these compressed formats, you can simply use the Sound Recorder application included with Windows 95.

After you've opened the file you want to convert into the Sound Recorder, then save it using the Save As command from the File menu. When the dialog box opens asking you to specify the name of the new sound file, click the Change button at the bottom of the window to change that file's format. This opens a window, shown in Figure 10.2, where you can select a new format to use when saving the audio information.

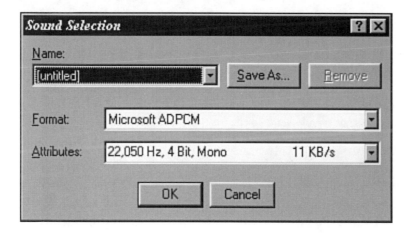

Figure 10.2.
*Audio files must be saved in a compressed format, such as ADPCM, to be used in the
ActiveMovie Stream Editor.*

Tip: The Microsoft ADPCM compressor for audio files works well with the
ActiveMovie Stream Editor. When converting sound files using the Sound
Recorder application, it doesn't matter what you choose for the file's compres-
sion attributes. When the audio file is imported into the ActiveMovie Stream
Editor, it's converted into a format suitable for playback at the bit rate you're
using for the movie.

Pictures stored in either Windows bitmap (.BMP) or JPEG (.JPG) formats may
be added to the file. To convert pictures to these formats, use a program such
as Paint Shop Pro, which is included on this book's CD-ROM. With Paint
Shop Pro, you can open a source graphic, then save it again as either a Windows bitmap or JPEG picture.

Tip: When converting pictures to use in the ActiveMovie Stream Editor,
consider changing some of the picture's qualities to reduce its final size. One
method for reducing an image's size is to save it as a JPEG file. JPEG is a
compression scheme that dramatically reduces the size of certain images. You

might also consider creating smaller pictures that use fewer pixels both in width and height because they load faster and, therefore, work better in an ActiveMovie stream.

Another method for reducing a picture's size is to reduce the number of colors it uses. Avoid using pictures that are full-color images (24-bit), or convert them to 256 color, or even lower color depths, to get smaller file sizes.

Coordinating Content

Once you have added the pictures and sound files you want to use in the ActiveMovie Stream Editor project, you can begin coordinating the sound and graphics for your presentation. This requires scheduling each picture or sound to occur at specific points in time by using the timeline window near the top of the Editor's screen.

To schedule a picture or sound file for a specific point in time, you can simply drag the source file you want to add from the list of files at the bottom of the Editor window onto the timeline. Once you have dragged the file onto the timeline, it's represented by a colored rectangle on the timeline—pictures are green; sounds are blue. In the example in Figure 10.1, a soundtrack, represented by a long rectangular bar, occupies the long bottom half of the timeline. Likewise, the pictures for the presentation are represented by the smaller rectangles just above the sound clip's rectangle.

Note that the timeline directly relates not only to the length of the final presentation, but also to the amount of information squeezed through the pipe at one time. For instance, the sound clip in this example is a little over twenty-six seconds in length, so the rectangle representing that sound in the ActiveMovie Stream file is wide enough to occupy twenty-six seconds on the timeline. Notice also that the height of this sound clip's rectangle is about half the height of the overall timeline window. The height of the timeline window represents the total *bandwidth* available for content. In this example, the ActiveMovie Stream file is created to run with a bit rate of 28.8Kbps. Therefore, the height of the timeline indicates the size of the pipe and how much information can be moved at one time. At a 28.8Kbps connection, roughly 3600 bytes can be moved per second of connect time. In this example, the audio file was compressed to use roughly 1800 bytes per second, or half the full bandwidth for the pipe.

The audio file plays constantly throughout the entire presentation, so half the pipe must be dedicated to playing the audio stream for the movie. As a result, the remaining portion of the pipe handles the pictures. In the example shown in Figure 10.1, you will notice that most of the pictures are displayed for longer than a second, according to the timeline, because the file size of these pictures is larger than the remaining size of the pipe. For example, a picture with a file size of 3600 bytes can't possibly be transferred in a single second, if only 1800 bytes are available per second in the pipe. Therefore, that image will automatically require at least two seconds to transfer; this can't be changed unless the bit rate is altered to accommodate a higher or lower bandwidth.

Pictures are displayed in the order in which they appear on the timeline. However, since some pictures need a predetermined amount of time to be transferred and displayed, it's hard to be creative when coordinating pictures with sound. You might find that to get the effect you want, you have to make much smaller pictures than you originally wanted.

Another method of reducing the amount of information passed through the pipe is to convert the files between compression formats. Often, if you drag a file from the project list at the bottom of the window onto the timeline and it requires more bandwidth than the ActiveMovie Stream can handle, the Editor will automatically prompt you to convert formats. You can also change the format used to compress data in the movie by clicking on the picture or sound file in the timeline and then selecting Convert from the Edit menu. Figures 10.3 and 10.4 illustrate the windows used for converting audio clips and pictures, respectively.

> **Tip:** Coordinating the pictures with your sound is difficult by viewing the timeline. If you want a picture to appear on a particular "hit" in the music, such as a cymbal crash, there is no way to determine where this crash is by using the timeline. Instead, you might want to try the Editor's Tap & Snap feature; it plays an audio clip and automatically advances through the pictures added to your project. However, it only advances the pictures when you tap on the "marker" button at the bottom of the window. The Editor stores the times at which you click this button and tries to synchronize the pictures with the audio in the timeline window, based on the taps you made.

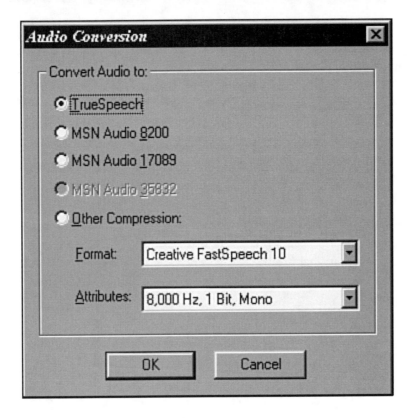

Figure 10.3.
The ActiveMovie Stream Editor software allows you to convert audio clips to use other compression formats.

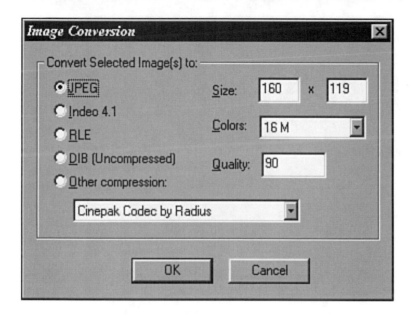

Figure 10.4.
Just as you can compress audio, you can also choose to compress pictures displayed in the
ActiveMovie Stream Editor.

Testing and Building the Movie

After you have arranged the sound and picture files on your timeline, you can
then test the final output of the movie by choosing Test from the Editor's
Stream menu. This "test" mode will simulate the speed at which pictures are
displayed as if you were connected to the movie using the bit rate you specify.
For instance, if you're creating a 28.8Kbps movie, the "test" mode displays
the pictures at the speed in which they would appear if you had connected and
streamed this movie using a modem.

Once you're satisfied with the movie's presentation, you can build the final
.ASF file. Before actually creating the file, you should first verify its properties.
To do this, select Properties from the Editor's File menu. In the window that
opens, you can set general information, such as the author who created the
file, and more detailed information, like the bit rate for displaying the file. Figure
10.5 shows this Properties dialog box.

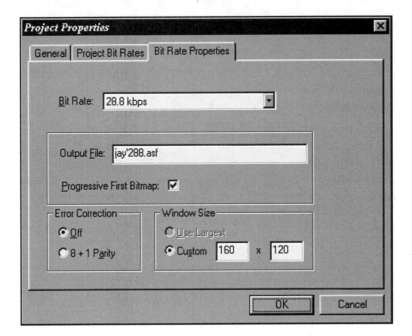

Figure 10.5.
You can set several properties for the ActiveMovie Stream before you build the final file.

After all the properties have been verified, you can create the ActiveMovie Stream file by choosing Build or Build All from the Stream menu. This final file (.ASF), as you will see shortly, can then be played by using the `ActiveMovie` ActiveX control in the context of a Web page.

ActiveMovie on the Web

Now that you have a familiarity with what `ActiveMovie` is and how to create ActiveMovie Stream files, you could include videos in your own Web pages. Since `ActiveMovie` is an ActiveX control, it can easily be embedded in a Web page and controlled through VBScript. This section explains how to embed an `ActiveMovie` control, discusses its properties, methods, and events for other programming languages, such as Visual Basic, Visual C++, and VBScript, to use, and reviews a complete example of a Web page with an `ActiveMovie` control and VBScript.

Embedding ActiveMovie on a Page

Since the ActiveMovie control is simply an ActiveX control, it can be embedded on a Web page just as any other ActiveX control can. For more information on embedding ActiveX controls in Web pages, you might want to refer to Chapter 9, "ActiveX Controls and VBScript."

To insert an ActiveMovie control, you must use the <OBJECT> tag within your HTML document for a Web page. Within that tag lies the class identifier, which indicates that the ActiveMovie ActiveX control is to be loaded. Again, as with other ActiveX controls, the class ID for the ActiveMovie control exists in your system registry. By running the Registry Editor (regedit.exe) included with Windows 95, you may find the ActiveMovie control under the following directory entry:

```
My Computer\HKEY_CLASSES_ROOT\AMOVIE.ActiveMovieCtrl\CLSID
```

The class ID for ActiveMovie may then be used in the <OBJECT> tag to create the control within the Web page. Listing 10.1 demonstrates how to embed an ActiveMovie control using the <OBJECT> tag.

Listing 10.1. The <OBJECT> **tag is used to embed an** ActiveMovie **control on a Web page.**

```
<OBJECT
    classid="clsid:{05589FA1-C356-11CE-BF01-00AA0055595A}"
    id=VideoWindow
    width=320
    height=340
    hspace=20
    vspace=0
>
<param name="filename" value="example\jay'288.asf">
<param name="ShowControls" value="false">
<param name="Balance" value="0">
</OBJECT>
```

As you can see in Listing 10.1, several parameters may be altered when the object is displayed initially on the Web page. These parameters are essentially the properties for the ActiveMovie control, and they can be easily set when the object is first loaded and easily changed through VBScript, as explained in the following section.

Controlling ActiveMovie with VBScript

Once the ActiveMovie control has been added to a Web page and given an appropriate ID to use within VBScript, that control can be easily modified or monitored through code created in VBScript for the Web page. Figure 10.6 illustrates a sample Web page containing an ActiveMovie control. In this example, there is an ActiveMovie window that displays the movie during playback, as well as three buttons to play the video, play an ActiveMovie stream, or stop the video playback altogether. In addition to these buttons, there are two sliders that control the volume and stereo balance of the audio track. These two sliders are created using VBScript and illustrate some of the dynamism of the ActiveMovie control.

Listing 10.2 is a complete listing of the HTML for this Web page, including the <OBJECT> definitions for the ActiveMovie and slider controls, as well as the VBScript needed to handle the events of sliding the sliders or clicking the buttons. You can see from the source code that several properties are set for the ActiveMovie control, as well as methods for running or stopping the media's playback.

Figure 10.6.
ActiveMovie *controls can be embedded on a Web page to create a more dynamic site.*

Listing 10.2. The Web page in Figure 10.6 requires several <OBJECT> definitions as well as VBScript routines.

```
<!--  ActiveMovie Example  -->

<HTML>
<TITLE>
ActiveMovie Example
```

continues

Listing 10.2. continued

```
</TITLE>
<BODY>

<OBJECT
    classid="clsid:{05589FA1-C356-11CE-BF01-00AA0055595A}"
    id=VideoWindow
    width=320
    height=340
    hspace=20
    vspace=0
>
<param name="filename" value="skiing.asf">
<param name="ShowControls" value="false">
<param name="Balance" value="0">
</OBJECT>

<P>
<P>
<SCRIPT LANGUAGE="VBS">
sub SetVolume(TheVolume)
    VideoWindow.Volume=(TheVolume-9)*250
end sub

sub SetBalance(TheBalance)
    VideoWindow.Balance=(TheBalance-1)*10000
end sub

sub BalanceControl_Click()
    Call SetBalance(BalanceControl.Value)
end sub

sub VolumeControl_Click()
    Call SetVolume(VolumeControl.Value)
end sub

sub PlayAVIContent()
    BalanceControl.enabled=true
    VolumeControl.enabled=true
    VideoWindow.filename="skiing.avi"
    VideoWindow.run
    Call SetBalance(BalanceControl.Value)
    Call SetVolume(VolumeControl.Value)
end sub

sub StopVideoWindow()
    VideoWindow.stop
end sub

sub PlayASFContent()
    BalanceControl.enabled=false
```

```
        VolumeControl.enabled=false
        VideoWindow.filename="skiing.asf"
        VideoWindow.run
end sub
</SCRIPT>

<FORM Name="MyForm">
<INPUT TYPE="BUTTON"
        VALUE="Play AVI Video"
        NAME="PlayAVI"
        onClick="PlayAVIContent"
>
<INPUT TYPE="BUTTON"
        VALUE="Play ActiveMovie Stream"
        NAME="PlayASF"
        onClick="PlayASFContent"
>
<INPUT TYPE="BUTTON"
        VALUE="STOP"
        NAME="StopIt"
        onClick="StopVideoWindow"
>
</FORM>

<P>Stereo Balance:<BR>
<OBJECT
    classid="clsid:{373FF7F0-EB8B-11CD-8820-08002B2F4F5A}"
    id=BalanceControl
    width=320
    height=25
    hspace=20
    vspace=0
>
<!-- Set the range for the slider from 0-2 (3 values total)
    3 values are used for: left, center and right -->
<param name="Max" value=2>
<param name="Value" value=1>
<param name="LargeChange" value=1>
<param name="Enabled" value="false">
</OBJECT>

<P>
<P>Volume:<BR>
<OBJECT
    classid="clsid:{373FF7F0-EB8B-11CD-8820-08002B2F4F5A}"
    id=VolumeControl
    width=320
    height=25
    hspace=20
    vspace=0
>
```

continues

Listing 10.2. continued

```
<!-- Set the range for the slider from 0-9 (10 values total) -->
<param name="Max" value=9>
<param name="Value" value=5>
<param name="LargeChange" value=2>
<param name="Enabled" value="false">
</OBJECT>

</BODY>
</HTML>
```

> Note: In Listing 10.2, there are many instances in which the slider controls for changing volume or stereo balance have been disabled and then enabled. In this example, the ActiveMovie video file allows you to dynamically change these properties. ActiveMovie Stream, on the other hand, does not. Therefore, to avoid any confusion and potential runtime errors, the sliders are disabled when their respective properties aren't supported. You should try to catch or avoid all errors when possible on your own Web pages.

Since the `ActiveMovie` control is an ActiveX control, it features properties, methods, and events just as other ActiveX controls do. Through these object-oriented techniques, a VBScript routine can interact with the `ActiveMovie` control.

Properties

Several properties are associated with an `ActiveMovie` control. The following list briefly describes each property and its function; they can all be either set or read by a VBScript routine.

> `AllowChangeDisplayMode`   If you want someone viewing the video to have the ability to change the display mode, set this property to TRUE. There are two modes available: by time or by frame. The ability to change the display mode is located on a context menu, as shown in Figure 10.7.

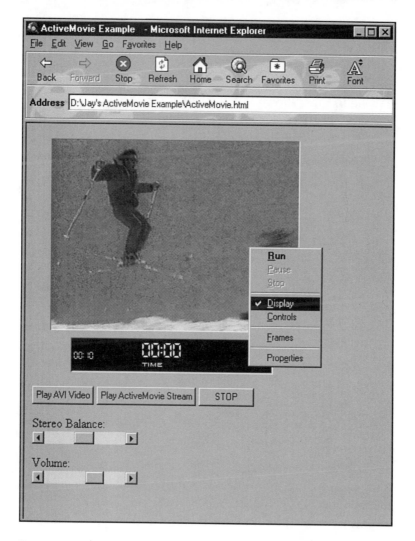

Figure 10.7.
The ActiveMovie *control supports a context menu, available by right-clicking within the control.*

AllowHideControls   Similar to `AllowChangeDisplayMode`, you can determine whether you want the user to have the ability to hide or display the VCR-like buttons at the bottom of the ActiveMovie window. Hiding or displaying the controls can be done by using a context menu like that shown in Figure 10.7.

AllowHideDisplay   This property determines whether the user playing a video file can display or hide the time display at the bottom of the ActiveMovie window. The display may be toggled on or off by using a menu choice in the context menu shown in Figure 10.7.

Author   Holds the name of the author for the video clip.

AutoRewind   If you want a video clip to automatically rewind to the starting position after it has finished playing, you can set this property to `TRUE`.

AutoStart   Once the ActiveMovie window has been displayed, the movie can automatically begin playing when this property is set to `TRUE`. Otherwise, you must start the video manually.

Balance   The stereo balance from left to right of the audio track for an ActiveMovie video can be adjusted dynamically. Values for this property range from `-10000` (far left) to `10000` (far right). A value of `0` indicates a balanced center.

Copyright   If the video clip contains copyright information, it can be extracted by using this property.

CurrentPosition   This property indicates the current position of the playback in the video stream, which depends on the mode currently used (frames or time). When this property is set with a new position, the ActiveMovie player moves to that position in the video stream.

CurrentState   This property can only be read by VBScript. It indicates the current status of the video content. The player's state may change when a routine in VBScript issues an appropriate command or when the user clicks the VCR buttons at the bottom of the ActiveMovie window. The status returned by this property may be any of the following:

  0   The video is stopped.
  1   The video is paused.
  2   The video is playing.

Description A brief description or comment can be attached to the multimedia content.

DisplayBackColor The VCR-like output for the display of the ActiveMovie window may be altered to use different colors. This property sets the background color to use for that display. Color values can be any RGB color between 0 and 16,777,215.

> Tip: To help with the selection of colors, the Web Helper application has been included on this book's CD-ROM. This application has color-conversion capability as well as a translator between degrees and radians (which is useful for the Virtual Reality Modeling Language).

DisplayForeColor Similar to the DisplayBackColor property, you can set the color to use when painting the numbers and text displayed in the VCR-like output window of the ActiveMovie control.

DisplayMode The position of the content being played may be displayed in measurements of time or frames; this property is used to change the mode. The following values are used with this property:

0 Use time for measuring position.

1 Use frames for measuring position.

Duration The overall length of the media content can be determined by reading this property. The value returned indicates the length of the content in seconds.

EnableContextMenu When a user right-clicks on the ActiveMovie control, a pop-up menu appears containing options a user can set for media playback. Setting this property to TRUE allows the user to right-click on the ActiveMovie window and display this menu. This menu is similar to the one shown in Figure 10.7.

EnablePositionControls With this property, you can determine whether users have the ability to change the current position of the video's playback. If this property is set to TRUE, then a user can "seek" to different positions in the media file; if this property is FALSE, the respective buttons are disabled in the ActiveMovie window.

EnableSelectionControls   You can establish starting and ending points for the media loaded in the ActiveMovie control. The content between these points is then referred to as the "selection." Additional selection buttons may be enabled or disabled in the ActiveMovie control to determine whether users can create selection ranges for playback. If this property is set to TRUE, then these additional buttons will be enabled. A value of FALSE will disable these buttons.

EnableTracker   Near the playback controls at the bottom of the ActiveMovie window, you may find a slider control referred to as a "tracker." This control can be enabled or disabled by setting this property to TRUE or FALSE, respectively.

EventNotification   There are several events associated with the ActiveMovie control. You can choose which of these events you want to trap in your application with this property. Each event is identified by a value. To trap multiple events, you may add those values together and set this property to the resulting value. For example, if you want to trap both keyboard and mouse clicks, you would use the value of 8+16, or 24. The following list describes valid events and their values:

eventNone	0	No events are triggered.
eventStateChange	1	Events are triggered when the state of the content changes; for example, stopping the current playback.
eventPositionChange	2	When the position updates, an event is triggered.
eventTimer	4	An event can be triggered each time a timer event occurs.
eventKeyboard	8	Pressing a key on the keyboard triggers this event.
eventMouseClick	16	When a mouse button is clicked, this event is triggered.
eventMouseMove	32	As the mouse is moved, this event is triggered.

FileName   The filename of the media content to be displayed must be supplied for playback to begin. This property contains the name of the file to load and display in the ActiveMovie window. Filenames are either video files (.AVI) or ActiveMovie Stream files (.ASF).

FilterGraph   In addition to being able to change volume and stereo balance dynamically, you can set or change other video playback attributes, such as brightness, contrast, or other special effects. These effects are established in a filter graph. If a filter graph has been designed, you may specify using it with this property.

FilterGraphDispatch   To use ActiveMovie filter graphs, you must provide a IDispatch object pointer. If you're using filter graphs, you specify this object pointer with this property.

ImageSourceHeight   Video content is created using varying resolutions for pixel height and width. This property contains the control's recorded height in pixels. This is not necessarily the same size as it is when the content is played.

ImageSourceWidth   Like ImageSourceHeight, it's possible to determine the original width for the content displayed in the ActiveMovie control.

MovieWindowSetting   As previously mentioned, you can play video content using a different height and width for the window than what it was when originally recorded. This property allows you to set the method by which the video playback will be scaled. The following are valid values for this property:

movieDefaultSize	0	Uses the size at which the video was recorded.
movieHalfSize	1	Displays the content as half the original recorded size.
movieDoubleSize	2	Displays the content as twice the original recorded size.
movieMaximizeSize	3	Displays the content using the full size of its parent's window.
movieFullScreen	4	Displays the content using the full screen.

| `moviePermitResizeWithAspect` | 5 | Allows the user to control playback size, but maintains the typical 4:3 aspect ratio. |
| `moviePermitResizeNoRestrict` | 6 | Allows the user to control playback size, ignoring aspect ratio. |

PlayCount   The multimedia content in an `ActiveMovie` control can be played repeatedly. This property establishes the number of times the content will repeat. A value of `0` for this property indicates that the content should repeat indefinitely.

Rate   The media content in an ActiveMovie window can be played faster or slower than it was originally intended by adjusting this property. A value of `1.0` indicates that playback should occur at the original recorded rate. Values higher than `1.0` indicate faster playback; values lower than `1.0` indicate slower playback. For example, a value of `2.0` instructs ActiveMovie to play the content at twice its original speed.

Rating   Multimedia content may be rated. If a particular media file is rated, this property will contain its rating.

SelectionStart/SelectionEnd   Instead of playing an entire media file from start to finish, you can set up a range for the playback. These properties indicate where the playback should start (`SelectionStart`) and stop (`SelectionEnd`). When the media content is played, only data between the start and end positions will be played.

ShowDisplay   The VCR display at the bottom of the ActiveMovie window can be displayed or hidden by setting this property to TRUE or FALSE, respectively.

ShowPositionControls   This property controls whether the position controls for seeking within a file are displayed or hidden. Setting this property's value to TRUE will display the position controls. This is similar to `EnablePositionControls`; however, this property controls whether the buttons are displayed or hidden. `EnablePositionControls` either disables or enables those buttons.

ShowSelectionControls   Like ShowPositionControls, this property determines whether the additional selection buttons should be displayed (TRUE) or hidden (FALSE).

ShowTracker   The slider at the bottom of the ActiveMovie window indicates the current position of the media playback and allows the user to seek to different positions within the file. This slider can be displayed or hidden by setting this property to TRUE or FALSE, respectively.

ShowControls   All VCR button controls at the bottom of the ActiveMovie screen can be displayed (TRUE) or hidden (FALSE) by setting this property appropriately.

Title   If the currently loaded media file has a title, it's stored as the value for this property.

Volume   As you can with balance, it's possible to adjust the volume of the media's playback dynamically. Volume values range from -10000 (minimum volume) to 0 (maximum volume).

Methods

Besides being able to read and set properties of an ActiveMovie control, there are several functions or methods that may be invoked. Unlike properties, these methods instruct the ActiveMovie control to perform a particular action instead of simply specifying or retrieving settings. The following is a list of methods available to VBScript for controlling an ActiveMovie control.

Run   This method starts the playback of a media file. If the file was stopped, then the Run method starts playing the content again from the beginning or from the beginning of the selection range. If the content is paused, the Run method will continue playback from the point at which it was paused.

Stop   This method stops the playback of a media file. When the media content is played again, it will begin at the start of the file or at the starting point for the selection range.

Pause   This method pauses the playback of a media file. It's similar to the Stop method, except when the playback is paused, it can resume from the point at which it was paused.

Events

Earlier you learned about the property that allows you to specify which events you would like to receive notification for when they occur. Your VBScript routines can then handle these events to perform specific actions. The following list describes the valid events that can be recognized by VBScript for the ActiveMovie control:

Error()   When an error occurs in the ActiveMovie control, this event can be triggered. If your VBScript contains a routine to handle this event, you can intercept errors and post your own messages or design code to act accordingly.

PositionChange()   This event is triggered when a user changes the current position of the media playback with the tracker control or seek buttons in the ActiveMovie window. It is not triggered when the CurrentPosition property is updated through VBScript.

StateChange()   When the current state of the media playback changes, this event is triggered. A state change may be the event of stopping a media file being played. The CurrentState property can be used to determine the current action of the media player.

Timer()   An event can be triggered on a regular basis as determined by the ActiveMovie control. Whenever this event occurs, a VBScript routine can be executed.

What's Next

In this chapter, you have learned about Microsoft's ActiveMovie ActiveX control and had an opportunity to learn more about using ActiveX as a video player and controlling playback of media through VBScript. You have also been introduced to the concept of streaming media content, particularly designed for low-bandwidth connections, such as those used for Internet access through a modem. A complete review of the ActiveMovie control interface would clearly extend beyond the scope of this chapter and certainly this book. However, you should now be at least acquainted with the technology and able to use ActiveMovie controls on your own Web pages.

In the next chapters, you will have the opportunity to learn about connecting Web pages with databases on a Web server (Chapters 12 and 13) and how to create an original ActiveX control that can be placed on a Web page (Chapter 11).

ActiveX DocObjects and Internet Explorer: Making Your Application Internet and Intranet Aware

by Daniel F. Wygant

Imagine editing a Microsoft Word document by selecting a hyperlink displayed by Internet Explorer. After clicking on a hyperlink to a Microsoft Word document, the document is displayed in Internet Explorer's window. The Word menus and toolbars are displayed along with those from Internet Explorer, as shown in Figure 11.1.

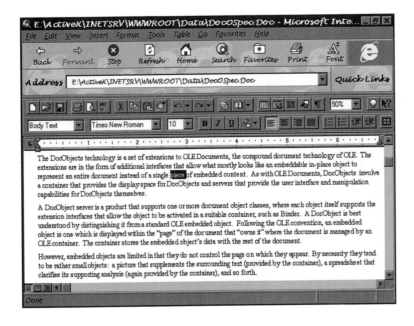

Figure 11.1.
Editing a Word document in Internet Explorer.

This is known as visual editing; Word becomes activated in Internet Explorer's window. The editing functions of both applications (Word and Internet Explorer) are coexisting on the Internet completely intact.

You can benefit greatly from this type of "online" document management and editing. It gives you a much greater maintenance capability, which doesn't exist for most file formats. The problem of distributing your documentation is also alleviated merely by putting the documents on the Web.

Tip: To try this on your own, you need Office95 and Internet Explorer 3.0. You can get the beta version of Internet Explorer 3.0 directly from Microsoft's Web site (`http://www.microsoft.com/ie` `The Internet Explorer Home Page`).

DocObject Technology

ActiveX DocObjects offer this new and powerful capability. They are intended for use in both Internet Explorer 3.0 and in the Office95 Binder for visually editing various file formats. The ActiveX DocObject technology uses a modified menu-sharing technique that more closely resembles the data's own standalone native editing application.

This chapter discusses how businesses can benefit from DocObject technology and gives a broader understanding of what the DocObject interfaces are. A sample DocObject OLE server, with source code, is presented to illustrate how this new ActiveX technology works. The chapter winds up by discussing ways ActiveX DocObject OLE servers could be used.

> Note: The source code for all this chapter's examples can be found on this book's CD-ROM.

Using this technology allows you to manage your company's documentation through the Internet. This is illustrated in Figure 11.2, which shows many users accessing documents over the network.

Editing a Word document in Internet Explorer

Figure 11.2.
Users accessing documents on a central HTTP server; the menus and toolbars for both Word and Internet Explorer are displayed.

ActiveX and Business

Most businesses maintain a lot of documentation in a variety of formats. The cost of maintaining, updating, and distributing this information can be astronomical. The Binder delivered with Office95 gives you a way to organize your documents into a sort of three-ring binder, as the name implies. Like the Internet Explorer, the Binder allows you to visually edit documents that are associated with DocObject-enabled applications. The ActiveX DocObject technology, both for Office95's Binder and Internet Explorer, offers some solutions to these problems. In addition, it paves the way for better online publishing techniques that haven't been available in the past.

By using DocObjects, a business can develop better viewing *and* editing applications for its various data formats. They will be better because DocObjects work in the context of the binder they're embedded in. As an added bonus to your business, Internet Explorer understands how to use DocObjects. That is, all DocObject applications display in the context of their binder complete with their usual menus—in this case, Internet Explorer.

For example, your business could give users of their data and documents a DocObject server. Some users, such as the author or maintenance person, could be given either write access to the document or an editing-enabled DocObject application. Other users of the information might be allowed only view access to it or given a viewing-only DocObject application.

In either case, all your business information can be made more accessible through HTML pages with hyperlink references to the data files. When the hyperlinks are activated, the DocObject application for that data format will activate inside the browser. All the data format's application menus will be merged with Internet Explorer's menus.

> **Note:** At present, only Internet Explorer has integrated ActiveX DocObject technology. However, Microsoft has agreed to provide an ActiveX plug-in for Netscape's browser in the near future. Other applications for DocObjects will undoubtedly soon follow.

The visual editing capabilities of ActiveX DocObject technology provides users with a consistent desktop, even while surfing the Internet. The familiar menus users are already comfortable with are displayed in the context of Internet Explorer's window, requiring less training time and encouraging higher productivity, something all businesses must be concerned with.

Another advantage of the DocObject's visual editing is that the documents can be stored in a central location. Your business could put all its documents on a central HTTP server, with massive data storage for speed, reliability, and centralized security. All users and maintenance personnel could then easily access the information stored there through their Internet Explorer browser. This is beneficial since the information can be easily found and either edited or viewed without moving around or copying the actual files. Figure 11.3 shows a sample configuration of an HTTP server.

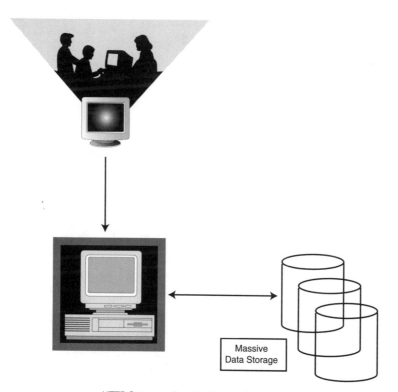

HTTP Server configuration for a business Intranet

Figure 11.3.
HTTP server configuration for a business intranet.

Deeper Explanation of ActiveX DocObjects and Their History

In this section, I'll let you in on the big secret—DocObjects are not really new; just their use on the Internet is new. You'll see where the DocObject concept initially evolved from, then take a look at just what the DocObject does to make it special before getting into the sample code in the next section. The deeper explanation shows you before and after shots of DocObjects at work to illustrate how they work and exactly what the benefits are.

The Origin of DocObjects: The Concord Specification and Windows 95 Binder

Originally, the DocObject technology was mentioned in the Concord specification for the next generation of OLE after OLE 2.0. I would have said OLE 3.0, which was the unofficial name for Concord, but Microsoft decided to stop numbering the various versions of OLE to avoid confusion. It isn't uncommon for a technology leader like Microsoft to look into the next few generations of their software years in advance of its actual introduction. That is the case with the Concord specification, in which Microsoft actually mentions the Office95 specification. Microsoft's work on the Concord specification paved the way for the Office95 Binder interfaces, presenting some of the ideas used for DocObjects.

The Binder interfaces in Office95 were created to allow for the binder-container (Binder.EXE) delivered with Office95. This useful container allows you to organize various documents into the equivalent of a three-ring binder—thus, the term "binder." Each of the DocObjects in the binder is embedded into distinct (OLE) storages. As the object is activated for visual editing in the Office95 Binder, its DocObject application is activated in the context of the Office95 Binder. The menu sharing, as discussed earlier, allows the DocObject to display its entire menu along with the Office95 Binder's menu. This menu merging was originally called in-place activation in OLE 2.0 terminology—Microsoft coined the phrase "visual editing" as a more descriptive term for in-place activation. Another reason for this choice in terminology is that the menu choice for in-place activation in an OLE 2.0 container is "Edit." You see the same kind of in-place activation, or visual editing, in Internet Explorer.

Once again, Microsoft used well-planned, well-designed, existing technology to pave the way for the future into other areas of computing. They borrowed the visual editing model from the Office95 Binder, which improved on the generic in-place activation model of OLE 2.0. Now your existing OLE applications can be retrofitted or redesigned to use the Binder-now-DocObject technology. Adding DocObject interfaces to your application instantly turns them into intranet/Internet applications—a significant but inexpensive added value. If you do add them, then Internet Explorer can use a hyperlinked document's application to perform visual editing.

Tip: Microsoft has hinted that Visual C++ 4.2 will support DocObject classes in Microsoft Foundation Classes, so they will probably either offer a DocObject Wizard or integrate the DocObject classes with their MFC AppWizard.

Edit Menu Merging Techniques of OLE 2.0 and DocObjects

Now look at a detailed example of using Office95 DocObjects. Note that you must have Office95 and Internet Explorer 3.0 (or better) installed. You start out with a click on a hyperlink in Internet Explorer, which references a Microsoft Word document (.doc). Microsoft Word is then activated in the context of the Internet Explorer for editing. Figure 11.4 shows Internet Explorer before and after Word is activated in-place to illustrate how the menus are merged.

Internet Explorer then looks in the registry to see what application is associated with (.doc) Word documents—namely Microsoft Word (the Word.Document.6 registry key for Word 6.0). Since Microsoft Word has registry entries indicating it supports DocObjects (the DocObject registry key), Internet Explorer knows it can activate the document. The Internet Explorer then uses Word's "class id" (the CLSID registry key) to create a Microsoft Word OLE server object to handle the document. After the initial Microsoft Word OLE server object creation, Internet Explorer tries to activate Word as an ActiveX Document by querying for Word's DocObject. Microsoft Word is then activated inside Internet Explorer's window with its usual complete set of commands and toolbars, just as though you were running Microsoft Word standalone. Figure 11.5 compares the menu and toolbars of Word running standalone and activated in Internet Explorer.

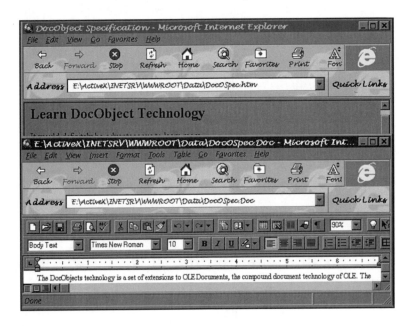

Figure 11.4.
Internet Explorer before and after Word menus are merged.

That's the magic of Microsoft's new ActiveX DocObject technology—your application runs in the *context* of the container it's activated in. This is similar to OLE's Edit verb, which equates to "in-place activation" in OLE 2.0 terms, or "visual editing" in DocObject terminology. Another OLE verb, Open, equates to running the native application standalone.

However, there is a difference between DocObject activation and OLE's in-place activation. With OLE's in-place activation, the menu is shared with the container the object is activated in. With DocObject activation, the menu is virtually taken over by the object. Some menu sharing still occurs, but all the native application's menus are "embedded" in the container's menu. Also, the Help menu item is shared between the two applications, with both container and DocObject applications providing submenus.

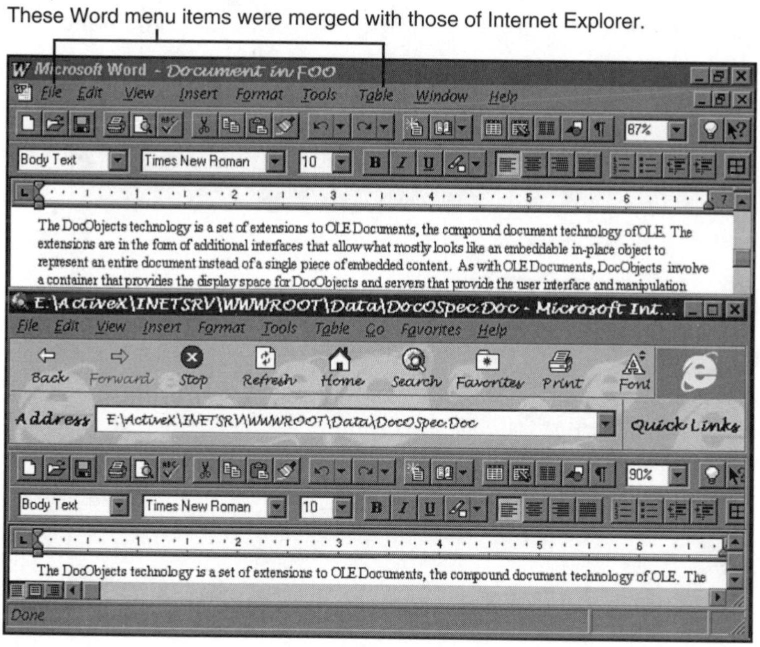

These Word menu items were merged with those of Internet Explorer.

Figure 11.5.
Comparing Word's menus and toolbars running standalone and in Internet Explorer.

With the MFC Scribble tutorial/example from Visual C++ 4.1, Microsoft has added the DocObject interfaces (look in \msdev\samples\mfc\ole\bindscrb where \msdev is the directory where you downloaded VC++). In fact, the sample code discussed in the next section uses the code from the Scribble example as a basis for its DocObject interfaces. The Scribble application is a simple drawing tool. It lets you draw lines of various thicknesses and save the lines to a file as a list of strokes (the CStroke class). The saved file (.osc) may be read to initialize Scribble as a standalone application, an OLE server, or a DocObject server. The file can be used by the standalone Scribble application, can be inserted into an OLE container, or can be activated in the Internet Explorer from a hyperlink. The OLE container can be an OLE 2.0 container or a Binder container, such as Office95 Binder. Scribble can run by itself in its own window, as a linked or embedded OLE Object in any OLE container (Microsoft Word for example), as a DocObject in any Office95 Binder–compliant application, or as a DocObject in Internet Explorer 3.0. The following lists the running scenarios for Scribble; Figures 11.6 through 11.9 illustrate all four cases:

- If you double-click on a file with an .osc extension, the standalone Scribble application runs.

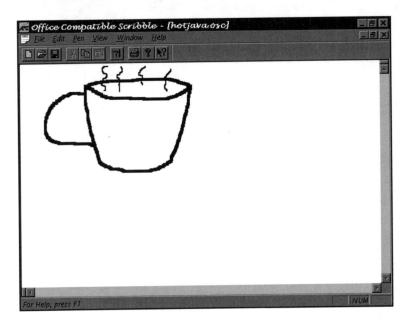

Figure 11.6.
Scribble running standalone.

- If you drag an .osc file into a Word document, it displays a picture of the Scribble strokes in the Word document (although I don't guarantee this part), making the Scribble file an embedded OLE object in the document. Alternatively, you can insert a new Scribble document or insert an existing .osc file, either embedded or linked.

- Using the Office95 Binder, you can embed a new or existing Scribble object into a binder file with the Binder's Section|Add or Section|Add from File commands, respectively. Alternatively, you can drag and drop an existing .osc file into the Binder. Currently, these will always be embedded files.

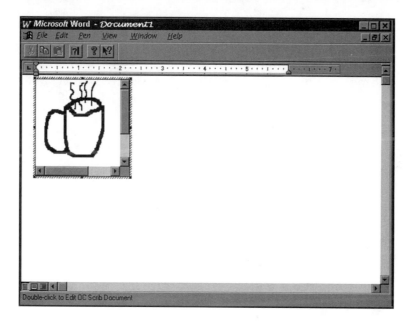

Figure 11.7.
Scribble running in Word.

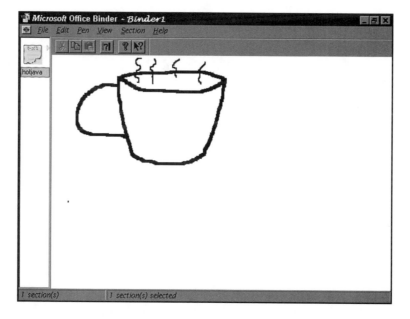

Figure 11.8.
Scribble running in Binder.

■ Finally, since Internet Explorer provides DocObject support, if you click on a hyperlink to a Scribble (.osc) file, the Scribble application runs in the context of Internet Explorer's window. This is neither embedding or linking, but when visually edited in Internet Explorer, the ActiveX Document is used as though it were a linked file.

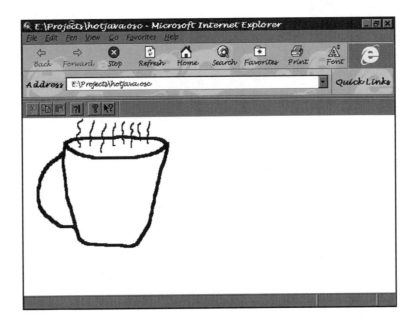

Figure 11.9.
Scribble running in Internet Explorer.

A typical application can easily be written to run in these four different ways. The real power here comes from using the MFC framework from Visual C++ 4.1; it makes building your own DocObject application very easy. Other methods are time-consuming, at best. The next section explains in more detail how to use the MFC framework to build an ActiveX Document server application.

An ActiveX DocObject Example

In this example, you write a simple DocObject application; it's a multi-document (MDI) application called TextView that displays text windows (the `CTextView` class) for keying in and editing text. The file can be saved with the

.tvi extension and read later to initialize the TextView application. In this example, you will focus only on the DocObject parts, although it can be used equally well as a standalone application, as an OLE server, or in the Office95 Binder.

The major features of the interfaces used are discussed first as a brief overview of how the TextView application was created and written. Next, the main interfaces are presented, introducing you to the DocObject interfaces. Following this is a presentation on the sequence of events that occur during initialization, activation, and deactivation, and, finally, saving and termination. Next are the implementation details of crucial interface methods pertinent to writing a DocObject application. After all this, you can finally deal with the setup and usage instructions, followed by a few notes on testing and debugging your DocObject application.

Major Features of Interfaces Used

There are two main interfaces in the TextView application. For a particular DocObject, or document instance, there is one `IOleDocument` object, hence the name Document Object, or DocObject for short. I relate the `IOleDocument` object to a document, so I will usually refer to it as just "the document" from here on.

Each document has one or more `IOleDocumentView` interfaces. Each one of these objects represents one view; each of these views is merely a different representation of the data in the document. Perhaps the document can be viewed at different levels of detail, like zooming in on a drawing or looking at your town from the street and then from the rooftop. At any rate, the different views are your DocObject's different views of its data or document. Figure 11.10 illustrates the ActiveX Document/View architecture.

A good example of multiple views might be an Excel spreadsheet. One set of views of the Excel spreadsheet could be views of the database with various options set, such as gridlines off and a background displayed. This would essentially just be a set of rows and columns with numbers, words, and other data in each slot. Another view may be a diagram view, or a picture of the data in the spreadsheet. For instance, the author can create a pie chart from the data in the Excel spreadsheet.

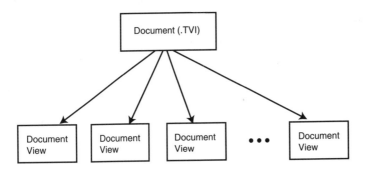

Figure 11.10.
ActiveX Document/View architecture.

On the client side—the container—there is an interface called IOleDocumentSite. It's just what it sounds like: the server's "view site" within the container. This interface represents where the server's ActiveX Document will "live" in the client's application, or where the DocObject will be placed. The IOleDocumentSite isn't really used in that manner, but rather tells your DocObject application that it's supposed to act like a DocObject and not like the typical OLE 2.0 server object. This makes a difference when the container asks your ActiveX Document to activate; you can tell the container to activate with a particular—favorite or default—view.

Most applications in the examples and tutorials from both the VC+ 4.1 samples and the ActiveX SDK samples provide only one view. If your DocObject server is an MDI application, then the implementation of the one view is fairly straightforward. However, if you *do* or *can* have multiple views (as in the preceding Excel example), there is an IEnumOleDocumentViews interface that you can support. The client may initially ask your document for a status flag that indicates, among other things, whether your DocObject supports multiple views. The client may also ask your document to return this document view enumeration, which is essentially a standardized list interface (or enumeration) of the views you support. If your DocObject has only one view, then it returns that view and NULL for the enumeration. In the sample code for this chapter, there is only one view, so this interface isn't supported.

There are a few other important ActiveX Document interfaces. Though not required, they are important parts of the ActiveX DocObject specification. The following is a brief description of each interface:

- The `IPrint` interface is used for printing through the client. In the Office95 Binder, in particular, it's used to create the binder in hardcopy form, which would have a real-life binder layout.

- The `IContinueCallback` interface, used with the `IPrint` interface, is designed to facilitate a generalized callback interface for a continue/interrupt paradigm yet to be implemented anywhere but in the `IPrint` interface.

- The last interface is the `IOleCommandTarget`. This interface must be used to perform a command handshake between client and server. In the specification, it's referred to as the "command dispatch interface" used for executing and querying commands.

Main Interfaces Used

Now draw yourself a BIG cup of coffee (with Scribble) and read on about the main interfaces used for this example:

- `IOleDocument`   This represents the file, or rather the "document." For both the Binder and Internet Explorer, all `QueryInterface()` calls go through this interface. It represents the DocObject and is one-to-one with the file. It has the following interface methods:

CreateView()   Returns a view object (`IOleDocumentView`), possibly pre-initializing it with a saved view state stored in a stream (`IStream`) passed in. Also the "view site" (`IOleInPlaceSite`) may be passed in.

Parameters

(input) `IOleInPlaceSite *pIPSite`

(input) `IStream *pstm`

(input) `DWORD dwReserved`

(output) `IOleDocumentView **ppView`

GetDocMiscStatus()   Returns a status flag, duplicated in the objects registry under the `DocObject` key. The client is responsible for using this status to determine how to communicate with the DocObject. The values are listed in Table 11.1.

Parameters

(output) DWORD *pdwStatus

Table 11.1. The values that may be assigned to the status word returned.

DOCMISC enumerations	=	Meaning Interfaces
DOCMISC_CANCREATEMULTIPLEVIEWS	1	Supports multiple `IEnumOleDocumentViews` (views interface supported)
DOCMISC_SUPPORTCOMPLEXRECTANGLES	2	Can use complex `IOleDocumentView`'s rectangles for `SetRectComplex` interface scrollbar method (not construction implemented)
DOCMISC_CANTOPENEDIT	4	Cannot "open" `IOleDocumentView`'s Open standalone view interface method (not application-implemented)
DOCMISC_NOFILESUPPORT	8	Cannot read/write `IPersistFile` interface (file not implemented, only `IPersistStorage` interface implemented)

EnumViews()   Returns either an enumeration of view objects (`IEnumOleDocumentViews`) if your DocObject supports multiple views, or a single-view object (`IOleDocumentView`) if not.

Parameters

(output) IEnumOleDocumentViews **ppEnum

(output) IOleDocumentView **ppView

■ **IOleDocumentView**   Represents a single view of your document. If your DocObject supports multiple views, there is a many-to-one relationship of views to document; otherwise, it's a one-to-one relationship. According to the specification in the ActiveX SDK, "this interface provides all the necessary operations for a container to manipulate, manage, and activate a view."

SetInPlaceSite()   Saves the view site's (IOleInPlaceSite) interface pointer in the container.

Parameter

(input) IOleInPlaceSite *pIPSite

GetInPlaceSite()   Returns the view site's (IOleInPlaceSite) interface pointer in the container.

Parameter

(output) IOleInPlaceSite **ppIPSite

GetDocument()   Returns an (IUnknown) interface pointer to the DocObject.

Parameter

(output) IUnknown **ppunk

SetRect()   Sets the view's rectangle for display inside the container or client.

Parameter

(input) LPRECT prcView

GetRect()   Returns the view's rectangle for display inside the container or client. An error (E_UNEXPECTED) is returned if no view rectangle has been set yet.

Parameter

(output) LPRECT prcView

SetRectComplex()   Same as SetRect() with additional rectangles for vertical and horizontal scrollbars.

Parameters

(input) LPRECT prcView

(input) LPRECT prcHScroll

(input) LPRECT prcVScroll

(input) LPRECT prcSizeBox

Show()   Either "Show" or "Hide." This is the same idea as OLE's "Show" and "Hide" verbs. To "Show" means to activate in-place the view without a user-interface (UI) activation *and* to show, or display, the view window. To "Hide" means to deactivate the user interface *and* hide the view.

Parameter

(input) BOOL fShow

UIActivate()   Activate or deactivate the user interface. Activating involves the menu merging/sharing, setting up the toolbar and accelerators, and so forth.

Parameter

(input) BOOL fUIActivate

Open()   Same as OLE's "Open" verb. Invokes the native application as a separate process or in a pop-up window.

Parameter

void; no parameters

CloseView()   Close down the view by hiding the view and user interface by calling Show(FALSE) and release the view site's (IOleInPlaceSite) interface pointer in the container by calling SetInPlaceSite(NULL).

Parameter

(input) DWORD dwReserved

SaveViewState()   Save view-specific data to a stream for use in reinitializing the view at a later time by ApplyViewState(). According to the DocObject specification, this interface "instructs the view to save its state into the given stream, where the state includes properties like the view type, zoom factor, insertion point, and so on."

Parameter

(input) IStream *pstm

ApplyViewState() Reinitialize the view from data in a stream previously saved by SaveViewState(). According to the DocObject specification, this interface "instructs a view to reinitialize itself according to the data in a stream that was previously written through IOleDocumentView::SaveViewState."

Parameter

(input) IStream *pstm

Clone() Create and return another view object exactly like itself.

Parameters

(input) IOleInPlaceSite *pIPSiteNew

(output) IOleDocumentView **ppViewNew

- **IOleObject** This is the main interface used by containers to communicate to all OLE objects. The only interface methods of interest to this discussion are SetClientSite() and DoVerb().

  SetClientSite() This interface method is called by the container to set up the "view site" interface pointer. If the "view site" passed in has the IOleDocumentSite interface, then the server is supposed to act like a DocObject as opposed to an ordinary OLE server.

  DoVerb() For an ActiveX Document server, this interface method is called by the container to allow your document to specify which view to use. This view would typically be the default or favorite view.

- **IPersistFile** This interface is a standard OLE server interface. The Load() interface method is called by the client with the filename to use for initialization.

- **IPersistStorage** This interface, also a standard OLE interface, is used for OLE embedding (as opposed to linking). The container calls the Save() interface method with a pointer to a structured storage (IStorage) to let the OLE server save—or embed—its data in the container's document. Likewise, the Load() interface method is later called to let the OLE server initialize itself from the embedded data.

Creating a DocObject Server with Visual C++ 4.1 AppWizard

Let me begin by saying, "Thanks, Microsoft." Once again, they've made life a bit easier—relatively speaking, of course. There is an example of the Scribble tutorial in the VC++ 4.1 sample code with the DocObject interfaces. The source for the Scribble-DocObject sample code is in \msdev\samples\mfc\ole\bindscrb, where \msdev\ is the directory where you download VC++. Alternatively, in the VC++ Project Workspace window on the InfoView tab, go to Samples\MFC Samples\MFC OLE Samples\BINDSCRB: Illustrates an MFC Document Binder.

What is exceptional is that this sample code is built by using the AppWizard and has just gained an extra parent class for DocObject interfaces. This extra level of parent classes in turn has the respective standard MFC classes you normally get from AppWizard as parent classes. In other words, they just slipped in an extra level of parent classes to enable the DocObject interfaces. Therefore, if *you* create an AppWizard project, all you have to do is change your classes to use these new parent classes supplied with the Scribble-DocObject sample code, instead of the standard MFC classes.

That is, the Scribble-DocObject extensions are subclasses from the classes used to create a project with the VC++ 4.1 AppWizard. When I looked at the new DocObject classes, it instantly occurred to me that they will probably be added to MFC in VC++ 4.2. The classes are meant to accommodate the DocObject/Binder interfaces that Internet Explorer 3.0 and Office95 introduce. In addition, they also seamlessly integrate with the class structure created through the AppWizard.

Whether I'm right or wrong about these classes, all I can say is that using these subclasses made writing a DocObject application a snap! Until VC++ 4.2 makes its long-awaited appearance, however, you're better off using this sample code as a basis. All I had to do was change the parent class that AppWizard sets up for you (of COleServerDoc, COleServerItem, and COleIPFrameWnd) and make global replacements for the parent class name in most places. The new parent classes are `CDocObjectServerDoc`, `CDocObjectServerItem`, and `CDocObjectIPFrameWnd`. The details are explained in the following numbered steps—the actual AppWizard process. Figure 11.11 shows where in the class structure these classes fit, illustrating what Microsoft has done in the Scribble-DocObject sample code.

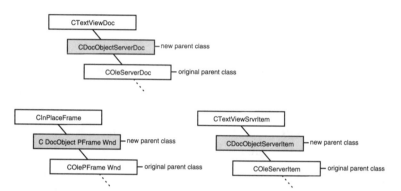

Figure 11.11.
Scribble-DocObject MFC extensions.

To start with, bring up Visual C++, choose File | New (or Ctrl+N), and select the Project Workspace option from the New dialog box. This will bring up the New Project Workspace dialog box. Select MFC AppWizard (exe), enter the name `TextView`, and click the Create button to start the MFC AppWizard. The following list explains what to do for each of the six "step" dialog boxes:

1. Check either the "Multiple documents" (default) or "Single document" checkbox, depending on which you prefer, then click the Next button.

2. Click the Next button again on this database support step, taking the default of "none".

3. Check the Full Server option. Make sure the "Yes, please" checkbox is selected under the "Would you like support for OLE compound files?" option, then click the Next button.

4. Check the Context-sensitive Help option under "What features would you like to include?" so that all options in this list are selected. Click the Advanced... button to bring up the Advanced Options dialog box.

On the Document Template Strings option tab in the File extension field, enter `tvi`—note that as you type, you see the letters being added to the "Filter name." You can edit the other fields as follows, but it isn't essential:

```
Doc type name = TxView
File new name (OLE short name) = TxVw
Main frame caption = Text Viewer
Filter name = Text View Files (*.tvi)
File type name (OLE long name) = TextView Document
```

Now click the Close button to close the Advanced Options dialog box, then click the Next button.

5. Click the Next button to go to the next step, taking the defaults for source file comments and using the shared MFC library.

6. Select the `CTextViewView` class, change the "Base class" to `CEditView`, and change the "Header file" and "Implementation file" to `TxVwView.h` and `TxVwView.cpp`, respectively, so they both have eight-character filenames. Next, select the `CTextViewDoc` class and change the "Header file" and "Implementation file" to `TxtVwDoc.h` and `TxtVwDoc.cpp`, respectively. Now click the Finish button to bring up the New Project Information dialog box, then click the OK button to complete the Wizardry.

Implementing Your Example

The AppWizard has done quite a bit of the work for you, and the classes you borrow from the Scribble-DocObject sample code essentially do the rest. To use this code, copy the following files into your project directory:

Binddcmt.cpp
Binddoc.cpp
Binddoc.h
Bindipfw.cpp
Bindipfw.h
Binditem.cpp
Binditem.h
Bindview.cpp
Mfcbind.cpp

Mfcbind.h
Oleobjct.cpp
Print.cpp

> **Tip:** An alternative to just copying files from the Scribble-DocObject sample code into each project is creating a dynamic-link library or a static library (using the New Project Workspace dialog box) from this code and using the library in multiple projects.

To include these files in your project, choose Insert|Files into Project... from the menu to bring up the Insert Files into Project dialog box. Select the following files (note only the .cpp files):

Binddcmt.cpp
Binddoc.cpp
Bindipfw.cpp
Binditem.cpp
Bindview.cpp
Mfcbind.cpp
Oleobjct.cpp
Print.cpp

To change the class hierarchy so you can use these DocObject MFC classes, edit and change the parent classes as indicated in the following files:

- **TxtVwDoc.h:** Change parent from `COleServerDoc` to `CDocObjectServerDoc`

  `class CTextViewDoc : public CDocObjectServerDoc`

- **SrvrItem.h:** Change parent from `COleServerItem` to `CDocObjectServerItem`

  `class CTextViewSrvrItem : public CDocObjectServerItem`

- **IpFrame.h:** Change parent from `COleIPFrameWnd` to `CDocObjectIPFrameWnd`

  `class CInPlaceFrame : public CDocObjectIPFrameWnd`

Now your classes are using the new parent classes which enable the DocObject interfaces. The next step is to use the Find in Files toolbar button and

Edit | Replace commands. Replace COleServerDoc with CDocObjectServerDoc, COleServerItem with CDocObjectServerItem, and COleIPFrameWnd with CDocObjectIPFrameWnd in all the source and header files. Use the Find In Files dialog box with each of the original class names to help find all instances that must be changed. The only exception is the OnGetEmbeddedItem() method, which requires that you return a COleServerItem.

Now add the required #include files, as follows:

- TxtVwDoc.cpp and SrvrItem.cpp:

  ```
  #include "binddoc.h"

  #include "binditem.h"
  ```

- IpFrame.cpp:

  ```
  #include "bindipfw.h"
  ```

- TextView.cpp:

  ```
  #include "mfcbind.h"

  #include "binddoc.h"

  #include "bindipfw.h"
  ```

- TxVwView.cpp:

  ```
  #include "binddoc.h"
  ```

To perform the extra required DocObject registration, edit the CTextViewApp::InitInstance() method in the TextView.cpp file and change the line

```
m_server.UpdateRegistry(OAT_INPLACE_SERVER);
```

to

```
MfcBinderUpdateRegistry(pDocTemplate, OAT_INPLACE_SERVER);
```

Modify the CTextViewSrvrItem::OnGetExtent() method in the SrvrItem.cpp file to return the correct extents by changing the line

```
rSize = CSize(3000, 3000);    // 3000 x 3000 HIMETRIC units
```

to

```
rSize = pDoc->GetDocSize();
CClientDC dc(NULL);
    // set a MM_LOENGLISH based on logical inches
// (we can't use MM_LOENGLISH because MM_LOENGLISH uses physical
➡inches)
```

```
dc.SetMapMode(MM_ANISOTROPIC);
```

```
dc.SetViewportExt(dc.GetDeviceCaps(LOGPIXELSX),
➥dc.GetDeviceCaps(LOGPIXELSY));
```

```
dc.SetWindowExt(100, -100);
```

```
dc.LPtoHIMETRIC(&rSize);
```

Now add a few things to the document class (CTextViewDoc) to initialize and provide the correct size. Add the following to the TxtVwDoc.h file:

```
protected:
```

```
CSize m_sizeDoc;
```

```
public:
```

```
    CSize GetDocSize() { return m_sizeDoc; }
```

```
protected:
```

```
    void InitDocument();
```

The InitDocument() method has only one line, used to initialize the document size:

```
m_sizeDoc = CSize(200,200);
```

The OnOpenDocument() method should be added to the document class (CTextViewDoc) through the built-in Class Wizard; you also add a call to the InitDocument() method to set the size. Open the TxtVwDoc.cpp file, and you'll notice that it has a built-in Class Wizard on the window's title bar. Select the OnOpenDocument method from the Messages pull-down menu, and a Microsoft Developer Studio dialog box prompts you to add this method: OnOpenDocument is not handled. Do you want to add a handler? Click the Yes button, and the method is "magically" added (that's why it's called a Class *Wizard!*). Your cursor is placed at the following line:

```
// TODO: Add your specialized creation code here
```

Change this to a call to the following:

```
InitDocument();
```

Then add a call to the InitDocument() method in the document's constructor (CTextViewDoc::CTextViewDoc()) and in the document's OnNewDocument() method.

A string must be added to the Resource file's String Table for the `MfcBinderUpdateRegistry()` function. Select ResourceView from the Project Workspace window, and add the `BIND_IDP_FAILED_TO_AUTO_REGISTER` ID with the associated string `Unable to add Binder-Compatible entries to registry`.

Before you try to compile and link the code, you must add the uuid3.lib library to the Object/library modules field in the Link option tab on the Project Settings dialog box to get the DocObject GUIDs. Choose Build | Settings from the menu to bring up the Project Settings dialog box, then select the Link tab. After adding the uuid3.lib, click in the Project Options field and enter the `/nodefaultlib:"LIBC"` option to avoid a link error.

Now you can compile and link your project.

Setup and Usage Instructions

The project is now ready to run. The TextView.exe executable must run standalone one time to perform the necessary registration. Once it has registered itself, the TextView application can be used to view its .tvi files in the context of Internet Explorer as a DocObject server.

First, run TextView standalone, and create and save a .tvi file with some text in it. Next, create an HTML file with a hyperlink reference to the .tvi file. The HTML file contains the following line, which references your new DocObj.tvi file:

```
<A HREF="DocObj.tvi">Text View DocObject test</a>
```

When you select this hyperlink in Internet Explorer, the TextView DocObject is invoked to display in-place activation in the context of Internet Explorer. Figure 11.12 shows TextView running both standalone and serving as a DocObject in Internet Explorer.

> Note: The TextView application can also be used as an OLE server in the Office95 Binder.

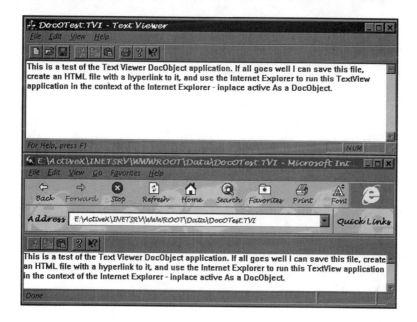

Figure 11.12.
The TextView application running standalone and as a DocObject server in Internet Explorer.

Implementation Ideas: How to Use This Technology

Your initial example was of an Office95 Word document displaying in the context of Internet Explorer. If you have your own data format viewer or editor, providing DocObject support can make your application much more usable. Using the techniques outlined in this chapter will make building a DocObject application based on Visual C++ 4.1 MFC very easy. Take a look at another possible implementation to get you thinking the DocObject way.

One area that I see as a good candidate, outside of Office95, is the CAD/CAM market. The various CAD/CAM formats, such as AutoCAD, MicroStation, Imagineer, and Solid Edge, to name but a few, could really benefit by providing viewer/editor DocObject applications. This would enable their viewing through Internet Explorer. Could this lead to groupware applications? Imagine providing the capability to people at remote places to view or edit data for a group design. It's evident that this market stands to gain a lot from the evolving and expanding DocObject approach.

Conclusion

Making your application Internet and intranet aware is as easy as using the DocObject interfaces and Visual C++ 4.1 MFC classes. This can be a boon to your business by making your formats more accessible. The Office95 Binder and Internet Explorer are just the first two areas that have applied the DocObject interfaces; more DocObject container and server applications should follow in the near future. These new applications stand to revolutionize how diverse groups of people can easily access the same data in a standardized, efficient manner. If your business starts considering how to make use of these new interfaces now, it will undoubtedly stand to benefit considerably in the near (and far) future.

The next two chapters deal with ISAPI extensions. Chapter 12, "Controlling the Internet Information Server Through ActiveX ISAPI Filters," discusses how your business can use ISAPI filters to help manage its Internet site. Chapter 13, "Developing Web Applications Using ISAPI Extensions," discusses the efficiency advantages of using ISAPI extensions to service CGI requests.

Controlling the Internet Information Server Through ActiveX ISAPI Filters

by Daniel F. Wygant

During normal business operations, files and data in different formats are often created and updated. Tremendous amounts of information are stored in files and databases—like gold waiting to be mined by your business. Just trying to manage access can be a daunting task. Part and parcel of managing information is dealing with a wide variety of viewers, editors, and other applications for dealing with the massive information stored. Filtering this information on-the-fly for display through a Web browser such as Internet Explorer solves both the access problem and the viewer problem.

Microsoft supplies sample code in the ActiveX SDK for an ActiveX ISAPI filter that does just that. It converts documents (Word, Excel, Text) to HTML documents when a hyperlink for the document is selected. The converted HTML document is then displayed in the browser.

Tip: The CVTDOC ISAPI filter sample and a Word document describing how to use it are available in the ActiveX SDK in the INetSDK\samples\Isapi\CvtDoc directory. To run this software, you need Windows NT Server 3.5.1 running Internet Information Server (IIS) 2.0. You can get IIS 2.0 free from Microsoft at `http://www.microsoft.com/infoserv/`.

ActiveX ISAPI Filter Technology

ActiveX ISAPI filter technology offers several different types of filtering; some are listed briefly here:

■ Enhanced/customized logging capabilities

■ Enhanced/customized authentication capabilities

■ Data conversion/compression/encryption on-the-fly

■ URL mapping

This chapter discusses how businesses can benefit from ActiveX ISAPI filter technology and gives a broader understanding of what the various filters can be used for. A sample URL-mapping filter, with source code, is presented to illustrate how this new ActiveX technology works. The example walks you through creating a filter with the VC 4.1 MFC ISAPI Filter Wizard and briefly examines the MFC subclass produced. The chapter winds up with a few application ideas for using ActiveX ISAPI filters.

There are innumerable possibilities for using this technology. This is illustrated in Figure 12.1, which shows a Windows NT Server being accessed through the Web. A "black-box" ISAPI filter stands between the Internet Information Server and the data on the NT Server providing "mystery" value add-ons.

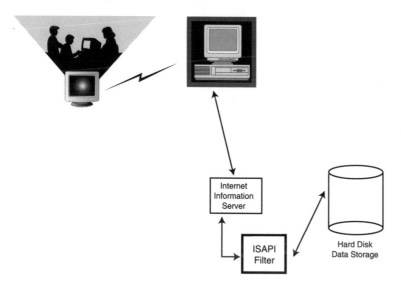

Figure 12.1.
A "black-box" ISAPI filter transforming data on-the-fly.

ActiveX and Business

To begin with, this new API is a very powerful, yet fast and easy, way to enhance your HTTP server's capabilities and security. With ActiveX ISAPI filters, you can provide new schemes for finding the data on the server, for custom logging of HTTP requests, for data encryption and compression, and for data conversion or preprocessing. The sample code developed for this chapter gives you an example of a URL Map ISAPI filter that modifies the URL requested by changing the directory name.

Note: The sample code presented later on in the chapter is on the CD-ROM included with this book. You can copy it, compile it if you like—provided you have Visual C++ 4.1 or later—and run or test it on a PC. The operating system this code was tested on was Windows NT Server 3.5.1 and IIS 2.0, since there was not a version available for any other operating system at the time of this writing in May 1996. As a matter of fact, the IIS this was tested with was the beta version. However, it is not likely that anything that would significantly affect the code will change since the MFC layer allows a layer of protective abstraction from the specification—another nice quality of using MFC.

Using a Dynamic Load Library (DLL) to process your HTTP requests is not only powerful, but also faster than using the Common Gateway Interface (CGI). With CGI, your HTTP server must invoke a separate process for every request, which may overload your server. However, with DLLs the only overhead is starting a new thread, which is very fast and inexpensive—both for processing and memory-wise—compared to starting a new CGI process.

Note: *Threading* means what it sounds like. A process can start a new "thread" to manage a chunk of processing while the main "thread" continues its normal processing. This is a particularly nice trick for a heavily user-interface–driven application or, in fact, any type of processing in which you want a fast response time. This allows the program to return to its main task while separate threads within its process space process requests. The main thread then spends most of its time processing requests—creating threads or communicating with other threads to have the other threads do the actual results processing. Typically, a threaded process can be broken into one main thread that processes requests and one or more additional threads for processing results and probably returning the results back to the main thread, which routes the results back to the requester. For a GUI application, this means you have immediate GUI response time—Internet Explorer and Netscape Navigator are good examples of this type of threading, allowing for asynchronous GUI and URL processing. Likewise, the IIS HTTP server uses this threading to process HTTP requests, hand them off to threads that communicate to their ISAPI extension and filter DLLs, and turn around and wait for the next HTTP request.

Overall, the ActiveX ISAPI filters are much more powerful and efficient tools than the CGI type currently in use. Creating new applications with the filter capabilities is easy, and retrofitting existing applications with filters isn't difficult. The payback in filter efficiency will clearly improve your business, and the new capabilities of these filters will put your business organization ahead of the Internet technology curve. In addition, Visual C++ 4.1 (VC 4.1) has MFC classes for ISAPI filters and an MFC ISAPI Extension Wizard that builds an initial class framework for an ISAPI filter using these MFC classes. The result of using MFC to build an ISAPI filter is a small ISAPI filter program (DLL), which is extremely easy to modify and extend to help efficiently manage your business's vast storage of information on its intranet and its connection to the Internet.

> Note: There is an equivalent CGI technology related to ISAPI filters called ISAPI extension DLLs. In Chapter 13, "Developing Web Applications Using ISAPI Extensions," you will find a sample ISAPI extension DLL with code.

As for actual business uses, start with a simple example: Say you would like to move your data, but there are links all over the Internet to data on your server. One easy solution is to provide an ISAPI filter to map URLs (Uniform Resource Locators) to point to the new location. Once the filter is installed and the server's IIS is restarted, any URLs requesting data in the old location can be mapped to the new location. This will save you the time of finding and rewriting all your HTML files, not to mention the problems finding and notifying any external Internet sites of the location change. Figure 12.2 illustrates the URL mapping process.

Another very powerful use, mentioned in the introduction, is data conversion or data preprocessing. You can essentially rewrite requested data on-the-fly. For example, you might have a particular set of files in a particular format that you want to make available in HTML format. Unfortunately, you don't have the resources to keep the HTML versions current or to manually perform the conversion to HTML format.

This is an excellent time to consider writing an ISAPI filter that processes URL Map events. The URL Map event occurs on your HTTP server any time it's requested to process a URL. When a URL Map event occurs, the HTTP server calls each ISAPI filter that had indicated an interest in URL Map events during initialization. Your ISAPI filter is called to process the URL Map event/request and, in this example, checks the file extension and directory name. If the file extension or directory name match the one(s) your filter wants to deal with, it converts the file to another format—for example, HTML. The path to the document-converted-to-HTML file is then returned in place of the input path to the original document. This, then, is an example of a URL mapping. The surfer/user requests the document and gets the document in an HTML format; the URL is mapped to an HTML file, which has been converted from the document originally requested. See Figure 12.3 for a diagram of this data-conversion process.

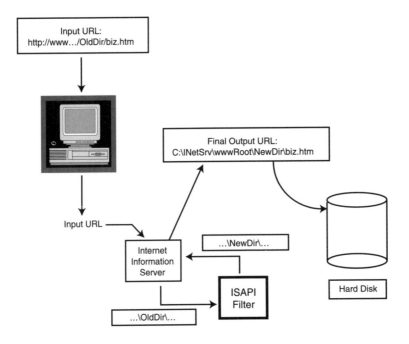

Figure 12.2.
ISAPI filter URL mapping process.

Note: Refer back to Chapter 5, "ActiveX Documents," for background on OLE DocObjects; Chapter 6, "ActiveX Controls," to review those controls; and Chapter 7, "ActiveX Scripting," for information on ActiveX scripting.

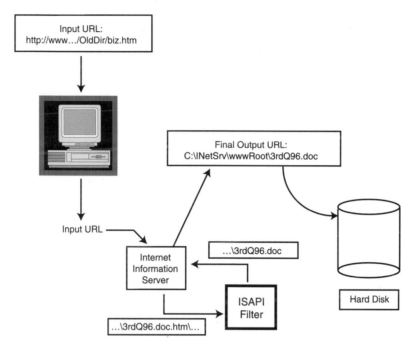

Figure 12.3.
ISAPI filter URL Map *file-conversion process.*

Other types of business uses for ISAPI filters are data encryption or compression for transmitting data in a custom format that only specific client browsers can interpret. For example, say you ran a stock-options business and had a set of clients that paid for high-speed access to sensitive market research information. You could allow access through a client-server architecture by passing the data back to the clients in a browsable or hyperlinked format.

An ISAPI filter can be used to transform the data before sending it to the client's browser. The client's browser would have to decrypt or decompress the data for display on the client side. In this way, your data is secured by encrypting the data before tranfer; by compressing the data, it can be transferred at higher speeds over the network. This is illustrated in Figure 12.4.

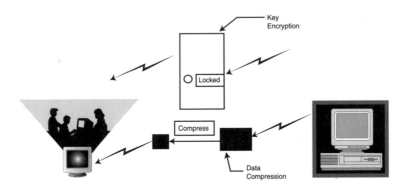

Figure 12.4.
Data encryption and compression on-the-fly.

You can create an ISAPI filter for a customized tracing mechanism of HTTP requests that pass through your HTTP server. You could then use the information this filter reports to make decisions affecting capabilities and security of your business intranet and its connection to the Internet. This alone is a good reason for creating an ISAPI filter—to offer a custom security scheme beyond what your current HTTP server can offer.

For instance, you may have certain files that only upper-level management should have access to, such as employee salaries or employee profiles. These files could be made accessible through the Web exclusively to upper-level management. You could write an ISAPI filter that would perform an authentication check before allowing access to the files.

When these files are accessed, your ISAPI filter would get an Authentication event. At this time, the filter would check the IDs against a database of the current upper-level management (since it changes so frequently). If the requester's ID is valid, then allow access; if not, he or she would get a "gentle" reminder in HTML format that this is (now) forbidden territory.

Your business can also use an ISAPI filter to modify certain documents for presentations. A filter could be used to change a file's data before the HTTP server passes it to the client's browser for display, or one could be written to convert any document references into HTML URL references. For example, assume a text file (FileStore\filelist.txt) is requested containing the following two lines:

```
Third Quarter 1996 Business Plan
```

```
c:\INetSrv\WWWRoot\FileStor\BusinessPlan3rdQ96.doc
```

A filter could be written to process the text file into an HTML file when it receives a URL Map event for the FileStore directory. For the sake of illustration, say the filter takes the second line and makes a hyperlink from it with the textual description on the first line being the URL's highlighted text, as follows:

```
<A HREF="FileStor\BusinessPlan3rdQ96.doc.htm">Third Quarter 1996
➥Business Plan</a><p>
```

This could certainly produce a nice business presentation, especially if you had the CVTDOC example, mentioned in the introduction, which takes *.doc.htm URL Maps and converts the *.doc file into an *.htm file (HTML). You could then click and get a Word-like display of the *.doc file in HTML. Figure 12.5 shows two screen shots illustrating the difference in appearance that converting the text file to HTML can make.

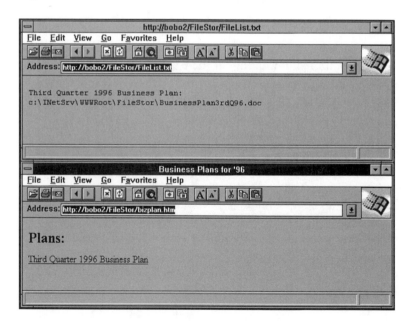

Figure 12.5.
Simple text file versus converting to HTML.

Event Notification Paradigm

The IIS HTTP server calls ISAPI filters for different types of HTTP-related requests. These are referred to as *events* and the process can be thought of as an event notification paradigm—the event notification paradigm for ActiveX ISAPI filters. The events sent to filter DLLs are specified by each individual DLL during initialization of IIS. When an IIS service is started, the DLLs listed in a special place in the registry are loaded. As each filter is loaded, an initialization routine (`GetFilterVersion()`) is called for each filter to return information; part of this information is which types of events it wants to be notified of. When IIS generates such events, it sends them to the filter DLLs that had expressed an interest in them. Your ISAPI filter DLL is listed in the registry in the following key:

```
"HKEY_LOCAL_MACHINE\System\CurrentControlSet\Services\W3Svc\
➥Parameters\"
```

under the value

```
"Filter DLLs"
```

The DLLs are separated by commas. The order in which filters are notified is based on priority: high, medium, or low. If there are two or more filters listed with the same priority, the order of notification is based on where the DLLs sit, left to right, as they are listed in this registry value. Once the DLL is initialized, you are notified—or called—for the events specified to IIS during server startup.

> Note: The priority is specified by the DLLs in a structure returned from the `GetFilterVersion()` entry point into the DLL. Initially, when an IIS service (WWW, FTP, or Gopher) is started, each of the filter DLLs are loaded; this entry point routine is called to collect information on each filter. The information returned includes the filter version, a descriptive string, and a bitmask flag indicating filter priority, what types of notifications to send it, and whether to be notified for secure and non-secure ports.

An "event" is triggered in IIS when a browser, such as Internet Explorer, Netscape, or Mosaic, tries to activate a hyperlink (URL) to your Windows NT Server's HTTP server. When your HTTP server, IIS, is contacted with a URL, the IIS HTTP server calls each of the ISAPI filters for a variety of events.

The events a particular filter is notified for are specified to IIS by a call to the filter during IIS startup. The initialization and event notification paradigm is illustrated in Figure 12.6. The list following explains the meanings of the notification flags, which are returned to IIS by the filter in a bitmask during initialization.

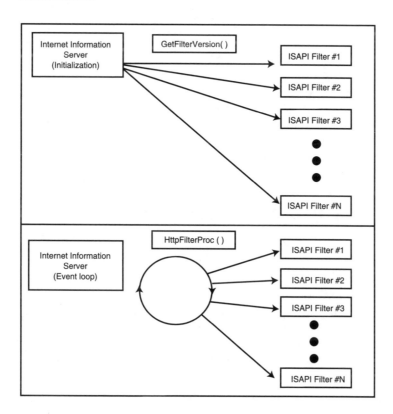

Figure 12.6.
Event notification paradigm for ISAPI filters.

Notification flags	Description
SF_NOTIFY_READ_RAW_DATA	Before data is read by the server
SF_NOTIFY_SEND_RAW_DATA	Before data is sent to the client
SF_NOTIFY_PREPROC_HEADERS	Before processing the client headers
SF_NOTIFY_AUTHENTICATION	Before secure client connection
SF_NOTIFY_URL_MAP	Before reading the data
SF_NOTIFY_LOG	For logging

> **Note:** The `HttpFilterProc()` entry point into the filter DLL is called for event notifications. Refer to Chapter 8, "ActiveX Internet Information Servers," for information on ISAPI filters and extension DLLs.

> **Tip:** During the event notification cycle, more than one filter may be called for the same event. If a particular ISAPI filter wants to be the only one dealing with a particular instance of an event, it may return `SF_STATUS_REQ_HANDLED_NOTIFICATION` to indicate that no other DLLs should be notified. This can apply to URL `Map` events; if your filter DLL handles the request, you probably don't want any other filter to further map the URL, but this is not the rule.

URL-Mapping ActiveX ISAPI Filter

This example shows you the basics of creating an ISAPI filter with Visual C++ 4.1 Microsoft Foundation Classes and walks you through using the VC++ 4.1 ISAPI Extension Wizard. For this simple example, you'll create a filter that maps URLs, which allows you to move data around on your Windows NT Server without having to modify the HTML files to point to the new location.

You'll also create a dynamic link library that's notified when a user selects a hyperlink from a browser, such as Internet Explorer. Your DLL will then filter the URL selected, modifying the file path if it contains the directory that has been moved.

Creating a Filter with VC++ 4.1 ISAPI Extension Wizard

Microsoft offers a set of C++ classes for creating ISAPI filters in Visual C++ 4.1, as well as an ISAPI Extension Wizard. To begin, bring up VC++, choose File|New (or press Ctrl+N), and select the Project Workspace option from the New dialog box to open the New Project Workspace dialog box. Select ISAPI Extension Wizard, enter the name UrlMapper, and click the Create button to start the ISAPI Extension Wizard. Check the "Generate a Filter object" checkbox and uncheck the "Generate a Server Extension object" checkbox.

> Caution: To be safe, you might want to select "As a statically-linked library" from the "How would you like to use the MFC library?" option because otherwise you would have to carry the MFC libraries with you and install them on the target Windows NT server. If you don't have VC++ 4.1 installed, then you have to install the shared DLL in the System32 directory, adding a level of complexity to your installation and debugging.

Figure 12.7 shows what the Wizard looks like after these selections have been made to the first page.

Figure 12.7.
ISAPI Extension Wizard—Step 1 of 2.

Now click the Next button, which opens the ISAPI Extension Wizard—Step 2 of 2 dialog box. Select the "URL mapping requests" checkbox and deselect the "End of connection" checkbox. (See Figure 12.8.)

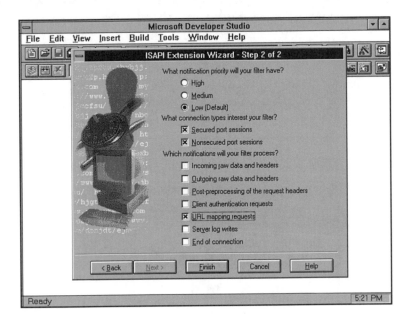

Figure 12.8.
ISAPI Extension Wizard—Step 2 of 2.

Now click the Finish button to bring up the New Project Information dialog box, then click the OK button to complete the Wizardry. Figure 12.9 shows VC++ 4.1 after this step. The initial filter, without any additional code, is ready to compile and debug.

Tip: There is a trick to debugging ISAPI filters. I found the information in Technical Note 63 using the integrated InfoView in VC++ 4.1. To find this information, go to the Project Workspace window, on the InfoView tab, under Visual C++ Books\MFC 4.1\MFC Technical Notes\MFC Technical Note Index\TN063: Debugging Internet Extension DLLs.

Basically the Technical Note says to use IIS directly as the program to debug. To set this up, choose Build|Settings from the menu to bring up the Project Settings dialog box and select the Debug tab. In the "Executable for debug session" field, enter the path to the IIS executable—the default install path is c:\INetsrv\Server\Inetinfo.exe. In the "Program arguments" field, enter -e W3Svc. You must also stop all three "publishing services" (WWW, Gopher, FTP) by using the Internet Information Server Manager or choosing Control Panel|Services from the menu.

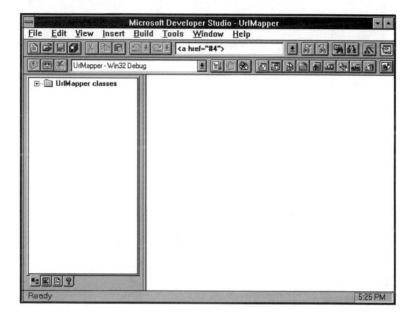

Figure 12.9.
The UrlMapper project after using the ISAPI Extension Wizard.

Implementing the Example

Since the ISAPI Extension Wizard did most of the work for you, all that's left to do is implement the call-back routine for URL mapping. The wizard-created class, `CUrlMapperFilter`, is subclassed from `CHttpFilter`. As you can see from Figure 12.10, the only method you have to implement is the `CUrlMapperFilter::OnUrlMap()`. Figure 12.10 shows the view after double-clicking on the `OnUrlMap()` method from the ClassView. You are positioned at the beginning of the `OnUrlMap()` method.

To implement the `OnUrlMap()` method, add the following code:

```
CString URLPath;
int index=0; // index of your old directory in the path

// copy into a CString for simple search
URLPath = pMapInfo->pszPhysicalPath;

// Find the start of the "\\OldDir\\" string
index = URLPath.Find ( "\\OldDir\\" );

// If the directory name was found; replace it
if (-1 != index)
```

```
{
// Get the left half of the directory path
CString newDir = URLPath.Left( index );

// Add the new directory
newDir += "\\NewDir\\";

// Add the right half of the directory path
newDir += URLPath.Mid ( index + strlen ( "\\OldDir\\" ) );

// copy the new directory path back into the input path
    strcpy ( pMapInfo->pszPhysicalPath, (LPCTSTR)newDir );
}
```

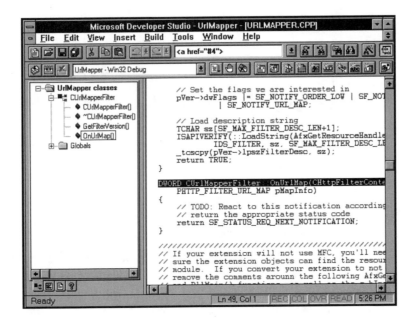

Figure 12.10.
ClassView of the UrlMapper class CUrlMapperFilter.

This code looks for the directory \OldDir\ and, if found, replaces it with the \NewDir\ directory. Note the paths are the same size. If the path passed to this method in the PHTTP_FILTER_URL_MAP structure had ended up being longer than cbPathBuff, you would have allocated a new chunk of memory for pszPhysicalPath and deallocated it in the OnEndOfNetSession() method. This reallocation scheme is substantially more difficult to manage and will not be addressed in this example.

> Note: After compiling the code, you have to add the path to your DLL to the `Filter DLLs` value in the registry under the following key:
>
> `"HKEY_LOCAL_MACHINE\System\CurrentControlSet\Services\W3Svc\`
> `➥Parameters\"`

Testing the Filter

To debug this filter, choose Build|Debug|Go (or press F5) from the VC++ menu bar. It's probably a good idea to set a break in the `CUrlMapperFilter::OnUrlMap()` method and perhaps in the `CUrlMapperFilter::GetFilterVersion()` method, as well. During the initialization, you should get a call to the `CUrlMapperFilter::GetFilterVersion()` method. If you don't, then you probably entered the wrong path under the `Filter DLLs` value or did not stop all three IIS publishing services before you started.

Note that the ISAPI Extension Wizard put the following lines of code in the `CUrlMapperFilter::GetFilterVersion()` method:

```
// Set the flags you are interested in
pVer->dwFlags |= SF_NOTIFY_ORDER_LOW

                  | SF_NOTIFY_SECURE_PORT

                  | SF_NOTIFY_NONSECURE_PORT

                  | SF_NOTIFY_URL_MAP;
```

This code sets the notification priority to low, indicates you want to deal with both secure and non-secure ports, and, most important, tells the server to notify your DLL for URL Map events. Since you've indicated that you want to be notified of URL Map events, you set a break in the `CUrlMapperFilter::OnUrlMap()` method. To cause IIS to call this method so you can generate a break, you must bring up a browser such as Internet Explorer and enter or select a hyperlink with a URL for your machine. The following is an example of HTML code that will cause the IIS server to call your filter for an URL Map event:

```
<a href="http://yourservername/OldDir/FileStore/filelist.txt">
The Biz</a>
```

Figure 12.11 shows this HTML code displayed in Internet Explorer.

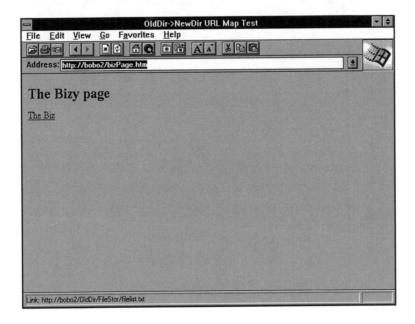

Figure 12.11.
HTML reference displayed in Internet Explorer.

When you are called for this URL Map event, the code in the CUrlMapperFilter::OnUrlMap() method will change the path from

c:\INetSrv\WWWRoot\OldDir\FileStore\filelist.txt

to

c:\INetSrv\WWWRoot\NewDir\FileStore\filelist.txt

Implementation Ideas: How to Use This Technology

As pointed out in the introduction, data conversion is one of the more powerful capabilities provided by ActiveX ISAPI filters. This section explores a few more possible implementation ideas for filters and discusses extending the sample ISAPI filter to preprocess data as well.

First, take a look at one of the filters provided as sample code in VC++ 4.1. The example from which I got the idea for the URL Map sample code is the MFCUCASE example in the directory c:\msdev\samples\mfc\internet\mfcucase.

This example receives URL Map and Send Raw Data events. The code in its OnUrlMap() method looks for URLs with \UC in the directory path, which triggers it to change everything to uppercase in the OnSendRawData() method. The OnUrlMap() method removes the \UC from the path so the browser can find the file; the \UC in the path is just an indicator that the text should be turned into uppercase. The following is a sample URL:

```
http://yourservername/FileStore/UC/FileList.htm
```

The actual file is in the c:\INetSrv\WWWRoot\FileStore\FileList.htm file. Suppose the file FileList.htm has the following lines in it:

```
<title>Upper Case Test</title>
<p><p><H3><HEAD><B>This code should appear in uppercase</B>
➡</HEAD></H3><p><p>
<A HREF="FileStor\BusinessPlan3rdQ96.doc.htm">
Third Quarter 1996 Business Plan</a><p>
```

Figure 12.12 shows what this will look like before and after selecting the hyperlink. Notice that the title, the header, and all the text, including the hyperlink, whose path is shown at the bottom, are in uppercase letters.

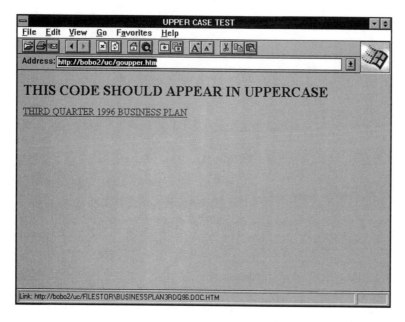

Figure 12.12.
Before and after selecting the sample \UC *hyperlink.*

Conclusion

Although there are currently some very powerful tools for the Web, the ActiveX ISAPI filters bring the Web closer to business applications. The Web is constantly evolving, providing new challenges to businesses who use it or actually live on it. With the capabilities of the filters and other ActiveX technologies, application programmers—and the people who increase their productivity by using their applications—are the beneficiaries.

What's Next

You will see the other half of the ISAPI story in the next chapter. Chapter 13, "Developing Web Applications Using ISAPI Extensions," explains how to write an ISAPI extension DLL that processes CGI. You'll even learn how to find information about avocados on the Internet!

Developing Web Applications Using ISAPI Extensions

by Kevin Walsh

My wife recently made an avocado salad, which left her with two light-tan avocado seeds, slightly larger than a robin's egg. She was reluctant to throw the seeds away and asked me if I knew how to grow an avocado tree from a seed. As it became clear to me that she was serious, my thoughts were ones of sadness as I pictured two forlorn seeds sitting alone, unloved and sterile in a pot, as unidentifiable organisms made themselves at home around them because she had no clue about how to make them grow. The next day, as a lark, I decided to conduct an Internet search on the topic.

As the well-connected user you no doubt are, you're probably familiar with the ever-expanding selection of Web search engines on the Internet. Just fire up your favorite Web browser, click the Search button, and you'll see at least five search tools to choose from, each with a slightly different approach to sifting through the vast amount of data on the Internet. These search engines are surprisingly fast, and my search on "avocado" resulted in hundreds of hits. To my naive astonishment, an awful lot of people care deeply enough about avocados to dedicate the time and effort to create some really quite attractive Web pages about the sublime pleasures and mercantile advantages of the strange green fruit. My wife got her instructions, and I became intrigued with these applications that somehow buried themselves in a Web page.

The Nature of Web Servers and CGI

Most people readily grasp the notion of HTML tags in a document and how they control the display of text. The language is simple and powerful, and after a few hours of applied study, even the most non-technical among us can construct nice-looking documents, complete with hyperlinks to other sections of the page and even to other pages. Technophiles, after playing with a browser for just a few minutes, intuitively understand that a Web browser is really an HTML interpreter and display engine, with a specific network protocol designed to transfer data contained in documents stored on a server—a souped-up FTP, if you will. Maybe it was its deceptive simplicity that caused many of us to dismiss the Web as a serious applications deployment environment; even Bill Gates admits that the explosive growth of the Web took Microsoft by surprise.

In retrospect, the clues were there almost from the beginning. As more and more server-based bits of magic like those search engines came online, I began to realize that suddenly, everything I knew was wrong. I had to find out what made that magic work, or get left behind. In a Web server, that magic is known as the Common Gateway Interface—CGI—and it's really not magic at all. Like browsers and HTML, it's surprisingly simple. Web server–based applications and CGI challenge developers to rethink how they implement and deploy client/server applications. This technology can save a great deal of the down-and-dirty grunt work now taken for granted as the price of getting two machines to talk to each other. It allows developers to forget about the nuts and bolts of network programming and concentrate on the job at hand.

As an example, I recently completed a job for a security firm that had installed employee ID card scanners to control access to a steel plant. They needed to gather information from the card readers to select employees for random drug testing. The question was, how would they get the computer at the medical clinic to connect to the server that runs the security system and get that computer to ask for a list of employees in the plant? I chose to implement a client/server application using the MFC CSocket classes. The client application sent a series of messages to the server, which in turn connected to the security controller. The controller shipped a list of people in the plant at that time to the server, which picked some people at random and passed the lucky winners back to the client. None of this was rocket science, but I did have to invent a small messaging protocol based on command/response packets, along with a simple state machine implementation at both ends to respond appropriately to incoming packets. After a lot of tweaking to ensure synchronization between the front and back ends, I finally got the thing installed and running, so I suppose the steel company now has a steady stream of onsite workers filling their quota. Although I was pretty pleased with the implementation, I wondered if perhaps there wasn't a better way. Well, there *is* a better way, and it's the Web.

How CGI Scripts Work

CGI is a relatively simple standard that defines how an HTTP server process can launch an application and pass data from the client's current HTML document to it by using environment variables and the standard input (stdin in Unix speak.) The application usually has the ability to get at resources the client either can't read or can't access because of security restrictions. The results of the application's work are passed back to the client by using the standard output (stdout) in the form of HTML tags generated on-the-fly to allow the user's browser to present the data. The application might be a standard executable, a batch file, or a Perl script; anything that can parse a command line or get environment variables can be a CGI extension. A typical CGI operation, such as a query command within an HTML document, might look something like the following:

```
Click <A HREF="http://BigServer/cgi-bin/
➥avosrch.exe?query=AllAvocados">here </A>
```

to find out just how many people care about avocados.

Embedded in the plain text is a URL that identifies the server `BigServer`. The string `cgi-bin` tells the server where to look for the script that can handle the request, and avosrch.exe is the script itself, in this case an executable file. The server uses the question mark after the script name to figure out where the filename ends and the data to be passed to the script begins. It's up to the script to figure out what the data means and what to do with it. The server creates a separate process for the executable to run and passes `query=AllAvocados` to it in the `QUERY_STRING` environment variable. Listing 13.1 shows another common way to pass data to a CGI script using HTML forms. Forms such as these gather user input with dialog controls like text fields and buttons.

Listing 13.1. Invoking a CGI script with HTML forms.

```
<H1>Choose which types of avocados you are desperately interested
➥in:</H1>
<FORM ACTION="http://BigServer/cgi-bin/avosrch.exe" METHOD=POST>
<INPUT TYPE="checkbox" name="c1" value="SmallAvocados"> Small
➥Avocados
<p>
<INPUT TYPE="checkbox" name="c2" value="LargeAvocados">
➥LargeAvocados
<p>
<INPUT TYPE="checkbox" name="c3" value="ReallyBigAvocados"> Really
➥Big Avocados <p>
<INPUT TYPE="checkbox" name="c4" value="AllAvocados"> All Avocados
➥<p>
<INPUT TYPE="submit" value="Submit">
<p>
</FORM>
```

Listing 13.1 shows a bit of HTML code that defines a command button and set of checkboxes and associates values with them. The <ACTION> tag tells the server what script to execute. The <METHOD> tag indicates a POST operation, which tells the server that the data should be placed on the standard input in the form `Name=Value`, where "Name" is the name of the input field and "Value" is the data associated with it. If, for example, the first checkbox is selected, the value `c1=SmallAvocados` is sent to the script. If the <METHOD> tag had indicated a GET operation, the HTTP server would place the data in an environment variable called `QUERY_STRING`. Other commonly used variable names include `REQUEST_METHOD`, `PATH_INFO`, and `PATH_TRANSLATED`.

How Extensions Are Microsoft's Answer to CGI

Simple though it is, the development of CGI has resulted in an extraordinarily rich and diverse set of applications deployed on Web servers worldwide, from efficient Web page search engines to an online phonebook for everyone in the United States. (I must admit that it's a little spooky to see my name pop up on a server available to anyone in the world.) The explosion in server applications has been more than matched by an explosion of users all clamoring to use these applications, which in turn has forced server administrators to beef up the machines running these applications to handle the load.

Compared to CGI, Microsoft's IIS (Internet Information Server) is quite new, but there are some advantages to joining the party late. IIS does implement CGI, so CGI scripts and their associated HTML documents will work just fine. To address the drawbacks inherent in the CGI process-based model, Microsoft has produced the ISAPI Extension architecture, which maintains the spirit of CGI even as it provides a much-needed performance boost, especially for heavily accessed servers.

Extension Architecture

Unlike CGI, an ISAPI extension is a standard Windows Dynamic Link Library (DLL) that runs in the process space of the IIS server, which avoids the overhead of creating a separate process for every connected user. The IIS server can load extensions on startup and can unload a particular extension if it's had no activity after a given period of time. The same instance of an extension DLL is used for all client connections, so as client connections increase in number, an IIS server uses far fewer resources than a comparable Unix-based CGI server.

There are some drawbacks to running in the server's address space. Because only a single instance of an extension DLL is ever loaded and several clients may be exercising your extension at exactly the same moment, your DLL must be multithread safe. This means that access to static or global data in a DLL must be synchronized using such things as semaphores, critical sections, or mutexes. (Microsoft suggests that you keep your extension processing as short as possible anyway, so that the client isn't waiting around too long for results.) Finally, a "buggy" extension can crash the server. That shouldn't cause too much of a problem, since no one writes buggy code, right?

Living in the server's address space calls for some different ways to pass client data to the extension. Happily, a CGI-based extension, if written as a native executable, can be easily modified to act as an ISAPI extension, usually by simply changing it to a DLL and adding a few required exported functions. If you have CGI extensions in some other form, such as batch files or Perl scripts, the ISAPI SDK offers a set of sample code that shows how an ISAPI extension can provide a wrapper for them so that they can run unchanged. As for the source HTML document, everything works the same way. When IIS sees a URL with an .exe or .bat filename extension, it launches it as a CGI script. If it's a .dll, it tries to load it as an ISA extension, so of course you need to change your CGI script name in the URL to reflect that it's a DLL.

To illustrate, try constructing a simple ISAPI extension that browses directories on the HTTP server. When you're done, you will have accomplished the following:

- Constructed an HTML home page that clients can access to generate requests.

- Constructed an Internet Server Application (ISA) DLL.

- Provided implementations and exports for the `GetExtensionVersion` and `HttpExtensionProc` functions required by the Internet Information Server (IIS).

- Exercised the small set of ISAPI functions to read and send data to the requester.

- Shown how to build HTML on-the-fly to communicate the results of the ISA's work.

Most of these features are required from any ISA DLL, no matter what task you have in mind. However, before you start the actual code, you need to know the tools, just like any good carpenter. Take a few minutes to review the ISAPI functions and data structures before you skip to the code. Also, if you haven't already done so, now would be a good time to install the INetSDK on your development machine and make sure the IIS server software is available to test your extensions. The ideal configuration is a machine with Windows NT Advanced Server, the IIS server software, the INetSDK, and your compiler of choice installed. After all, disk space is cheap nowadays.

The Extension API Set and Associated Data Structures

All extension APIs and data structures are defined in httpext.h in the INetSDK\Include directory. When the ISA server loads an extension for the first time, it looks for an exported function called GetExtensionVersion, which all extensions must implement. This function indicates to the server which version of the ISA specification the extension was written for to provide backward compatibility in future ISA releases. Here is the function prototype:

```
BOOL WINAPI GetExtensionVersion(HSE_VERSION_INFO *pVer);
```

The pVer argument is a pointer to a buffer containing a structure called HSE_VERSION_INFO. The actual definition of the structure, shown in Listing 13.2, is quite simple.

Listing 13.2. HSE_VERSION_INFO structure definition.

```
typedef struct _HSE_VERSION_INFO
{
    DWORD dwExtensionVersion;
    CHAR  lpszExtensionDesc[HSE_MAX_EXT_DLL_NAME_LEN];
}HSE_VERSION_INFO, *LPHSE_VERSION_INFO;
```

All implementations of this function should set the dwExtensionVersion member of the structure to a constant supplied in the INetSDK header file. The other member is a string for including some descriptive information about your extension. A sample suitable for cutting and pasting is shown in Listing 13.3.

Listing 13.3. Sample implementation of GetExtensionVersion.

```
BOOL WINAPI GetExtensionVersion(HSE_VERSION_INFO *pVer)
{
    pVer->dwExtensionVersion = MAKELONG(HSE_VERSION_MINOR,
➥HSE_VERSION_MAJOR);
    lstrcpyn(pVer->lpszExtensionDesc, "Copyright 1996, MuchoAvocado
➥Inc.",
HSE_MAX_EXT_DLL_NAME_LEN);
    return TRUE;
}
```

You've seen that CGI communicates with its extensions by loading up a known set of environment variables with data from the client. Since ISAPI extensions are DLLs that run in the address space of the HTTP server, there's no need for such a roundabout mechanism. Instead, ISA communicates with extension DLLs through a data structure called an Extension Control Block (ECB). The ECB is passed to extensions with the function HttpExtensionProc, which all extensions must export:

```
DWORD HttpExtensionProc( LPEXTENSION_CONTROL_BLOCK *lpEcb);
```

This function is called when the server determines that a client has a request the extension should handle.

The only argument is a pointer to a server-provided buffer containing the Extension Control Block. For most applications, the ECB will contain all the information needed to carry out the client's request. The structure in Listing 13.4 will look pretty familiar to CGI developers. The members are described in Table 13.1.

Listing 13.4. Extension Control Block structure definition.

```
typedef struct _EXTENSION_CONTROL_BLOCK
{
    DWORD     cbSize;
    DWORD     dwVersion;
    DWORD     connID;
    DWORD     dwHttpStatusCode;
    LPSTR     lpszLogData;
    LPSTR     lpszMethod;
    LPSTR     lpszQueryString;
    LPSTR     lpszPathInfo;
    LPSTR     lpszPathTranslated;
    DWORD     cbTotalBytes;
    DWORD     cbAvailable;
    LPBYTE    lpbData;
    LPSTR     lpszContentType;
    BOOL (WINAPI * GetServerVariable) (HCONN hConn,
                                       LPSTR lpszVariableName,
                                       LPVOID lpvBuffer,
                                       LPDWORD lpdwSize);
    BOOL (WINAPI * WriteClient) (HCONN ConnID,
                                 LPVOID Buffer,
                                 LPDWORD lpdwBytes,
                                 DWORD dwReserved);
    BOOL (WINAPI * ReadClient) (HCONN ConnID,
                                LPVOID lpvBuffer,
                                LPDWORD lpdwSize);
```

```
        BOOL (WINAPI * ServerSupportFunction) (HCONN hConn,
                                               DWORD dwHSERequest,
                                               LPVOID lpvBuffer,
                                               LPDWORD lpdwSize,
                                               LPDWORD lpdwDataType);
}EXTENSION_CONTROL_BLOCK, *LPEXTENSION_CONTROL_BLOCK;
```

Table 13.1. Extension Control Block structure definition.

Type	Name	I/O	Description
DWORD	cbSize	In	The size of the structure.
DWORD	dwVersion	In	The version number of the ISA specification that the ISA server implements. The major version number is in the HIWORD, and the minor version number is in the LOWORD. Extensions can use this value to gracefully degrade their functionality to older server versions' capabilities.
HCONN	connID	In	A number, referred to as a connection handle, that

continues

Table 13.1. continued

Type	Name	I/O	Description
			uniquely identifies the session. The handle is provided by the HTTP server; Microsoft says it should not be modified by an extension. Extensions will use this identifier as an argument to some server APIs.
DWORD	dwHttpStatusCode	Out	A value indicating the completion status of the requested operation.
CHAR	lpszLogData[HSE_LOG_BUFFER_LEN]	Out	A buffer containing a null-terminated string that will be posted to the ISA server log. This buffer is fixed at the size specified by the constant HSE_LOG_BUFFER_LEN. Extensions can post useful information in

Type	Name	I/O	Description
			the HTTP server log file with this member.
LPSTR	lpszMethod	In	A buffer containing a string specifying the method used to make the request. This member corresponds to the `REQUEST_METHOD` variable in CGI. This is typically `GET` or `POST`.
LPSTR	lpszQueryString	In	A buffer containing a null-terminated string representing the command requested by the client. In typical CGI applications, such as search engines, this represents a query string, but is application-specific and may be anything. This member corresponds to

continues

Table 13.1. continued

Type	Name	I/O	Description
			the QUERY_STRING variable in CGI.
LPSTR	lpszPathInfo	In	A buffer containing a null-terminated string representing a path in relation to the server's document root. This string typically identifies a particular document that should be returned to the client.
LPSTR	lpszPathTranslated	In	Similar to lpszPathInfo, this null-terminated string indicates the absolute server path to the document. The server generates this string.
DWORD	cbTotalBytes	In	The total number of bytes the extension has to receive from the client.

Type	Name	I/O	Description
			This value corresponds to the CGI variable CONTENT_LENGTH. Further, if this value is 0xFFFFFFFF, there are at least (and maybe more than) four gigabytes of data to read. The extension should use the ReadClient API to fetch the data available.
DWORD	cbAvailable	In	The number of client bytes available for reading. This may be the same as cbTotalBytes, in which case all the data will be in lpbData (below.) If it's less than cbTotalBytes, the extension should call ReadClient until all the data is read.

continues

Table 13.1. continued

Type	Name	I/O	Description
LPBYTE	lpbData	In	The buffer of data from the client.
LPSTR	lpszContentType	In	Indicates the content type of the data from the client. This null-terminated string corresponds to the CGI variable CONTENT_TYPE.

Four structure members are actually pointers to the ISA APIs you need to communicate with the server and the client. Extensions call these functions through the ECB. For example, a call to the ReadClient API might look like the following:

```
pEcb->ReadClient(hConn, pBuffer, dwSize);
```

You can get other variables not represented in the ECB that CGI defines by using the ISAPI GetServerVariable. These variables can contain information about the connection or the implementation of the server. Unless your extension needs to perform some type of security authentication, you probably won't need anything more than what's in the ECB, so your example won't use this API. If you do need to perform authentication, use this API to access the AUTH_TYPE and REMOTE_USER variables. Refer to the appropriate CGI and HTTP specifications for details on how to implement secure extensions or for information on any other CGI-defined variables. This is the prototype for GetServerVariable:

```
BOOL WINAPI GetServerVariable(HCONN hCOnn,

                  LPSTR lpszVariableName,

                  LPVOID lpvBuffer,

                  LPDWORD lpdwSizeOfBuffer);
```

The HCONN parameter indicates the connection handle and is provided by the server as the ConnID member in the ECB structure. You supply a string containing the name of the variable you want in lpszVariableName, and the server copies it into a buffer you supply in lpvBuffer. You must tell the server the size of your buffer with the lpdwSizeOfBuffer parameter, and the server will reset the value of that parameter with the number of bytes actually copied. If the buffer isn't large enough, the call returns FALSE, and a call to GetLastError() indicates ERROR_INSUFFICIENT_BUFFER.

Your implementation of HttpExtensionProc is the main entry point for your extension and is called by the server when a client has a request. Extensions parse the data in the lpszQueryString member if the HTML <METHOD> tag is a GET operation. Alternatively, if the client requests a POST operation, the ReadClient API can get the data. This API is analogous to a CGI's use of the standard input stream and the CONTENT_LENGTH environment variable. For most client requests, a single call to ReadClient, such as

```
BOOL ReadClient(HCONN hConn, LPVOID lpvBuffer, LPDWORD lpdwSize);
```

will get all the input, but the API supports multiple calls to fetch larger blocks.

Just as you do with GetServerVariable, you give the connection handle, a buffer to store the data in, and a value indicating the size of the buffer. If there is more data to fetch, GetLastError will indicate ERROR_INSUFFICIENT_BUFFER. An important thing to remember is that ReadClient will block and wait on the client until the amount of data you specify is available. Also, if the network socket has been closed, ReadClient returns TRUE, but the lpdwSize variable indicates that zero bytes have been read. An extension generally posts data back to the client in the form of HTML. In CGI, a script would indicate the format of the return data by writing a response header to the standard output. Instead, an extension uses the ServerSupportFunction API. The following line is the prototype of the function:

```
BOOL ServerSupportFunction(HCONN hConn,
               DWORD dwHSERequest,
               LPVOID lpvBuffer,
               LPDWORD lpdwSizeOfBuffer,
               LPDWORD lpdwDataType);
```

The hConn argument is the connection handle, and the dwHSERequest argument tells the server what the extension wants it to do. Refer to Table 13.1 for a list of the possible values. Nearly all extensions use only the

HSE_REQ_SEND_RESPONSE_HEADER command. The lpvBuffer argument changes meaning based on the type of server request you send. When using the HSE_REQ_SEND_RESPONSE_HEADER request, extensions put an optional status message to send back to the client, such as the ever-annoying but always useful 401 Access Denied message. If you set this argument to NULL, the server will handily send the message 200 OK for you. Use the lpdwSizeOfBuffer argument to indicate the size of the string in lpvBuffer.

Note that you should include the terminating NULL character at the end of the lpvBuffer string. The lpdwDataType argument is used to send a NULL-terminated string containing optional header information. This string nearly always contains the Content-type keyword to indicate the type of information you're sending back. The following shows a typical use of this API:

```
TCHAR lpszBuff[] = "Content-type: text/html\r\n";
DWORD dwSize = sizeof(lpszBuff);
pEcb->ServerSupportFunction(hConn, HSE_REQ_SEND_RESPONSE_HEADER,
➥NULL, &dwSize, (LPDWORD)lpszBuff);
```

Once the extension has determined what the client wants to do, either by getting the command string from QUERY_STRING or by using ReadClient, it performs the task it was asked to do and returns the results. It does this by forming HTML strings and using the WriteClient API. The following shows the prototype of this function, which is nearly identical to ReadClient:

```
BOOL WINAPI WriteClient(HCONN ConnID, LPVOID Buffer, LPDWORD
➥lpdwBytes, DWORD dwReserved);
```

After the connection handle, the argument Buffer is a pointer to a buffer containing the data to send to the client. For this example, you send NULL-terminated text data, but the type of data should match the Content-type string sent earlier. If the data in the buffer is a string, it should be null-terminated. The lpdwBytes argument tells the server how many bytes are in the buffer. This argument is also used by the server to indicate how many bytes were actually sent, which should always equal the number of bytes in the buffer. If the count of bytes is any amount less than that, then something bad happened, such as an interruption in the client/network connection. Also, if you are sending back a NULL-terminated string, the variable should be set to the string length minus the NULL terminator.

REGBROWSE: A Server Directory Browser

I've harped on the fact that an extension is a DLL that runs in the server's address space. Since the server loads the extension either on demand or at startup, it must load the extension dynamically. To do this, the server executes the LoadLibrary Win32 function, specifying the module's name in the HTML document's URL.

Once the library is in memory, the server will use GetProcAddress, using the symbol names for the functions it needs to call—namely, GetExtensionVersion and HttpExtensionProc. This means you must export these functions by creating an export definition module (see Listing 13.5) with the names of these functions in the EXPORTS section. (There are other ways of exporting functions, but this is the most common way.) Most DLLs also export a default entry point called DllMain that's called by the operating system when LoadLibrary is executed; it gives you a convenient place to handle any initialization your extension needs, such as loading state information from disk or initializing global variables. DllMain is not strictly required, but Microsoft recommends that you create one. In your sample extension, however, you'll go against that recommendation because you have no global data or state information to load.

Listing 13.5. REGBROWSE.DEF: The Exports File.

```
LIBRARY     regbrowse
DESCRIPTION  'Internet Server Extension DLL'
EXPORTS
    GetExtensionVersion
    HttpExtensionProc
```

I call this extension REGBROWSE, short for "A Regular Browser." The purpose of REGBROWSE is to allow clients to browse the server's file system. To that end, the extension has a very simple structure. You've already seen how GetExtensionVersion works, so there's no need to go over that again. Listing 13.6 shows REGBROWSE's implementation of HttpExtensionProc. Several variables are defined up front to handle the directory browsing, and an object called CISHelper is declared locally, with a pointer to the ECB structure as an argument to the constructor.

The `CISHelper` class (see Listing 13.6) was created to help you parse incoming data and communicate with the server. It stores the ECB in its private member data to simplify its other calls. `CISHelper`'s functionality is simple but useful—it handles reading commands from the client and sending data to it. It could also have handled the generation of HTML for you, but I chose to leave it in the main body. The INetSDK sample code contains a bonanza of APIs that make tasks like generating HTML much easier, and I leave it as an exercise to the reader to find and play with it. Once you've finished here, you'll have everything you need to know to understand the SDK's extension examples.

Listing 13.6. A partial listing of `HttpExtensionProc`.

```
DWORD WINAPI HttpExtensionProc(EXTENSION_CONTROL_BLOCK *pEcb)
{
    TCHAR    lpszDirectoryName[MAX_DIRECTORY_ENTRY+1];
    TCHAR    lpszDirectoryEntry[MAX_DIRECTORY_ENTRY];
    TCHAR    lpszDataBuffer[MAX_DIRECTORY_ENTRY];
    TCHAR    lpszFindString[MAX_DIRECTORY_ENTRY];
    CISHelper cHelper(pEcb);

    // Start the page
    cHelper.SendResponseHeader();
    cHelper.WriteClient(TEXT("<HEAD><TITLE>"));
    cHelper.WriteClient(TEXT("The Big Browser Page"));
    cHelper.WriteClient(TEXT("</TITLE></HEAD>\r\n\r\n"));
    cHelper.WriteClient(TEXT("<BODY>\r\n\r\n"));
    cHelper.WriteClient(TEXT("<h1>Server File System Browser</
➥h1>"));
```

The first real piece of work `HttpExtensionProc` does is to send the response header back to the client. You'll recall that the response header informs the client about the extension output format. Once that business is taken care of, the extension begins HTML generation by sending the title of the generated page. It then calls the `CISHelper` method `GetCommand`. This method bears looking into a little deeper because of the ways it deals with the various input methods available to the client. (See Listing 13.7.)

`GetCommand` first determines what the input method is by checking the value of `m_pEcb->lpszMethod` for `"GET"`. Since I created the HTML page that drives the extension, I know beyond a shadow of a doubt that you will get only a GET or POST. If it's a GET, call the `ConvertHtmlEscapes` method (I'll get to that in a minute) and return the resulting string back to `HttpExtensionProc`. If it's a

POST, check the value of m_pEcb->cbTotalBytes to see if no data was sent. If so, then HttpExtensionProc prints a nasty little message and returns it to the client.

Listing 13.7. Parsing the command string.

```
BOOL CISHelper::GetCommand(LPTSTR lpszData, LPDWORD lpdwSize)
{
    if(!m_pEcb)
    {
        return FALSE;
    }

    // It's a GET method. No URL escapes to process.
// Just copy the string and get out.
    if (!stricmp(m_pEcb->lpszMethod, "GET"))
    {
        ConvertHtmlEscapes(lpszData, (char *)m_pEcb-
➥>lpszQueryString);
        // lstrcpy(lpszData, (char *)m_pEcb->lpszQueryString);
        *lpdwSize = lstrlen(lpszData);
        return TRUE;
    }
    else
    {
        if(m_pEcb->cbTotalBytes == 0)      // No query at all
        {
            *lpdwSize = 0;
            return FALSE;
        }
        else
        {
            DWORD dwCount = 0;
            char lpszTemp[1024];
            char *s = NULL;

            lstrcpy(lpszTemp, (char *)m_pEcb->lpbData);

            if(m_pEcb->cbTotalBytes - m_pEcb->cbAvailable > 0)
            {
                m_pEcb->ReadClient(m_pEcb->ConnID,
                        (LPVOID) (lpszTemp + m_pEcb->cbAvailable),
                        &dwCount);
            }
            // Do escape char substitution
            s = strchr(lpszTemp, '=');
            if(!s)
            {
                return FALSE;
```

continues

Listing 13.7. continued

```
                }
                ++s;
                ConvertHtmlEscapes(lpszData, s);
                *lpdwSize = strlen(lpszData);
            }
        }

    return TRUE;
}
```

If there is data, `m_pEcb->cbTotalBytes` will be greater than zero and you handle two stages of input. In the first case, `cbTotalBytes` will be greater than `cbAvailableBytes`. If that happens, it means the server has given you only part of the data in the `lpbData` member variable, so you must call `ReadClient` to get the rest. If `cbTotalBytes` and `cbAvailableBytes` are the same, all the data the client ships is available in `lpbData`. In this example, you will probably never be called upon to exercise the `ReadClient` logic, but it's there just in case. Once you have the data, call `ConvertHtmlEscapes` again and return the string.

Now is a good time to talk about what `ConvertHtmlEscapes` does (refer to Listing 13.8). Windows directory paths contain at the very least two special characters (and possibly more) that have special meaning to HTTP, so for you to get the data unscathed, it's delivered to the extension in a special format. The : and \ characters are replaced with the ASCII characters `&3A` and `&5C`, respectively. Referring to your handy ASCII character set table, you see that these are the hexadecimal codes for these characters. You can't make much use of them this way, so you have to convert them to real hex numbers to build a directory search string later. Other characters are mangled as well, although they are easier to handle. For example, any spaces in the string are converted to a + character. `ConvertHtmlEscapes` takes as input two buffers, the destination and source strings. It scans through the source string looking for escape sequences and + characters and makes the appropriate conversions. It also dispenses with any carriage returns and line feeds. Once it returns, you have a string suitable for `HttpExtensionProc`'s use.

Listing 13.8. Converting HTML escape sequences.

```
void CISHelper::ConvertHtmlEscapes(LPSTR lpszDest, LPSTR
➡lpszSource)
{
```

```
int i = 0;
TCHAR *pChar = lpszSource;
TCHAR *pDestChar = lpszDest;

while(*pChar)
{
    switch(*pChar)
    {
        case 0x0a:
        case 0x0d:
            pChar++;
            break;

        // The plus sign is really a space character
        case '+':
            *pDestChar++ = ' ';
            pChar++;
            break;
        // Percent indicates a hex code. You need to
        // convert a two-byte ascii into an equivalent
        // hex number. For example, %3A == 0x3a
        case '%':
            // skip over the percent sign
            pChar++;
            if (*pChar >= '0' && *pChar <= '9')
            {
                *pDestChar = *pChar - '0';
            }
            else
            {
                *pDestChar = *pChar + 0x0A - 'A';
            }
            // You've converted the high order byte;
            // now shift it to its proper place
            // in the output
            *pDestChar <<= 4;

            // Next!
            pChar++;
            if (*pChar >= '0' && *pChar <= '9')
            {
                *pDestChar |= *pChar - '0';
            }
            else
            {
                *pDestChar |= *pChar + 0x0A - 'A';
            }

            pChar++;
            pDestChar++;
            break;
```

continues

Listing 13.8. continued

```
            default:
                *pDestChar++ = *pChar++;
                break;
        }
        *pDestChar = '\0';
    }
}
```

The next thing `HttpExtensionProc` does is to generate HTML representing the values contained in some of the more important ECB members. This will become useful to you when you start making modifications to the extension. Once you know what directory the user wants, concatenate the filter `*.*` to the end of the directory name and get a search handle by calling the Win32 function `FindFirstFile`. This function returns everything you ever wanted to know about a file, except whether it's a file or a directory. If it's a directory, you want to generate an HTML hyperlink so that the user can click on it to list its contents too. You do that by getting the attributes of the file and, if it's a directory, generating an HTML hyperlink that specifies a URL pointing to your script with the new directory appended to the string.

Refer to Listing 13.9 to see how the URL is generated. Note that the URL you generate results in a GET method. If it's a regular file, you print out the name, creation date, and file size as regular text. In both cases, you use the `CISHelper` method `WriteClient` to send text back to the server. Once you've finished listing the directory, generate an end-of-page HTML sequence and return a successful status to the server. Recall that your DLL remains in memory until the server decides there's no longer any need for it.

Listing 13.9. Generating a URL for a directory.

```
// Convert the file's creation date so you can print it
        FileTimeToSystemTime(&stFindData.ftCreationTime,
➥&stSysTime);
        dwFileAttr = GetFileAttributes(lpszDirectoryEntry);
        // if this is a directory, you want to create a bookmark
        // to allow the user to browse it. Otherwise,
        // you print the file data in plain text.
        if(dwFileAttr & FILE_ATTRIBUTE_DIRECTORY )
        {
            TCHAR lpszLine[MAX_DIRECTORY_ENTRY];
```

```
                        wsprintf(lpszDataBuffer,
                                "http://%s/scripts/regbrows.dll?%s",
                                SERVERNAME,
                                lpszDirectoryEntry);
                        wsprintf(lpszLine,
                                TEXT("<code><A HREF=\"%s\">%s</
➥A><code><p>\r\n"),
                                lpszDataBuffer,
                                stFindData.cFileName);
                        cHelper.WriteClient(lpszLine);
                }
                else
                {
                    wsprintf(lpszDataBuffer,
                    "<code>%25s     %02d-%02d-%02d%d</code>\r\n",
                    stFindData.cFileName,
                    stSysTime.wMonth,
                    stSysTime.wDay,
                    stSysTime.wYear,
                    stFindData.nFileSizeLow);
                    cHelper.WriteClient(lpszDataBuffer);
                    cHelper.WriteClient(TEXT("<p>\r\n"));
                }
```

Now take a look at the HTML that drives the extension. The salient features here are the two ways you can send requests to the server. The first one is a URL (see listing 13.10), which generates a request in the form of a GET method. I've hard-coded a directory path in the URL to give the user a starting point. The other is a FORM section that uses the POST method. The user can enter the desired starting directory and click the Submit button. Figure 13.1 shows a view of the REGBROWSE Web page user interface, and Figure 13.2 shows the results of the request.

Listing 13.10. HTML source for the REGBROWSE Web page interface.

```
<h2>Select the default directory link below. </h2>
<p>
<A HREF="http://kevpc/scripts/
➥regbrows.dll?c:\inetsrv\scripts">C:\InetSrv\Scripts</A>
<FORM Action="http://kevpc/scripts/regbrows.dll" method=post>
<p>
Or enter a starting path in the field below.
<p>
<INPUT Name="Path" Value="c:\">
<INPUT TYPE="SUBMIT" VALUE="Submit">
</FORM>
```

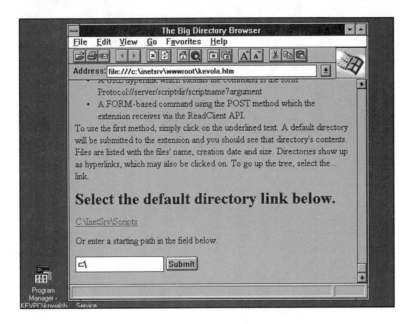

Figure 13.1.
The REGBROWSE Web page user interface.

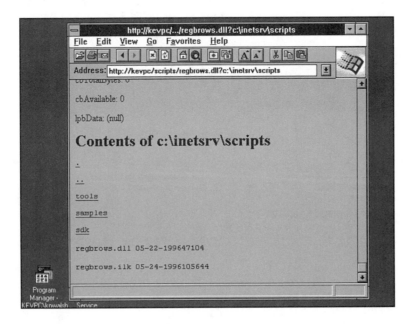

Figure 13.2.
A REGBROWSE-generated Web page.

Getting the Extension Running

To run the example, copy the DLL into your server's scripts root. If you took all the defaults when you installed the IIS software, this will be in C:\inetsrv\scripts. You must also allow scripts to read and execute from the directory. (See Figure 13.3.) The Internet Service Manager applet allows you to choose the system account that clients will use when accessing server resources and what permissions they have. The very nature of this example requires more permissions than most applications require. You might want to set the client account to one that has permission to browse the directory tree. Doing this would cause most of the system administrators I know to have a fit of monstrous proportions, so make sure you don't install the example on a production machine.

Once you have the DLL in the scripts directory, make sure you make any needed modifications to the HTML file to point to the correct server. As shipped, it's hardcoded to use my development machine. (Don't even try to connect to it; you can't.) The code that generates URLs for directories also needs to be changed to point to your server. Once all that is done, use the Internet Service Manager applet to make sure the WWW service is running. You can then use your favorite browser to load up the HTML file and begin to play.

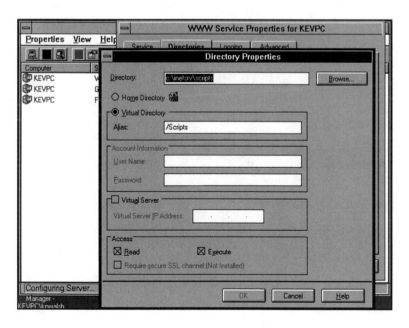

Figure 13.3.
Setting server directory permissions.

Debugging ISA Extensions

Since the ISA server is the parent process of an ISA extension, it probably isn't immediately clear how one goes about setting up a debugging environment. The INetSDK does give you a pretty good answer to that problem, though it's not immediately apparent that it's there.

Under the ISAPI sample code tree, there's an innocuous little project called ISMoke. When you run this example, you see a dialog box where you enter your DLL extension name, a query string to send to the extension, and the method to use to send the request. (See Figure 13.4.) A checkbox allows you to quickly load and unload the DLL so that you can rebuild your project and run it again. I should also point out that, in the version of the SDK I have, ISMoke generates only GET methods. It always nulls out the cbBytesAvailable, cbTotalBytes, and lpvData members, so that even if you do send a POST, you'll get no data. Listing 13.11 shows a simple modification to the CISmokeDlg::Submit method in ismokedlg.cpp to make posts work.

> Caution: By the time you read this, I expect Microsoft will have significantly polished its ISA development tools, but if they haven't, you've been warned!

Listing 13.11. Getting ISmoke to support POST methods.

```
    ...
    ecb.lpszMethod = szMeth;
    // This is the modification to fix the post method
    if(stricmp(szMeth, "get") == 0)
    {
        ecb.lpszQueryString = szStmnt;
        ecb.cbTotalBytes = 0;
        ecb.cbAvailable = 0;
        ecb.lpbData = NULL;
    }
    else
    {
        ecb.cbTotalBytes = strlen(szStmnt)+1;
        ecb.cbAvailable = ecb.cbTotalBytes;
        ecb.lpbData = (unsigned char *)szStmnt;
    }
    ...
}
```

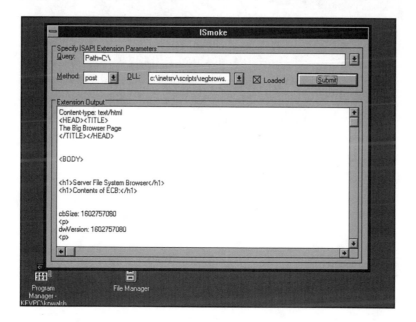

Figure 13.4.
The ISmoke *extension debugging tool.*

As a final debugging alternative, you can make use of the lpszLogData member of the ECB structure to write debug information to the server log file. It might seem, in these days of high-powered graphical development tools, a little like grabbing a stone axe to hunt up some dinner, but you can also look at it this way: When you want raw performance, you don't buy a big, plush car with leather seats.

Moving On

The techniques described here will help you produce some surprisingly powerful applications in a relatively short time. All that's needed is an extension DLL that exports the functions GetExtensionVersion and HttpExtensionProc, an HTML front end that submits requests through either GET or POST methods, and a mechanism for generating HTML output for the client to view the results. Use the REGBROWSE server DLL implementation as a framework to implement applications, such as database query engines or data entry tools, commonly done today with client/server technology.

Of course, a much richer set of ActiveX tools than simple HTML is available for creating really jazzy client pages. In the next couple of chapters, you'll learn about 3-D views of information using Active VRML, online multimedia, and some practical development strategies. You shouldn't throw away your super-duper sockets class libraries just yet, but as you dig into ISAPI extensions and ActiveX controls, you'll soon find that those other fancy client/server tools are starting to gather dust. I expect to see a new crop of interesting and exciting Web server applications make their way onto the Internet. Until then, I'll be staring at that avocado seed.

Issues and the Future of ActiveX

CHAPTER 14

Applications of ActiveX

by Warren Ernst

When use of the Internet and World Wide Web started to take off in early 1995, most people were using their browsers to retrieve text-based information to their screens, with perhaps only the occasional drawing or photograph along with it. Nobody had a problem with this lack of multimedia on the Web because first, nobody was really expecting anything more, and second, most people didn't have a direct LAN, ISDN, or 28.8 modem connection. Now, most people have Internet access at speeds only fantasized about in early 1995, and the bandwidth currently exists to widen how the Internet is used, far beyond relatively simple text.

However, access to high-speed connections is only part of the solution to moving beyond basic text-file transfer; there needs to be a common methodology to expand these horizons—and ActiveX is the answer. By using ActiveX controls and documents, almost anything that's *not* simple text can be transferred, used, and interacted with through the Internet more easily than it is now. This data includes not only new forms of files and information, such as audio, video, three-dimensional modeling, or whatever new forms of multimedia come along, but even new ways of using the Internet. ActiveX controls and documents pave the way to create applications for which the Internet is a vital information-gathering and transmitting pathway and that work within popular Web browsers. In short, ActiveX technologies can transform mere Web page sites into Web-based applications that run within your browser and calculate, manipulate, or create new information at your command.

This chapter demonstrates some of the new forms of multimedia and Web-based applications available today by using ActiveX controls and ActiveX documents.

Online Multimedia with ActiveX

Multimedia without ActiveX can be tricky at times—perhaps unnecessarily so. To enjoy multimedia with today's conventional Web browsers, plug-in modules or helper applications need to be installed and sometimes run in another window on the desktop, before users can enjoy video or audio feeds, virtual reality, or any of the other interesting new file formats.

ActiveX controls and documents reduce the burden on both the programmer and user of new multimedia programs and formats, enabling programmers to create programs and files more easily and users to retrieve and manipulate them more simply. Plus, they allow new formats to be directly embedded in Web pages for a truly new, online experience. This chapter reviews some of the new multimedia formats, ActiveX controls, and documents currently online that demonstrate the power of ActiveX-enabled multimedia.

Singing and Dancing Web Pages: ActiveX Eye Candy

One of the early experiments involving Java applets included simply making Web pages "stand out" from the rest of the world—normally by programming a little something that was animated, complete with lots of motion and bright colors. These little splashes of ingenuity have come to be called *eye candy*.

Now that ActiveX has recently been made available to the public, programmers have been devising ways to use ActiveX controls (either those bundled with Internet Explorer 3.0, or new ones of their design) to make eye candy, too. One clever and simple use of the included Label control can be found at Nuke's ActiveX Showcase page at `http://www.nuke.com/vbscript/vbscript.htm`. Once you get there, click the Matching Game link in the left frame, then follow the links to play the matching game in the right frame until you see something similar to Figure 14.1.

Figure 14.1.
Although the point of this page is to show off the Matching game, the entire game is an ActiveX VBScript!

I encourage you to play the Matching game itself, but make sure you notice the spinning, scrolling, multicolored text *above* the game. This text dances because of the Label control that comes with Internet Explorer.

New Types of Web-Based Multimedia

Full, 360-degree images with embedded hypertext hotspots have never been seen side-by-side with Web page text before, but with the Surround Video ActiveX control, they appear together now! By jumping to the Black Diamond Consulting site at `http://www.bdiamond.com/` and following the Surround Video Page links, you can manually download and install the Surround Video control and view the page in Figure 14.2.

Figure 14.2.
Embedded 360-degree images combine with hypertext with Black Diamond's Surround Video ActiveX control.

Once you install it and jump to the Surround Video demo page at `http://www.bdiamond.com/surround/demo/demo2.htm`, you can pan around the image by dragging the cursor left or right. The cursor will change to a "pointing hand" when it's positioned over a hypertext hotspot; clicking it loads another image.

Replacing Traditional Helper Applications with ActiveX

One of the problems associated with new types of multimedia files is the different programs required to use them, with one of these new formats being generically referred to as "Virtual Reality." The Virtual Reality Modeling Language (VRML) is currently being used to allow online users to walk through a three-dimensional landscape or manipulate three-dimensional objects onscreen as if they were holding them in their hands. This ActiveX module, referred to as Active VRML, allows Web surfers to seamlessly cruise these new VRML worlds while within the ActiveX-containing Internet Explorer 3.0, and it offers a relatively simple way for programmers to embed VRML technology into their own applications.

The sample site at `http://www.microsoft.com/INTDEV/avr/beta/default.htm` provides both samples and Active VRML itself.

Another useful ActiveX control lets the Web distribute Microsoft PowerPoint animation files directly to Internet Explorer, complete with transitions and other presentation attributes, but without the need for PowerPoint itself. Currently, the ActiveX control needs to be manually downloaded and installed from Microsoft at `http://www.microsoft.com/mspowerpoint/internet/player/default.htm`, but once you do, you can interactively work with PowerPoint files directly with your Web browser. (You'll find examples of how to create Web-based special effects for PowerPoint files in this site as well.) Once installed, you'll find a good set of presentations at `http://home.sprynet.com/sprynet/bjjohnson/xanimate.htm`, as well as at Microsoft itself.

PowerPoint animations run directly within Internet Explorer just as though they were HTML pages, but since the content is based on PowerPoint, there can be sounds, transitions, and a specific order to the presented information—in other words, there is intentionally no variable path that hypertext normally offers. When making a presentation, however, this is usually beneficial because it enforces the idea of one fact building into another.

The presentation at `http://www.threedgraphics.com/compadre/comp_live.html` is a good example of what PowerPoint Animations can do. Once you get to this page, click on "Click here to see a full-size (640×480) version of the presentation," and enjoy the show (it might take a minute or two to download). You'll witness smooth, scrolling text or transitions, hear embedded sounds, and follow a presentation just as though you were using PowerPoint, but within Internet Explorer. You can advance the slides by clicking the mouse in the content area or let them advance at their preprogrammed rate.

Web-Based Applications with ActiveX

One of the goals of ActiveX technologies is to change the way you use the Internet. Microsoft envisions ActiveX changing the Web from merely a source of static information to a place you jump to and fro to use Web-based applications, almost as though the Web were an extension of your local hard drive. For example, if you wanted to buy airline tickets yourself, you would jump to an airline's Web-based program through a conventional URL, "run" it through your Web browser, and book your flight. The transmittable nature of ActiveX makes this scenario possible.

Unfortunately, there are no ActiveX-based programs on the Web that perform such complicated actions…yet. In the meantime, there are several smaller, "test" Web-based applications available to play with right now, and "play with" is the operative term. As in the early days of Java applets, many developers have been testing the new technology by creating Web-based, online games using ActiveX controls.

Searching the Real World with the Web

Most people use programs to search for things in the online world, but did you know there's an ActiveX-enabled site that lets you search the real world? MapQuest, from GeoSystems Global Corp., is just such a site. Using ActiveX controls, you can send the MapQuest program any street address in the United States; in response, MapQuest displays a map of the location you want. You can also change the magnification of the map to 10 different levels, and interactively pan the map in four directions. Figure 14.3 illustrates what this innovative program looks like.

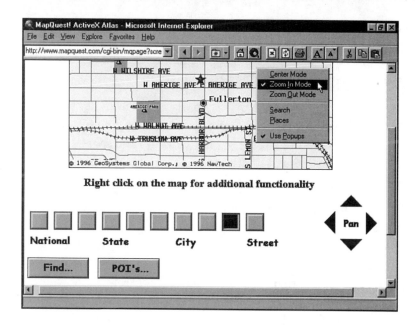

Figure 14.3.
Finding the location of an address has never been so easy! Give MapQuest an address, and it returns with a map. The star indicates the address's actual location.

To try MapQuest yourself, jump to http://www.mapquest.com/ and follow the links to the ActiveX version. Once it loads, click the Find button and enter an address in the Search dialog box (ZIP codes aren't always required, so if you don't know it, don't panic). Once you click OK, the map in the center of the page will automatically display the map with the entered address. To pan up, down, left, or right, click any of the pan arrows. To zoom in or out of the map, click any of the 10 magnification buttons to a state, city, or street level.

> Tip: If you really need the ZIP code of an address and don't have it handy, you can search for it at the United States Post Office Web site ZIP Code Lookup page at http://www.usps.gov/ncsc/lookups/lookup_zip+4.html.

This site also offers a version of MapQuest that doesn't use ActiveX technologies; instead, it uses the conventional Web page/server approach of constantly sending entire Web pages for even a simple panning of the map. Once you check out this alternative version, you'll have a firsthand look at the speed increases to be gained by using ActiveX controls.

Playing Games on the Web

The Web is certainly no stranger to users goofing around online, but never before has the online gaming within a Web page been so fast and furious, with the speed and graphics rivaling arcade games. In fact, ActiveX technologies enable this sort of time-wasting, but also pave the way for graphically intensive Web applications to be built in the future.

An example of this new, graphically intensive program class can be found at the NCompass ActiveX Netscape plug-in sample site at `http://www.ncompasslabs.com/ActiveX/index.html`. Once there, click the Multi Player Game icon to load the Tank Duel game (along with a new ActiveX control) in the Web page frame on the right. The new ActiveX control that downloads automatically is almost 350K in size, so plan on waiting according to your connection speed, but once it downloads and activates, a Duel image appears.

When it does, click the image and press the Enter key on your keyboard. From the resulting Choose Connection Mechanism dialog box, select Local Network (TCP) and click OK, then click the Create button in the resulting Create Game or Connect to Game dialog box. After a moment of initialization, the game starts and you can begin controlling the red tank in the upper-right corner of the playfield. (See Figure 14.4.)

To play the game by yourself, rotate the tank with your keyboard's left- and right-arrow keys, and thrust it forward or backward with the up- and down-arrow keys. Fire your gun with the spacebar. Once you're done moving around and shooting buildings, the Esc key ends the game. Another player can join your game by clicking the Connect button in the Create Game or Connect to Game dialog box, and selecting your computer from the resulting list.

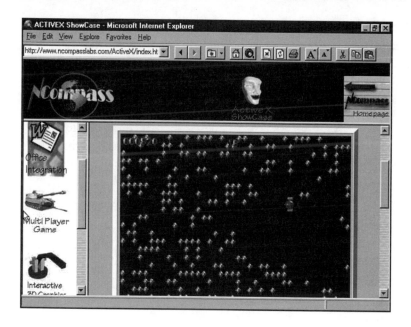

Figure 14.4.
The Tank Duel game represents the first Web-based arcade game with any amount of speed and excitement.

Educational Kiosks Through ActiveX

One of the immediate uses of the World Wide Web has been to educate people, and educators have been taking advantage of this resource to deliver text and graphical images to students from across the world. ActiveX technology takes this one step further, since information sources can truly be enabled to interact with people.

Two excellent examples of the kind of interactive kiosks that are possible are located in the previously mentioned NCompass site at http://www.ncompasslabs.com/ActiveX/index.html. If you are still there from the previous example, click the Interactive 3D Graphics icon in the left frame; when queried, allow the two new ActiveX controls to install in your system. Once they do, the right frame poses two different ActiveX controls that can communicate with each other, resulting in an accurate, three-dimensional rendering of a robotic arm and control panel. (See Figure 14.5.) To control the arm interactively, repeatedly click the directional arrows next to the arm.

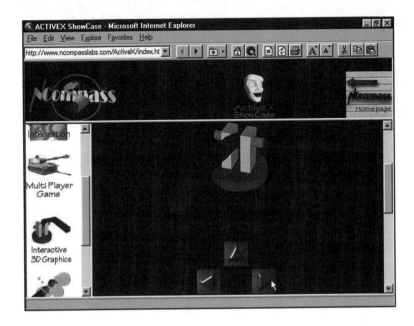

Figure 14.5.
The robotic arm rotates and lifts by clicking the buttons in its control panel, almost like the real thing.

If you click the Interactive 3D Graphics icon in the left frame (just below the Art Gallery icon), a new control loads that automatically rotates a three-dimensional cube and lets you rotate the cube by dragging the mouse. (See Figure 14.6.) This cube could be a construct of any three-dimensional object, such as a molecule or animal, embedded directly within a descriptive Web page. As a tool for educators, ActiveX controls allow these kiosks to be made widely available across the Internet, permitting common lessons over a wide geographic area.

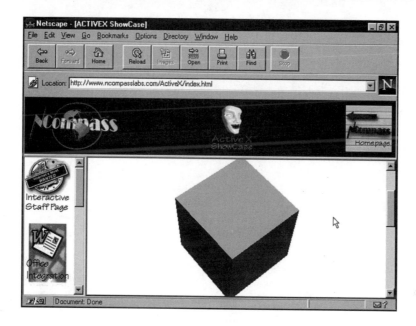

Figure 14.6.
Even though this cube rotates by itself, you can easily change its rotation with your mouse.

Moving On

This chapter has explored some of the more interesting ActiveX-enabled Web sites available today. In the next chapters, you'll see the similarities and differences between Java and ActiveX (Chapter 15) and the expected evolution of ActiveX and Nashville, the next version of Windows 95, in Chapter 16.

ActiveX Versus Java

by Michael Morrison

It's pretty much impossible to discuss ActiveX without bringing up its relationship to Java. Although you've already learned about some of the differences between ActiveX and Java, it's time to take a closer look at exactly where each technology is positioned in the whole of the interactive Web. With all the hype associated with both Java and ActiveX, it's easy to get confused over where each is headed. Even more important to Web developers is the issue of deciding which technology to embrace and whether that decision can even be made.

The goal of this chapter is to give you some perspective on the relationship between Java and ActiveX. In doing so, you learn the details surrounding what each technology offers and why they don't necessarily have to be viewed as direct competitors. In fact, you learn that the stage is being set for the two technologies to complement each other in a variety of ways.

Technological Goals

In a general sense, Java and ActiveX are both trying to achieve the same goal: to bring interactivity to the Web. This is a very general goal, and, as you probably realize, many different approaches can be taken to reach it. Java and ActiveX definitely take different routes to delivering interactivity to the Web, and for good reason; they're widely divergent technologies that come from two unique companies. First, take a look at each technology and see what it accomplishes in its pursuit to liven up the Web.

Java Pursuits

First and foremost, Java is a programming language. It certainly is other things as well, but the underlying strength of the Java technology is the structure and design of the Java language itself. The architects at Sun wanted to take many of the powerful features in C++ and build a tighter, easier to use, and more secure object-oriented language. They succeeded in a big way; Java is indeed a very clean, easy-to-use language with lots of advanced security features. The time spent designing the Java language is paying off well for Sun, since the language's structure is the primary cause of the C++ programmer migration to Java.

However, without its standard class libraries and Internet support, the Java language would be nothing more than competition for C++. In fact, the Java language, as cleverly designed as it is, would probably fail in a head-to-head match with C++, strictly from a language perspective. This is because C++ is firmly established in the professional development community, and programmers need a compelling reason to learn an entirely new language. Fortunately for Sun, Java has been presented as much more than just another programming language.

The basic Java technology consists of the Java language, the Java class libraries, the Java runtime system, and the JavaScript scripting language. It's the combination of all these parts that makes the Java technology so exciting. Java is the first large-scale effort at creating a truly cross-platform programming language with lots of functionality from the start. Couple the slick language and cross-platform aspects of Java with the ability to seamlessly integrate Java programs into the Web environment, and you can easily see the appeal.

This integration of the Web into the Java technology is no accident; Sun simply saw the potential to capitalize on a technology they had been developing for a while by fitting it to the Internet's rapidly growing needs. This pretty much sums up the aim of Java: to give you a means to safely integrate cross-platform interactive applications into the Web environment by using an object-oriented language.

ActiveX Pursuits

Microsoft has different ideas for the Internet than Sun does. Unlike Sun, Microsoft initially didn't realize the immediate potential of the Internet, or at least they didn't see how fast it was all happening. In fact, it wasn't until the excitement surrounding Java that Microsoft finally decided they had to rethink the Internet and the Web.

The connection was finally made somewhere in Redmond that the Internet would significantly affect personal computing. They couldn't just sit idly by and see what happened; they could either take action to capitalize on the Internet or get "burned" by not accepting it as a major shift in the way computers are used. When Microsoft finally came to terms with the Internet rapidly changing the face of computing—even personal computing—they quickly regrouped and decided to figure out a way to get a piece of the Internet action. Keep in mind that Microsoft has never been content with just a piece of the action; they want the largest piece of the action!

Unlike Sun, Microsoft already had a wide range of successful commercial software technologies; they just had to figure out which one would adapt best to the Internet. It turned out that one of their most successful technologies was ideally suited for the Internet: OLE. They saw OLE as a powerful, stable technology with lots of potential for the Internet, and they were right; ActiveX is basically OLE revamped for the Internet.

Unlike Java, however, ActiveX isn't just meant to be a way to add interactivity to the Web. Sure, that's part of it, but Microsoft isn't the type of company to just hand out technologies for the good of humanity. OLE is a technology deeply ingrained in most of Microsoft's commercial products, as well as many other commercial Windows applications. By simply migrating OLE to the Internet (ActiveX), Microsoft can effectively assume a huge market share of Internet products overnight. Suddenly, every piece of code based on OLE can now be considered ActiveX-enabled with little extra work. Microsoft's new goal of migrating desktop software to the Internet suddenly looks quite attainable!

Although Microsoft is certainly looking to bring interactive applications to the Web through ActiveX, they are making sure that many of those interactive applications are Microsoft applications. This situation also ensures that Windows remains a strong presence on the Internet, since OLE is essentially a Windows-derived technology. Although strategically ideal, selecting OLE as the technological underpinnings for ActiveX has much more to do with OLE being a slick technology already tweaked for distributed computing; it's just the icing on the cake that OLE is already firmly established in the PC development community.

Microsoft isn't the only company to benefit from the positioning of ActiveX. Every PC software developer that uses OLE in its applications will benefit from ActiveX just as easily as Microsoft will. Because the PC development community is by far the largest in the industry, end users will also benefit greatly, since many software companies will be building ActiveX applications from existing OLE code that's already stable.

So far in this discussion of ActiveX, little has been said about programming languages. Unlike Java, ActiveX has nothing to do with a specific programming language; you can write ActiveX code in any language you choose that supports Microsoft's COM specification. Just in case you don't realize it, this is a big deal! Although Java is a very powerful language, many programmers don't like being forced to learn a new language just to exploit the capabilities of the Internet. On the other hand, writing ActiveX controls in C++ is a little messier than writing Java applets in Java.

In many ways, the ActiveX technology extends beyond the reach of Java. For example, as you've already learned, ActiveX offers Microsoft's answer to CGI scripting with ISAPI applications and filters. Additionally, the whole concept of ActiveX documents is far beyond anything Java has to offer.

At this point in the discussion, what's important is that although Java and ActiveX both serve the same ends of bringing interactive applications to the Web, they do so for different reasons and use two distinct approaches. Ultimately, ActiveX is a more complete technology, even if it's more complex to learn and use at the programming level.

Ante Up

OK, so you have an idea what each technology is trying to accomplish, but what does each actually deliver? It turns out that Java and ActiveX are surprisingly different in their implementations, especially considering how similar their ultimate goals are.

What Java Brings to the Game

The Java technology can be broken down into these four major components

- The Java language
- The Java class libraries
- The Java runtime system
- The JavaScript scripting language

The Java language supplies the programmatic underpinnings that make the whole Java system possible. It's the Java language that shines brightest when comparing Java to ActiveX. The Java class libraries, which go hand-in-hand with the language, offer a wide array of features guaranteed to work on any platform. This is a huge advantage Java has over almost every other programming language in existence. Never before has a tight, powerful language been delivered that offers a rich set of standard classes in a cross-platform manner.

The Java runtime system is the component of Java that gets the least press attention, but ultimately makes many of Java's features a reality. The Java runtime system includes a virtual machine, which stands in the middle between Java bytecode programs and the specific processor inside a computer system. It's the responsibility of the virtual machine to translate platform-independent bytecodes to platform-specific native machine code. In doing so, the virtual machine supplies the mechanism that makes Java platform-independent. Unfortunately, the virtual machine is also responsible for the performance problems associated with Java. These problems will more than likely disappear, however, when just-in-time Java compilers become prevalent.

The JavaScript scripting language is the component you use to place Java programs directly into HTML code. The primary purpose of JavaScript is to allow Web developers who aren't necessarily programmers to add interactivity to their Web pages in a straightforward manner.

What ActiveX Brings to the Game

Although you've already learned about each ActiveX component in detail in previous chapters, quickly review the following major components that compose the ActiveX technology:

- ActiveX controls
- ActiveX scripting (VBScript)
- ActiveX documents
- ActiveX server scripting (ISAPI)

ActiveX controls are self-contained executable programs that can be embedded within a Web page or a standalone application. Acting as an extension to OLE controls, ActiveX controls can be used to perform a wide range of functions, both with or without specific support for the Internet. ActiveX controls are essentially Microsoft's answer to Java applets.

ActiveX controls are Microsoft's answer to Java applets; VBScript is Microsoft's answer to JavaScript. Built on the highly successful Visual Basic programming language, VBScript gives you much of the same functionality as JavaScript, but in an environment already familiar to many PC developers.

ActiveX documents are similar to ActiveX controls, except they're focused on representing and manipulating a particular data format, such as a Word document or an Excel spreadsheet. There's no logical equivalent in Java to ActiveX documents; ActiveX documents are a piece of the ActiveX technology that's completely foreign to Java.

The final component of ActiveX is the ISAPI scripting language and server support. ISAPI provides a more powerful answer to CGI scripting, which has long been used to supply pseudo-interactivity for Web pages. ISAPI goes a step further by giving you a means to build filters into Web servers. Again, Java offers nothing comparable to this aspect of ActiveX.

You might be beginning to understand how ActiveX is aimed at being a more complete Internet technology than Java. Java certainly has its strengths, but it's somewhat limited as a complete Web solution. ActiveX, on the other hand, tries to provide an answer for every major aspect of Web development.

What Does It All Mean?

By now, you not only understand what Java and ActiveX are trying to accomplish, but you have a good idea of how each are delivering on their promises. I've mentioned some of the differences between each technology while describing its relevant aspects, but it's time to dig in and take a look at what these differences really mean.

Although ActiveX, as a technology, delivers more than Java as far as individual components, the primary interest for most developers is how ActiveX and Java stack up from the standpoint of adding interactivity to Web pages. This interest forces you to analyze the differences between ActiveX controls and Java applets, since they are the primary aspects of each technology that deliver Web page interactivity.

Security

Probably the most significant divisive issue between ActiveX and Java is security. No one argues the fact that security is an enormous issue when it comes to the Internet. Both Sun and Microsoft saw the importance of security and took appropriate actions in designing their respective technologies. However, they each took a different approach, resulting in drastically different usage issues. Consider Sun's approach: Java's security consists primarily of verifying the bytecodes as a program is being interpreted on the client end, as well as not allowing applets access to a client user's hard drive. The first solution of verifying bytecodes, although imposing somewhat of a performance hit, is reasonable. However, the limitation of not being able to access the hard drive is pretty harsh. No doubt, Sun took the safest route—it's very unlikely anyone can corrupt a user's hard drive using Java, considering he or she isn't allowed access to it. Because of this limitation, it's also equally unlikely that developers could write Java applets that perform any significant function beyond working with data on a server.

Now consider Microsoft's security approach with ActiveX: ActiveX uses a digital signature attached to each control, which specifies the control's original author. The signature is designed so that any tampering with an executable after its release will invalidate the signature. What this means is that you have the ability to know who the original author of a control is and, therefore, limit controls' use to only those written by established software vendors. If some-one hacks into a control developed by an established vendor, the signature will protect you. Granted, this approach pushes some responsibility back onto the user, but it's a practical reality that freedom never comes without a certain degree of added responsibility.

When it comes to security, I think Microsoft has capitalized on what a lot of people are starting to perceive as a major flaw in Java. For the record, Microsoft implemented the signature approach in ActiveX after the release of Java, meaning that they had the advantage of seeing how Sun tackled the security issue and could then improve on it. There's nothing wrong with this—it's just an example of how every technology, no matter how powerful and popular, is always susceptible to another one coming along and taking things a step further.

Practical Usage

When I initially heard about the security limitations of Java, it all sounded plausible. Why not just go the distance and be completely safe about every-thing? For the purposes of livening up the Web, writing to a user's hard drive just didn't seem like that big of a deal. However, ActiveX has ushered in a new way of thinking about the whole issue of adding interactivity to the Web; it's not just about showing neat animations and creating more exciting marketing promotions. ActiveX is attempting to take interactivity to a whole new level, simply by moving desktop software to the Internet.

This is another critical difference between ActiveX and Java: the ability to build practical applications for the Internet. Currently, although some exciting things are being done in Java, little has surfaced in the way of full-blown practical applications or applets. To be fair, applications take a while to develop and Java is certainly new enough that many developers are just getting used to the idea. Nevertheless, the fact that nothing of significant practicality has been built using Java should at least make you take notice. ActiveX, on the other hand, is practically bursting with practicality. Most major Windows productivity soft-ware is based on OLE, which is the backbone for ActiveX. Therefore, ActiveX immediately inherits a wide assortment of very practical applications and con-trols.

The issue of practicality isn't all that important when you just think in terms of making Web pages a little more exciting. However, when you shift your mode of thinking about the Internet to encompass software in general, you start to understand why it's so important. Microsoft has benefited greatly by being a late participant in the Internet game. Without being caught up in the immediacy of making Web pages more interesting, Microsoft could rethink the big picture of how the Internet and the Web affects software as a whole. Consequently, ActiveX addresses software migration to the Internet from a much wider perspective. Microsoft's goal with ActiveX is no less than moving desktop software to the Internet. It's a pretty ambitious goal, but ActiveX has the substance to put them on track to achieve it.

Development Strategy

In all the recent excitement surrounding programming and the Web, which has basically revolved around Java, I've been concerned about what it will all mean to software developers. Being a Windows programmer myself, I've always been frustrated that writing networked applications has been so much more difficult than writing desktop applications. The difference has been so drastic that you practically have to specialize in one type of programming or the other.

When Java came along, I suddenly saw a language as powerful and useful as C++, but with enough interesting networking support built-in that I could write both types of applications without developing an ulcer. I think this accounts for much of the excitement among developers quickly jumping on the Java bandwagon. And rightly so! Software developers deserve a break from the headaches of network programming, and Java delivers in this area quite nicely. However, when you approach Java from the perspective of someone who has been developing commercial software, you can't help but feel like there's something missing. The lack of decent development tools is rapidly changing, so that's not a long-term problem. Ultimately, the inability to see a use for Java beyond flashy applets is causing many developers to at least reconsider what Java has to offer.

ActiveX, on the other hand, offers a solution to the problem of merging two different programming disciplines and provides a powerful and practical framework to build real applications for the Web. Microsoft realized the problem of having to take two different approaches to writing networked applications and non-networked applications, and they are addressing it directly with ActiveX. With ActiveX, you can write controls and applications just as you did before, then gain the benefits of Internet support by adding a minimal amount of extra code.

Decisions, Decisions

Even though I've been leaning toward ActiveX in comparing the two technologies so far, please understand that I don't see Java and ActiveX as existing in an either/or situation. The software development community is far too diverse to try to say that one technology surpasses another in every possible way. In addition, you have to consider that both of these technologies are in a constant state of flux, with new announcements and releases popping up weekly.

In my opinion, it's foolish to think that a single software technology will take the Internet by storm and eliminate all others. Java will naturally find its way to where it's best suited, as will ActiveX. Likewise, smart software developers will keep up with both technologies and learn to apply each when the benefits of one outweigh the other. My goal is just to try to shed some light on where the differences between the two technologies lie and hopefully give you some insight into determining what each has to offer you.

The Crossroads

Just in case you're getting nervous about having to learn two completely new types of programming, here's some reassuring news: Microsoft has released a technology allowing developers to integrate Java applets with ActiveX controls. What does that mean? Well, since ActiveX is language-independent, it means you can write ActiveX controls in Java. Furthermore, it means you can access ActiveX controls from Java applets and vice versa. To me, this is a very exciting prospect: the ability to mix two extremely powerful yet seemingly divergent technologies as you see fit.

The technology I'm talking about is an ActiveX control that acts as a Java virtual machine. What is a Java virtual machine? A Java virtual machine is basically a Java interpreter, which means it's ultimately responsible for how Java programs are executed. By implementing a Java virtual machine in an ActiveX control, Microsoft has effectively integrated Java into the ActiveX environment. This integration goes well beyond just being able to execute Java applets as though they were ActiveX controls; it provides a means for both ActiveX controls and Java applets to interact with each other.

Microsoft's willingness to embrace Java as a means of developing ActiveX objects should give you a clue about the uniqueness of each technology. It could well end up that Java emerges as the dominant programming language for the Internet, while ActiveX emerges as the distributed interactive application standard. I know this seems like a confusing situation, but it does capitalize on the strengths of both Java and ActiveX.

The main point I'm trying to make is that ActiveX and Java are both strong in different ways, which puts them on a collision course of sorts. The software development community is pretty objective; if programmers can have the best of both worlds by integrating ActiveX and Java, then why not do it? No doubt both Sun and Microsoft will have a lot to say about this prospect in the near future. The ActiveX Java virtual machine is a major step in the right direction. My plan is to just sit back and enjoy the show!

Summary

This chapter focuses on ActiveX as it relates to Java. ActiveX tackles so many of the same issues as Java that it's important to understand the similarities and differences between the two technologies. You have learned how ActiveX and Java overlap, along with a surprising number of differences between them. Keep in mind that ActiveX and Java don't necessarily need to be considered rivals, simply because each shines in different situations. This point is hammered home when you realize there are future plans for a mixing of ActiveX and Java. It's an exciting and often unnerving situation for Web developers, but these two technologies are laying the groundwork for a whole new generation of software.

If you think the idea of mixing ActiveX and Java is exciting, wait until you find out how ActiveX is being used to bring the Internet to the Windows desktop. The next chapter, "ActiveX Goes to Nashville," tackles this very topic by exploring how ActiveX is integrating the Internet with the new Windows shell, code-named Nashville.

ActiveX Goes to Nashville

by Michael Morrison

What could ActiveX possibly have in common with Music City, USA? Being born and raised in Nashville, Tennessee myself, I feel pretty qualified to provide an answer: absolutely nothing! Seriously, Nashville is the code name of the new Windows shell that plans to integrate the Internet into the Windows interface. This chapter takes a look at ActiveX and the role it plays in the new Windows shell. You begin with a brief look at how ActiveX came to be, which will help you understand the role it plays on the road to Nashville.

Understand, as you read this chapter, that Nashville is a very new technology that is still in development. Many of the specifics on Nashville have yet to be revealed. Knowing this, my goal in this chapter is to paint a general picture of the role ActiveX plays in the evolution of Windows to the new Nashville interface.

The Evolution of ActiveX

To fully understand the circumstances surrounding the Nashville interface and its dependence on ActiveX, you have to go back a few years and take a peek at the evolution of it all. The road to Nashville begins thousands of miles away in Redmond, Washington, home of Microsoft.

COM

Back before ActiveX or OLE meant anything, some insightful software engineers at Microsoft had an idea about developing a language-independent standard for distributed software objects. They called the specification COM, which stands for Component Object Model. The COM specification provides a binary standard for how software objects are represented in memory and a programming model that effectively hides an object's inner workings. It does this in a language-independent manner, meaning that COM objects can be developed using a variety of different programming languages.

At first glance, COM may not seem like that big of a deal; it's such a low-level technology that it's hard to see the practicality of it. However, consider the effect of designing all the software objects in a system to support the COM standard. Since the objects all share the same layout in memory, they all understand how to communicate with each other, resulting in a system composed of objects that know how to interact with each other. This creates some very powerful opportunities. Even though object communication within a system is powerful in itself, COM goes much further; COM defines a standard for objects to communicate with each other in any environment, including distributed networks.

At the center of COM is the concept of a *software component*, which is a reusable piece of software in binary form that can be easily integrated with other components with relatively little effort. Additionally, software components can be mixed and matched with components from other vendors. For example, a spellchecking component from one vendor could be plugged into several different word processing applications from other vendors. As simple and logical as this scenario sounds, it has yet to be realized in the realm of computer software. The COM standard aims to change that.

The primary responsibility of COM is to ensure that software components behave consistently without limiting how programmers use different components. Objects written to support COM are collectively called COM components, or COM objects. COM offers a way to address both the problems of application complexity and future enhancements to functionality, and it does so in a completely open way so that all software vendors can adopt it and put it to use immediately. Microsoft made the entire COM specification fully available to the public; it was never positioned as a proprietary technology.

OLE

Following quickly on the heels of COM, Microsoft unveiled its OLE technology, which stands for "object linking and embedding." Although object linking and embedding correctly identifies the original releases of OLE, the technology eventually grew far beyond its original intentions. OLE's original goal was to provide a more document-centric architecture for Windows, but it has since evolved into a rich set of object-oriented system interfaces and services forming a standard framework for building reusable, integrated software components.

It should come as no surprise that OLE is built on top of COM; it is an open, extensible architecture built on the foundation of COM. OLE and COM are so intertwined that they are often used interchangeably when discussing component software technology. In fact, because OLE is based on the underlying object architecture of COM, it forms the basis of the strategic evolution of the Windows operating system family into fully object-based operating systems. Every feature of OLE depends on COM to provide basic interobject communication. In other words, COM provides the "plumbing and wiring" of OLE.

The OLE technology supplies a wide range of services, including application automation, reusable controls, version management, standardized drag-and-drop, documents, object linking and embedding, and visual editing. These services have shared great success and account for much of the power and ease of use evident in the Windows operating systems.

ActiveX

When Microsoft finally decided to turn their attention to the Internet, they decided that OLE was the technology to focus their efforts on. Since they had put so much into OLE, it was already a very stable and powerful technology, with a broad range of industry support. Therefore, their approach was to just figure out ways to extend OLE to support the Internet. The new, revamped OLE for the Internet was renamed ActiveX. ActiveX builds on the success of OLE, and takes it to a new level by giving it the ability to thrive in the online world of the Internet.

DCOM

Although COM is certainly a sound technology at its core and a good basis for ActiveX, Microsoft realized that it still lacked some of the support necessary for the widely distributed type of computing presented by the Internet. So, they went back to the drawing board and came up with DCOM (Distributed COM). DCOM picks up where COM left off and focuses on the communication protocols between distributed objects. Where COM fleshes out the low-level physical issues for distributed binary objects themselves, DCOM addresses the communication protocols necessary to transfer information between these objects.

Like COM, DCOM is also designed as a component of the ActiveX technology. The difference is that DCOM addresses the application-level issue of handling remote communication between objects, and COM specifies the binary makeup of the objects. The goal of DCOM is to provide a reliable, secure, and efficient means for software components to communicate in a distributed environment such as the Internet. DCOM is implemented as a generic protocol layered on the DCE (Distributed Computing Environment) RPC (Remote Procedure Call) specification. Because of its relationship to the RPC specification, DCOM is sometimes also referred to as Object RPC, or ORPC.

Internet Explorer 3.0

Since ActiveX essentially defines an Internet component technology, you often think in terms of client software when you think of ActiveX. This implies the need for a client application that supports ActiveX components. Microsoft's primary ActiveX client application is Internet Explorer 3.0, a Web browser that fully supports embedded ActiveX components. (See Figure 16.1.)

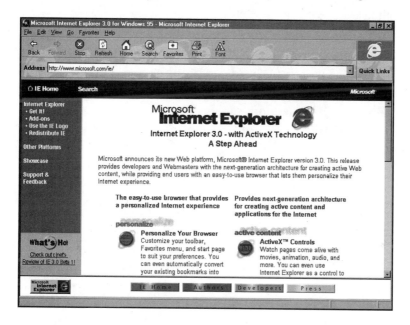

Figure 16.1.
Microsoft's Internet Explorer 3.0.

Internet Explorer is Microsoft's answer to Netscape Navigator, and they're doing all they can to make sure it succeeds. ActiveX is a significant part of the Internet Explorer strategy; Microsoft is aiming to provide a smooth integration of popular desktop applications with Internet Explorer through ActiveX. In doing so, Microsoft is attempting to redefine the whole concept of Internet computing. Their goal is to take things a significant step further than both static Web pages and dynamic Java applets by allowing users to work with familiar data types and full-blown client applications within Internet Explorer.

The idea of Internet Explorer is to create a universal client capable of understanding and responding to a wide variety of content types. To better understand this, consider the capabilities of a browser such as Netscape Navigator. Navigator is primarily used to view HTML documents, but it can also view other document types, such as text documents and FTP directory listings.

Navigator also supports plug-in modules, which allow it to support an unlimited variety of content types. However, Navigator plug-ins are specific to Navigator and can't really be used in any other context.

Internet Explorer, on the other hand, supports both ActiveX controls and documents, which also encompass an unlimited range of content types. However, since ActiveX is based on OLE, ActiveX controls and documents have a practical use beyond Internet Explorer; you can integrate them into your own standalone applications. Furthermore, support for a wide range of content types has already been implemented in OLE documents and controls, which are already being converted to ActiveX. Because of this, Internet Explorer will immediately support a wide range of content types and ultimately be far more extensible than any other Web browser.

This approach of making Internet Explorer a universal client fits in well with Microsoft's movement toward a document-centric computing environment. Understand that when I say Internet Explorer serves as a client for a particular document type, I don't just mean it's capable of only viewing documents. The nature of ActiveX makes it just as easy for Internet Explorer to also serve as an in-place editor for a wide range of documents. If you have any experience with using OLE in-place editing, you already know what I'm talking about. Basically, in-place editing allows you to edit a document within a client application as though you were using the originating application, such as Word.

Beyond the issue of ActiveX, it's clear that Microsoft is directly challenging Netscape with Internet Explorer. Although Microsoft is late to the game, they are gaining ground fast. Internet Explorer 3.0 contains a lot of interesting features, such as extensive customization options, a Web site ratings system, browsing with the keyboard, and an administration kit for building custom versions of the browser. Furthermore, Internet Explorer 3.0 offers complete support for both ActiveX and Java, along with secure communications, code signing, and multilingual support.

Nashville

Once Microsoft realized the power inherent in combining all their software component technology with the Internet and with an Internet browser, they took yet another step back to examine things again. It occurred to them that merely providing a universal client for different types of content wasn't enough. There still existed a clear distinction between accessing information on the Internet and information located on the local hard drive or network. Although this distinction is widely accepted by the current Web-using community, Microsoft was looking at things from a larger perspective. Why not make accessing computer information the same regardless of its origin? That problem became the basis for the Nashville project.

Fortunately for Microsoft, this problem wasn't entirely new; they had tackled a similar problem on a smaller scale years earlier when they developed Windows for Workgroups. Windows 3.1 provided weak support for accessing data on a network, so Microsoft developed a version with network extensions called Windows for Workgroups. Windows for Workgroups managed to successfully expand the Windows 3.1 File Manager to allow smooth access to network computers.

Windows 95 Explorer, which superseded File Manager, included this same functionality but with a much cleaner interface. With Windows 95 Explorer, you can easily examine other computers on a network and copy and move files around just as though they were on your local hard drive. This consistency in file access is important and has helped make Windows much easier to use.

When it comes to the Internet, the problem of consistent data access rears its head again in a big way. To access information on the Web, you have to launch a Web browser and work within it entirely. To work with things on your local hard drive, you launch Windows Explorer and run an application that works that particular type of information. Figure 16.2 shows the current situation for working with information on the Internet versus working with it locally.

Notice in the figure that access to local data is provided both by Windows Explorer and by client applications. Additionally, you can launch client applications from Windows Explorer. This scenario is familiar to most Windows users, and ultimately goes back to the File Manager/Program Manager approach in earlier versions of Windows. Now look at how Internet data is accessed in the figure; the only way to access Internet data is through a Web browser, which is ultimately a specialized application. This rift between accessing local data and Internet data presents a significant problem to the open-ended approach of data access promoted by Windows.

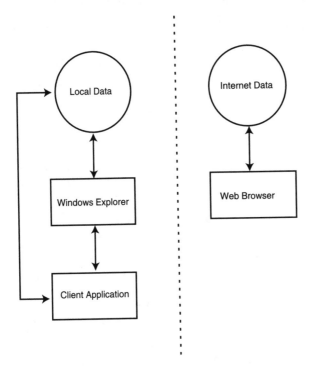

Figure 16.2.
The current problem of information access.

Microsoft realized that the most logical solution to this problem was to expand on the Windows Explorer concept to incorporate browsing information on the Internet. Since they already had a Web browser with a lot of potential (Internet Explorer), it made sense to somehow combine the two Explorers into a single application that handles both hierarchical directory/file management and Internet content browsing.

Note: In reality, the whole concept of "Internet content" or "Web content" will eventually disappear. Even though HTML is the standard document type for Web pages, as the Internet becomes more integrated with the desktop, you will see HTML being used more in local situations. Additionally, many local data types will see more use on the Internet as the support for them becomes available.

Integrating Internet Explorer with the Windows 95 shell is a Microsoft project that has been code-named Nashville. Nashville marks the first attempt by a major software company to integrate full-blown Internet services into an operating system. The Nashville project will no doubt change the way everyone views working with the Internet, since it mixes two entirely different modes of computing. The end result will hopefully be a more seamless computing environment, in which accessing information on the Web will be much like opening a folder on your hard drive. The Nashville interface will likely rear its head in the next major release of Windows.

Figure 16.3 shows how the information access problem is solved by the Nashville interface.

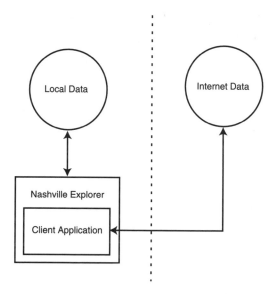

Figure 16.3.
Information access through the Nashville interface.

If you contrast this figure with Figure 16.2, you see how the Nashville Explorer solves the problem of inconsistent data access. By providing a unified means to access both local and Internet data, the Nashville Explorer successfully extends the Windows interface to incorporate the Internet.

The success of the Nashville interface is highly dependent on the component and document-centric aspects of Internet Explorer, which is directly attributed to ActiveX. In this way, you can see how ActiveX is an even more important technology than OLE, residing at the heart of all of Microsoft's Internet efforts.

Summary

Although brief, this chapter tries to give you some perspective on ActiveX as it applies to Microsoft's plans to integrate the Internet into Windows. You have reviewed a brief history of ActiveX, which gives you some insight into the push for component technology. You then learned about Internet Explorer and how it makes use of ActiveX to provide support for a wide range of content types. This chapter concludes with a discussion of Nashville, Microsoft's new Windows interface that integrates Internet Explorer into the Windows 95 shell.

PART V

Appendixes

ActiveX Online Resources

by Warren Ernst

This appendix gives you some sources for more online information on ActiveX, the Web and the Internet, and related topics. When this book was written, ActiveX was in the earliest stages of development with some portions still awaiting final approval from either Microsoft or the Internet community, and this appendix gives you some launching points to read and retrieve the latest on ActiveX technologies.

ActiveX (Official) Information Sources

Naturally, the major "official" ActiveX site is hosted on the Microsoft Web server at `http://www.microsoft.com`, but since you might have trouble wandering through one of the largest Web servers on the Internet without some guidance, here are some of the high points:

The Internet Development Home Page
(`http://www.microsoft.com/intdev/`) is Microsoft's top-level page that encompasses all its Internet development programs, including (but not limited to) ActiveX technologies. You can further refine your search for ActiveX information by using the search engine on the left side of the page.

The Microsoft Internet Explorer Home Page
(`http://www.microsoft.com/ie/default.htm`) is the official home of Microsoft's Internet Explorer 3.0 and includes links for downloading, bug notices, feature lists, and technical notes.

The ActiveX Table of Contents
(`http://www.microsoft.com/intdev/toc1.htm`) is a complete listing and description of every ActiveX-related document with hyperlinks on the Microsoft Web site.

The ActiveX Component Connection Page
(`http://www.microsoft.com/devonly/community/cbisv_9.htm`) is a fairly complete listing of the various software vendors that either are, or soon will be, offering ActiveX technology components for sale (or free use, although this is not clear at some sites). Links to the vendor's own pages are supplied.

The Internet Component Download Page
(`http://www.microsoft.com/intdev/signcode/codedwld.htm`) discusses the different proposed solutions for the issue of downloading and installing ActiveX controls on-the-fly while browsing Web pages. As the specification gets more solid, this will be a page you'll want to look at frequently.

The Visual Basic Scripting Edition Page
(`http://www.microsoft.com/vbscript/default.htm`) is the springboard for all queries about VBScript, including implementation schedules, programming tips, and new products.

The ActiveVRML Page
(`http://www.microsoft.com/INTDEV/avr/beta/default.htm`) provides links to examples, release notes, the installable test programs, and

tutorials for creating and navigating through VMRL worlds with Active VRML.

Unofficial ActiveX Information Sources

Just because Microsoft makes ActiveX doesn't mean they have the market on information about it. Here are some of the more interesting alternative sources of information:

NCompass might be doing more to make ActiveX successful than Microsoft by making the NCompass ActiveX plug-in module freely available at `http://www.ncompasslabs.com/`. Also available are the specifications for writing ActiveX controls for the NCompass plug-in.

There are probably at least 40 Usenet newsgroups that deal with certain aspects of ActiveX technology, and Microsoft has compiled a thorough list of the most useful. This list is on the Newsgroups page at `http://www.microsoft.com/intdev/resource/news.htm`.

Brian Johnson has created The Visual Basic Script Information Page, a nice compilation of VBScript information, at his Web pages at `http://home.sprynet.com/sprynet/bjjohnson/vbs.htm`.

Vijay Mukhi's Technology Watch Page (`http://www.neca.com/~vmis/`) has some interesting information about ActiveX from the standpoint of someone who is dabbling in it, as well as a nice comparison of ActiveX to Java.

General Web/Internet Information

If you've been using the Web and the Internet for a while but never really learned the nuts, bolts, ins, and outs that make it all work together, here are some sites that explain some of the gory details:

The Web Overview/W³C (`http://www.ww3.org/`) is an overview of the World Wide Web from the World Wide Web Consortium.

Web Info/EARN (`http://www.earn.com/gnrt/wwww.html`), from the European Academic Research Network Association, is a somewhat lighthearted overview of the Web that makes a good read.

The Web FAQ (`http://sunsite.unc.edu/boutell/faq/www_faq.html`) is the Frequently Asked Questions (and answers) list about the Web. This FAQ is maintained by Thomas Boutell.

Yahoo - Web (`http://www.yahoo.com/Computers/World_Wide_Web/`) gives you a comprehensive set of links that describe the World Wide Web in one way or another.

Yahoo - Internet (`http://www.yahoo.com/Computers/Internet/`) provides another comprehensive set of links about the broader topic of the Internet.

HyperText Markup Language Specification 3.0 (`http://www.hpl.hp.co.uk/people/dsr/html/Contents.html`) is the most thorough breakdown of HTML you'll find anywhere. Sometimes it gets very detailed, but it can be considered an exhaustive listing.

OneWorld/SingNet WWW and HTML Developer's Jumpstation (`http://oneworld.wa.com/htmldev/devpage/dev-page1.html`) is a nice set of links that covers the different aspects of writing Web pages.

Glossary

by Michael Morrison

ActiveMovie   An ActiveX control that allows developers to easily control and modify the playback of video content as well as streaming video content.

ActiveMovie Stream Editor   An application that allows you to create simple streaming content for use with ActiveMovie on the Internet.

ActiveX   A family of technologies developed by Microsoft to combine computing ability with Internet connectivity.

ActiveX Control   A software module with OLE capabilities that can easily be embedded within Web pages or programs.

ActiveX Control Container   A program capable of running an ActiveX control.

ActiveX Document   A computer file with OLE links to enable the automatic launching of a program that can interact with it.

ActiveX Document Container   A program capable of running an ActiveX document.

applet   A Java program that can be embedded within an HTML page with the APP element and run within a Java-enabled browser.

bandwidth   How much "stuff" you can send through a connection, usually measured in bits per second (bps). A full page of English text is about 16,000 bits. A fast modem can move about 15,000 bits in one second. Full-motion, full-screen video would require roughly 10,000,000 bps, depending on compression.

binder   A DocObject container; a new type of OLE container that can embed DocObject servers.

browser   A computer program used to view Web pages written in HTML and other languages. Also referred to as a client.

bytecode   An intermediate form of a Java program that's between the source code and a native executable. Bytecode Java programs are interpreted by the Java runtime system.

CGI (Common Gateway Interface)   The connectivity between the Web browser (client) and the Web server. CGI allows information to pass between the server and the client. An example would be a user filling in a form and submitting the results to a server.

chatting   Talking in real time to other network users from any and all parts of the world, either through text or multimedia-based methods.

client-server architecture   An environment where the client uses a server application to host various requests for data or services.

CODEC (COmpressor/DECompressor)   Data files such as video require enormous amounts of space. To conserve space, such content is compressed and decompressed as needed. Examples of CODECs are Cinepak, Indeo, and MPEG.

COM (Component Object Model)   A binary standard developed by Microsoft for representing software components in a distributed environment.

container   An application that can "contain" OLE objects.

cross-platform   A term used to indicate that a piece of software can run on any operating system platform.

digital signature   A security technique consisting of attaching a code to a software component that identifies the vendor of the component.

DNS (Domain Name System)   A system for translating computer names into numeric Internet addresses.

DocObject   Document Object; an OLE server with view-saving extensions that allow it to be used by the Office95 Binder and online through Internet Explorer.

document-centric   A term used to describe a type of environment, such as OLE, where the focus is placed on documents containing information, rather than applications that act on the information.

domain name   The unique name that identifies an Internet site. A given machine may have more than one domain name, but a given domain name points to only one machine.

embedded object   An OLE object may be embedded as opposed to *linked*. To embed, the OLE object is asked to save its data (a file, for instance) into a structured storage area in (or embed its data into) the container's storage. The OLE object then runs from the data in the storage, instead of from data in a (linked) file.

encryption   Converting data into an unreadable, unusable form, until it has been decrypted. The purpose of encryption is to protect information from being accessed by parties other than the intended receiver. For example, encrypted e-mail can only be viewed by the person it's addressed to, who typically has a code used to decrypt the message.

event   Particular objects allow user interaction or monitor actions of the computer program or system. When something "happens," an event is triggered. For instance, when using a button object, the process of actually clicking on the button triggers a "click" event.

function   Like a subroutine, functions allow you to assemble a series of commands together. Functions may then be invoked from anywhere else within a program. Functions are identified by names and often read parameters. However, functions also return a resulting value.

GUID (Globally Unique ID)   Each OLE component registered on your computer system may be uniquely identified by its GUID. When embedding OLE objects in Web pages, this ID specifies which objects are to be used. These IDs may be found in the Windows 95 or NT system registries.

HTML (Hypertext Markup Language)   The convention (some call it a language) used to create conventional Web pages; see **hypertext**.

HTTP (Hypertext Transfer Protocol)   The native communications scheme of the World Wide Web, initially used to transfer hypertext documents, though this is being expanded.

home page   The first Web page that appears in a Web browser when it's started.

HTTP Server   Hypertext Transfer Protocol Server; a computer (server) that serves HTML documents.

hyperlink   A reference in HTML to another hypertext segment.

hypertext   A system of writing and displaying text that enables the text to be linked in several ways. Hypertext documents can also contain links to related documents, such as those referred to in footnotes. Hypermedia can also contain pictures, sounds, and /or video.

imagemap   A graphic image embedded within a Web page that supplies different links, based on where the cursor is clicked within its borders.

in-place activation   A technique that allows you to view and manipulate information within the context of different applications. For example, by using in-place activation, you can view and edit Microsoft Excel spreadsheets within a Microsoft Word document.

Internet   The global "network of networks" that communicates through the suite of protocols encompassed by the TCP/IP specification.

intranet   A local area network, within a company's firewall. Used for network traffic inside the company.

Internet Explorer 3.0   An advanced Web browser written by Microsoft that is an ActiveX control and document container.

ISAPI (Internet Server Application Programming Interface)   A standard method to write programs that communicate with Web servers through OLE.

Java   A development language that allows Web developers to create Windows-type applications for the Internet. Java is based on the C++ development language, and the resulting applications can be executed on any computer platform: Macintosh, PC, or UNIX.

JavaScript   A language that can be used to expand the capabilities of a Web page. Like VBScript, JavaScript instructions are embedded within an HTML document for a page. JavaScript is based on the Java language, which is similar to C++.

JPEG (Joint Photographic Experts Group)   A standard compression algorithm used for minimizing the amount of data required to display graphic files, particularly those used on the Internet. It was named for the group that devised the standard.

LAN (Local Area Network)   A group of connected computers, usually located close to one another (such as the same building or floor of the building) so that data can be passed among them rapidly.

language-independent   A term used to indicate that a piece of software can be developed in any programming language.

linked object   An OLE object may be linked as opposed to *embedded*. For a link, the container merely saves the actual filename, as opposed to the whole file.

loop   When programming, it's sometimes necessary to repeat steps of a program. The process of repeating program instructions is referred to as "looping."

method   Similar to properties in an object-oriented world; however, instead of merely setting the characteristics of an object, methods invoke an action for that object. For instance, a Web browser object may have a method you invoke for connecting to and displaying a Web site.

MIME (Multipurpose Internet Mail Extension)   A set of schemes for transmitting various file formats (usually multimedia) across the Internet.

MPEG (Motion Pictures Expert Group)   A standard compression algorithm for storing digital video content. Like JPEG, it was named for the group that created the standard.

Nashville   The new Microsoft Windows interface that merges Internet browsing with the Windows 95 Explorer application.

native   A term used to identify software that runs only on a particular platform.

object-oriented   A term specifying that a piece of software is composed of *objects*, which are self-contained modules that contain both data and procedures that act on the data.

OLE (Object Linking and Embedding)   A COM-based technology developed by Microsoft that offers a wide range of services, including application automation, reusable controls, version management, standardized drag-and-drop, documents, object linking and embedding, and visual editing.

page   A document, or collection of information, available through the World Wide Web. A page may contain text, graphics, video, and/or sound files.

parameter   When creating an ActiveX control for the first time within a Web page, it's possible to establish its default settings by using parameters. A parameter is simply a value passed to an object or to a function.

property   In an object-oriented environment, an object's properties describe the characteristics of that object. For instance, an object's foreground color would be a property for a text object.

registry   A database within the Windows 95 and NT operating systems that contains information about your computer and its configuration.

server   A software package connected to a network that supplies information or services based on the requests of a connecting client program.

ShockWave   An extension for the Web that allows users to view multimedia content originally authored with Macromedia's Director tool.

site   An area within an Internet server that provides information.

software component   A reusable piece of software in binary form that can be easily integrated with other components with relatively little effort.

streaming   Instead of being required to transfer a file in its entirety before viewing it, streaming allows data to be downloaded in the background. Data appears to be displayed more quickly as a result. For instance, instead of being required to transfer an entire video file before playing it, streaming allows the beginning of the video to play while additional information is transferred for playback in the background.

subroutine   If a series of instructions are to be used many times in other sections of a program, it's possible to group these instructions together as a subroutine. Other portions of the program can execute the batch of instructions within the subroutine by merely calling that subroutine. Subroutines are identified by names and can often accept parameters to make their functions more generic.

surfing   The act of following hypertext (or other) links across the World Wide Web to collect the information you want.

tag   The format code that defines portions of an HTML file or embedded applets, controls, or scripts.

TCP/IP (Transmission Control Protocol/Internet Protocol)   The set of communications protocols the Internet uses to communicate.

URL (Uniform Resource Locator)   The site and file-addressing scheme for the World Wide Web.

virtual machine   The environment created by a Java-enabled Web browser that Java applets run within.

visual editing   The act of modifying an object or program in a visual manner using graphical software tools; this technique is usually more intuitive than other non-visual techniques and typically involves using the mouse.

VBScript (Visual Basic Script, or VBS)   An OLE-enabled scripting language based on the Visual Basic programming language, used to write ActiveX scripts within Web pages.

VRML (Virtual Reality Modeling Language)   A specification for defining three-dimensional landscapes or objects to be used on the Web.

WWW (World Wide Web, or simply "the Web")   A popular hypertext-based system of transmitting textual and multimedia-based information through the Internet.

VBScript Syntax Quick Reference

by Keith Brophy and Timothy Koets

VBScript is composed of a great deal of syntax you need to keep straight. You will probably use many elements of the syntax so often that you will easily remember what they do. However, even an experienced programmer uses some of the syntax elements infrequently. When you come across those elements in your code or strain to remember if you have the syntax exactly right, a good reference can serve as a welcome relief.

Languages such as Visual Basic 4.0 come complete with a very useful context-sensitive help facility. VBScript provides no such inherent support. It is a hosted language that comes along for the ride with the environment that supports it, such as a browser. It is not a separate product with its own development environment and the help that is typical of such an environment. You can turn to other places for help on the

Internet, however. At the time of this writing, Microsoft had a very helpful VBScript language reference that could be reached under `http://www.microsoft.com/vbscript`.

This appendix is intended to supplement the VBScript information available from the Web location. Unlike some of the other language references available, the information in this appendix is presented in a strict alphabetical fashion, intermixing functions, statements, See Prior Notes, and major properties in the same list. A brief description of each element is provided, but it's not enough to replace the official reference material—just enough to give you a quick high-level understanding of what that element does.

You'll develop a common way to refer to information as you work your way through a new book or sample programs. You might find a language element that is unfamiliar, but all you need to do to quickly get back on course is see a brief description of what it does and find out if it is a property, function, or other type of construct. This appendix can serve as a quick first resort for such information.

Table C.1. Summary of VBScript syntax.

Symbol	Type	Description
+ (addition)	Operator	Adds two numbers together. You can also use this to concatenate strings.
' (comment indicator)	Keyword	What follows this symbol on the line is a comment.
" (double quote)	Keyword	Denotes the start and end of a literal string.
& (string concatenation)	Operator	Performs the concatenation of two string expressions.
/ (division, floating point)	Operator	Divides two numbers and returns a floating-point result.

Symbol	Type	Description
\ (division, integer)	Operator	Divides two numbers and returns an integer result.
= (equals) comparison		Checks whether two expressions are equivalent.
^ (exponent)	Operator	Raises a number to the power of an exponent.
> (greater than)	Comparison	Checks whether the left-side expression is greater than the right-side expression.
>= (greater than or equal)	Comparison	Checks whether the left-side expression is greater than or equal to the right-side expression.
< (less than)	Comparison	Checks whether the left-side expression is less than the right-side expression.
<= (less than or equal)	Comparison	Checks whether the left-side expression is less than or equal to the right-side expression.
_ (line continuation character)	Keyword	Indicates that the current line continues onto the next line.
* (multiplication)	Operator	Multiplies two numbers.

continues

Table C.1. continued

Symbol	Type	Description
- (subtraction or negation)	Operator	Finds the difference between two numbers, or when applied to one operand, treats it as a negative value.
: (colon)		Indicates line separation, as in `A = A + 1 : B = C + 1`.
<> (not equal)	Comparison	Checks whether two expressions are not equivalent.
`Abs`	Function	Returns the absolute value of a number.
`And`	Logical operator	Performs a logical conjunction on two expressions.
`Array`	Function	Returns a variant comprising an array.
`Asc`	Function	Provides the character code corresponding to the first letter in a string as a return code.
`AscB`	Function	Like `Asc`, but it returns the first byte rather than the first character of a string.
`Atn`	Function	Provides the arctangent of a number as a return code.
`Call`	Statement	Calls a procedure.
`CBool`	Function	Provides as a return code an expression that

Symbol	Type	Description
		has been converted to a variant of subtype `Boolean`.
Cbyte	Function	Provides as a return code an expression that has been converted to a variant of subtype `Byte`.
CDate	Function	Provides as a return code an expression that has been converted to a variant of subtype `Date`.
CDbl	Function	Provides as a return code an expression that has been converted to a variant of subtype `Double`.
Chr	Function	Provides as a return code the character associated with the ASCII code. This function can return one or two bytes.
ChrB	Function	Returns the byte associated with the ASCII code.
Cint	Function	Provides as a return code an expression that has been converted to a variant of subtype `Integer`.

continues

Table C.1. continued

Symbol	Type	Description
Clear	Method for the Err object	Results in resetting all the Err object's properties to a no-error state.
CLng	Function	Provides as a return code an expression that has been converted to a variant of subtype Long.
Cos	Function	Provides as a return code the cosine of an angle.
CSng	Function	Provides as a return code an expression that has been converted to a variant of subtype Single.
CStr	Function	Provides as a return code an expression that has been converted to a variant of subtype String.
CVErr	Function	Provides as a return code a variant of subtype Error containing a user-provided error code.
Date	Function	Returns the current system date.
DateSerial	Function	Provides as a return code a variant of subtype Date for the given month, day, and year.

Symbol	Type	Description
DateValue	Function	Provides as a return code a variant of subtype Date for the given string.
Day	Function	Provides as a return code a whole number of 1 through 31, representing the day of the month for the given date string.
Description	Property for the Err object	The string that describes the current error.
Dim	Statement	Declares variables.
Do…Loop	Statement	Repeats a block of code while a condition is True or until a condition becomes True.
Empty	Literal	Signifies that a variable is uninitialized.
Erase	Statement	Reinitializes fixed-size array elements and frees the storage space of dynamic arrays.
Err	Object	Provides information about runtime errors.
Eqv	Logical operator	Performs logical equivalence for the two expressions provided as operands.
Exit Do	Statement	Exits a Do…Loop code block.

continues

Table C.1. continued

Symbol	Type	Description
Exit For	Statement	Exits a For…Next code block.
Exit Function	Statement	Exits a function.
Exit Sub	Statement	Exits a procedure.
Exp	Function	Returns *e* (the base of natural logarithms) raised to a power.
Fix	Function	Provides the integer portion of a number as a return code; if the number is negative, it provides the first number greater than the operand.
For…Next	Statement	Repeats a group of statements a designated number of times.
For Each…Next	Statement	Repeats a group of statements for each element in an array or collection.
Function	Statement	Declares a procedure-level block of code that returns a value when called.
HelpContext	Property for the Err object	The context ID in a corresponding help file for the current error.
HelpFile	Property for the Err object	The corresponding help file for the current error.

Symbol	Type	Description
Hex	Function	Provides as a return code a string representing the hexadecimal value of a number.
Hour	Function	Provides as a return code a whole number from 0 through 23, representing the hour of the day.
If…Then…Else	Statement	Executes a group of statements, depending on the value of an expression.
Imp	Logical operator	Performs a logical implication on the two operands provided.
InputBox	Function	Displays a dialog box with a prompt, appropriate buttons, and an input text box and then returns the input text and button response to calling program.
Int	Function	Provides the integer portion of a number as a return code; if the number is negative, it provides the first number less than the operand.
InStr	Function	Provides the position indicator of the first character of the target

continues

Table C.1. continued

Symbol	Type	Description
		string within the search string.
InstrB	Function	Provides the position indicator of the first byte of the target string within the search string.
Is	Operator	Compares two object reference variables.
IsArray	Function	Provides as a return code a Boolean value signifying whether a variable is an array.
IsDate	Function	Provides as a return code a Boolean value signifying whether an expression can be converted to a date.
IsEmpty	Function	Provides as a return code a Boolean value signifying whether a variable has been initialized.
IsError	Function	Provides as a return code a Boolean value signifying whether an expression is an error value.
IsNull	Function	Provides as a return code a Boolean value signifying whether an expression contains no valid data (Null).

Symbol	Type	Description
IsNumeric	Function	Provides as a return code a `Boolean` value signifying whether an expression can be evaluated as a number.
IsObject	Function	Provides as a return code a `Boolean` value signifying whether an expression represents an OLE automation object.
LBound	Function	Provides as a return code the smallest available subscript for the stated dimension of an array.
Lcase	Function	Provides as a return code a string that has been converted to lowercase.
Left	Function	Provides as a return code a specified number of characters from the left side of a string.
Len	Function	Provides as a return code the number of characters in a string or the number of bytes required to store a variable.
LenB	Function	Provides as a return code the number of

continues

Table C.1. continued

Symbol	Type	Description
		bytes in a string or the number of bytes required to store a variable.
Log	Function	Provides as a return code the natural logarithm of a number.
Ltrim	Function	Provides a string that has leading (leftmost) spaces removed.
Mid	Function	Provides as a return code a described number of characters from a string.
Minute	Function	Provides as a return code a whole number from 0 through 59, representing the minute of the hour.
Mod	Operator	Divides two numbers and returns only the remainder.
Month	Function	Provides as a return code a whole number from 1 through 12, representing the month of the year.
MsgBox	Function	Shows a given prompt in a message dialog box with a button and returns the user's button response.

Symbol	Type	Description
Not	Logical operator	Checks for logical not equivalent condition.
Nothing	Literal	Removes reference and frees memory.
Now	Function	Returns the current setting of your computer's system date and time.
Null	Literal	Indicates no valid data state, as opposed to Empty, which indicates no data was ever assigned.
Number	Property for the Err object	The numeric error code for the current error.
Oct	Function	Provides as a return code a string representing the octal value of a number.
On Error Resume Next	Statement	Indicates that if an error occurs, control should resume at next statement.
Option Explicit	Statement	Indicates that variables must be declared.
Or	Operator	Performs a logical disjunction on two expressions.
Raise	Method for the Err object	Forces a runtime error to be raised.

continues

Table C.1. continued

Symbol	Type	Description
Randomize	Statement	Starts a sequence for the random-number generator.
ReDim	Statement	Allocates or reallocates storage space and declares dynamic-array variables at the procedure level.
Rem	Statement	Used to include comments in a program. The single quote that achieves the same purpose is used more often.
Right	Function	Provides as a return code a described number of characters from the right side of a string.
Rnd	Function	Provides a random number as a return code.
Rtrim	Function	Provides a string that has trailing (rightmost) spaces removed.
Second	Function	Provides as a return code a whole number from 0 through 59, representing the second of the minute.
Set	Statement	Assigns an object reference.

Symbol	Type	Description
Sgn	Function	Provides as a return code an integer disclosing the sign of a number.
Sin	Function	Provides as a return code the sine of an angle.
Source	Property for the Err object	The source of the error for the current error.
Space	Function	Returns the given number of spaces.
Sqr	Function	Provides as a return code the square root of a number.
Static	Statement (Procedure-level)	Declares a persistent variable. Contents will be retained from one call to the next.
StrComp	Function	Returns a value signifying the outcome of a string comparison.
String	Function	Returns a repeating character string of the number of characters described.
Sub	Statement	Declares procedures that do not provide a return code.
Tan	Function	Provides as a return code the tangent of an angle.
Time	Function	Returns a variant of subtype Date showing

continues

Table C.1. continued

Symbol	Type	Description
		the current system time.
TimeSerial	Function	Returns a variant of subtype Date comprising the time for a specific hour, minute, and second.
TimeValue	Function	Returns a variant of subtype Date containing the time.
Trim	Function	Provides as a return code a duplicate of a string without leading spaces (LTrim), trailing spaces (RTrim), or both leading and trailing spaces (Trim).
Ubound	Function	Provides as a return code the largest available subscript for the indicated dimension of an array.
Ucase	Function	Returns a string that has been converted to uppercase.
Val	Function	Returns the numbers enclosed in a string. Not supported in current beta.
VarType	Function	Returns a value disclosing the subtype of a variable.

Symbol	Type	Description
vbAbort*	(See footnote*)	Applies to the MsgBox function; Value = 3 indicates abort.
vbAbortRetryIgnore	(See footnote*)	Applies to the MsgBox function; Value = 2 displays Abort, Retry, and Ignore buttons
vbApplicationModal	(See footnote*)	Applies to the MsgBox function; Value = 0 indicates that the application is modal. The user must respond to the message box before continuing work in the current application.
vbArray	(See footnote*)	Applies to the VarType function; Value = 8192 indicates array.
vbBoolean	(See footnote*)	Applies to the VarType function; Value = 11 indicates Boolean.
vbByte	(See footnote*)	Applies to the VarType function; Value = 17 indicates byte.
vbCancel	(See footnote*)	Applies to the MsgBox function; Value = 2 indicates cancel.
vbCr	(See footnote*)	General purpose; indicates carriage-return character.
vbCritical	(See footnote*)	Applies to the MsgBox function; Value = 16

continues

Table C.1. continued

Symbol	Type	Description
		displays critical message icon.
vbCrLf	(See footnote*)	General purpose; indicates carriage-return and line-feed characters.
vbCurrency	(See footnote*)	Applies to the VarType function; Value = 6 indicates currency.
vbDataObject	(See footnote*)	Applies to the VarType function; Value = 13 indicates non-OLE automation object.
vbDate	(See footnote*)	Applies to the VarType function; Value = 7 indicates date.
vbDefaultButton1	(See footnote*)	Applies to the MsgBox function; Value = 0 indicates the first button is the default.
vbDefaultButton2	(See footnote*)	Applies to the MsgBox function; Value = 256 indicates the second button is the default.
vbDefaultButton3	(See footnote*)	Applies to the MsgBox function; Value = 512 indicates the third button is the default.
vbDouble	(See footnote*)	Applies to the VarType function; Value = 5 indicates a double-precision, floating-point number.

Symbol	Type	Description
vbEmpty	(See footnote*)	Applies to the VarType function, Value = 0 indicates empty.
vbError	(See footnote*)	Applies to the VarType function; Value = 10 indicates error.
vbExclamation	(See footnote*)	Applies to the MsgBox function; Value = 48 displays the warning message icon.
vbFalse	(See footnote*)	General purpose; indicates Boolean value represented by 0.
vbFriday	(See footnote*)	Applies to the Weekday function; Value = 6 indicates Friday.
vbIgnore	(See footnote*)	Applies to the MsgBox function; Value = 5 indicates Ignore.
vbInformation	(See footnote*)	Applies to the MsgBox function; Value = 64 displays information message icon.
vbInteger	(See footnote*)	Applies to the VarType function; Value = 2 indicates integer.
vbLf	(See footnote*)	General purpose; indicates line-feed character.
vbLong	(See footnote*)	Applies to the VarType function; Value = 3 indicates long integer.

continues

Table C.1. continued

Symbol	Type	Description
vbMonday	(See footnote*)	Applies to the Weekday function; Value = 2 indicates Monday.
vbNo	(See footnote*)	Applies to the MsgBox function; Value = 7 indicates no.
vbNull	(See footnote*)	Applies to the VarType function; Value = 1 indicates null.
vbObject	(See footnote*)	Applies to the VarType function; Value = 9 indicates OLE automation object.
vbObjectError	(See footnote*)	Indicates an object-generated error.
vbOK	(See footnote*)	Applies to the MsgBox function; Value = 1 indicates OK.
vbOKCancel	(See footnote*)	Applies to MsgBox function; Value = 1 displays OK and Cancel buttons.
vbOKOnly	(See footnote*)	Applies to the MsgBox function; Value = 0 displays OK button only.
vbQuestion	(See footnote*)	Applies to the MsgBox function; Value = 32 displays warning query icon.
vbRetry	(See footnote*)	Applies to the MsgBox function; Value = 4 indicates retry.

Symbol	Type	Description
vbRetryCancel	(See footnote*)	Applies to the MsgBox function; Value = 5 displays Retry and Cancel buttons.
vbSaturday	(See footnote*)	Applies to the Weekday function; Value = 7 indicates Saturday.
vbSingle	(See footnote*)	Applies to the VarType function; Value = 4 indicates single-precision, floating-point number.
vbString	(See footnote*)	Applies to the VarType function; Value = 8 indicates string.
vbSunday	(See footnote*)	Applies to the Weekday function; Value = 1 indicates Sunday.
vbSystemModal	(See footnote*)	Applies to the MsgBox function; Value = 4096 indicates system modal. All applications are suspended until the user responds to the message box.
vbThursday	(See footnote*)	Applies to the Weekday function; Value = 5 indicates Thursday.
vbTrue	(See footnote*)	General purpose; indicates Boolean value represented by -1.

continues

Table C.1. continued

Symbol	Type	Description
vbTuesday	(See footnote*)	Applies to the Weekday function; Value = 3 indicates Tuesday.
vbUseSystem	(See footnote*)	Applies to the Weekday function; Value = 0 uses the NLS API setting.
vbVariant	(See footnote*)	Applies to the VarType function; Value = 12 indicates variant.
vbWednesday	(See footnote*)	Applies to the Weekday function; Value = 4 indicates Wednesday.
vbYes	(See footnote*)	Applies to the MsgBox function; Value = 6 indicates yes.
vbYesNo	(See footnote*)	Applies to the MsgBox function; Value = 4 displays Yes and No buttons.
vbYesNoCancel	(See footnote*)	Applies to the MsgBox function; Value = 3 displays Yes, No, and Cancel buttons.
Weekday	Function	Returns a whole number showing the day of the week.
While…Wend	Statement	Performs a series of statements as long as a given condition is True.

Symbol	Type	Description
Xor	Logical operator	Performs logical exclusion on the operands.
Year	Function	Returns a whole number showing the year for the date string representation.

*The symbols with the vb prefix are values expected by various VBScript functions. In Visual Basic, these are intrinsic contants. In VBScript, you must declare these as variables if you want to treat them as constants since there is no direct constant support.

What's on the CD-ROM?

The CD-ROM contains all the sample files that have been presented in this book, along with a variety of other applications and utilities. This appendix presents the applications found on the CD-ROM and their location.

To begin installation, run the setup program located in the root directory of the CD-ROM. This installs a Presenting ActiveX Group to your Program Manager and places several icons within it. When that's completed, you can launch the **CD Guide** and choose to do any of the following:

- learn more about the third-party applications on the CD-ROM
- install the sample code from the book
- launch an ActiveX Web Tour

■ read the book, *Presenting Java,* also from Sams.net Publishing

■ install Sun's Java Developer's Kit with sample applets and scripts

Use the **CD Guide** to install the programs and view the `readme` file. Each program's individual setup guides you through the steps necessary to finish installing the software. Some files (the ones with a `.exe` extension) are self-extracting archives. You can always reinstall the software directly from the CD-ROM without using the interface, if necessary. The remainder of this appendix lists the programs in the third-party subdirectory.

\clients

■ `\eudora`—Eudora Light v1.5.4 e-mail client, 16-bit and 32-bit

■ `\explorer`—Microsoft Internet Explorer v2.0 Web browser for Windows

■ `\newsxprs`—News Xpress v1.0b4 Usenet newsreader client application

■ `\winftp`—WinFTP v1.2 32-bit FTP client application

\controls

■ `\imglib`—ImgLib is a 32-bit DLL for developers who would like to support reading, converting, and manipulating of all popular graphics image formats

■ `\visfax`—Visual Fax is a Visual Basic custom control that allows developers to rapidly build high-volume, Windows-based, multi-line fax applications such as fax servers and fax broadcast systems

■ `\vspell`—VisualSpeller by Visual Components is a high-performance spell-checking component

\graphics

■ `\acdsee`—ACDSEE v1.3 is a fast Windows image viewer that supports BMP, GIF, JPEG, PCX, Photo-CD, PNG, TGA, and TIFF files

■ `\thmpls`—ThumbsPlus is a popular image viewer and browser

\html

- \hotdog32—Hot Dog is an HTML editor
- \hotm1new—HoTMetaL is an HTML editor
- \mapthis—An imagemap utility for creating map files
- \webedit—WebEdit Pro is an HTML editor

\utils

- \acrobat—Adobe Acrobat viewer
- \uedit32—UltraEdit-32 is a Windows™ disk-based text or Hex editor taking full advantage of the multiple document interface (MDI)
- \winzip95—WinZip for Windows NT/95

Note: You'll need WinZip95 to unzip program files that use long filenames.

- \winzipse—WinZip Self-Extractor is a utility program that creates native Windows self-extracting .zip files

Please check in the \book directory on the CD-ROM for the following sample files.

\book\ch11

- Sample file from Chapter 11

\book\ch12

- Sample file from Chapter 12

\book\ch13

- Sample file from Chapter 13

Please check the \java directory on the CD-ROM for the following Java resources:

- `\java\jdk`—Sun's Java Developer's Kit version 1.02
- `\java\scripts`—Sample Java scripts

Bonus Book!

Check out the `\presjava` directory on the CD-ROM for the complete text of the Sams.net title, *Presenting Java.*

- `\java\presjava\httoc.htm`

Check in the `\tour` directory on the CD-ROM for an HTML document that directs you to the Microsoft and third-party Web pages dealing with ActiveX.

- `\tour\tour.htm`

About Shareware

Shareware is not free. Please read all documentation associated with a third-party product (usually contained with files named `readme.txt` or `license.txt`) and follow all guidelines.

Index

SYMBOLS

A

A VIACOM SERVICE

The Information SuperLibrary™

| Bookstore | Search | What's New | Reference | Software | Newsletter | Company Overviews |

| Yellow Pages | Internet Starter Kit | HTML Workshop | Win a Free T-Shirt! | Macmillan Computer Publishing | Site Map | Talk to Us |

CHECK OUT THE BOOKS IN THIS LIBRARY.

You'll find thousands of shareware files and over 1,600 computer books designed for both technowizards and technophobes. You can browse through 700 sample chapters, get the latest news on the Net, and find just about anything using our massive search directories.

All Macmillan Computer Publishing books are available at your local bookstore.

We're open 24-hours a day, 365 days a year.

You don't need a card.

We don't charge fines.

And you can be as **LOUD** as you want.

The Information SuperLibrary

http://www.mcp.com/mcp/ftp.mcp.com

Copyright © 1996, Macmillan Computer Publishing-USA. A Simon & Schuster Company

Presenting Java

John December

This book teaches readers how to incorporate sound, video, and animation into their Web pages. Through the design of "applets," programmers can enhance their own Web page. Java is the hottest new technology on the World Wide Web, and this book shows programmers how to tap into Java's power.

- Teaches how to design and program "applets" into Web pages
- Readers will learn how to enhance their own Web pages
- Covers the latest version of Java

$25.00 USA, $35.95 CDN, 1-57521-039-8, 224 pp.   *New—Casual—Accomplished*

Tricks of the Visual Basic 4 Gurus

James Bettone, et al.   *Internet Programming*

Microsoft is betting that the new release of Visual Basic 4 will create a mass migration from other compilers, including its own Visual Basic 3 compiler. Therefore, *Tricks of the Visual Basic Gurus* gives developers the "inside scoop" on the latest shortcuts and techniques to VB programming. Both 16-bit and 32-bit developing is covered.

- Covers Windows 32-bit programming for Windows 95
- Teaches OLE and the Win32 API
- Programmers learn to port between 16-bit OCX controls and 32-bit OLE controls

The CD-ROM contains source code from the book and the complete referenced applications.

$49.99 USA, $70.95 CDN, 0-672-30929-7, 744 pp.   *Accomplished—Expert*

Teach Yourself Web Publishing with HTML 3.2 in 14 Days, Professional Reference Edition

Laura Lemay   *Internet Programming*

This is the updated edition of Lemay's previous bestseller, *Teach Yourself Web Publishing with HTML in 14 Days, Premier Edition*. Readers will find advanced topics and updates—including adding audio, video, and animation—to Web page creation.

- Explores the use of CGI scripts, tables, HTML 3.0, the Netscape and Internet Explorer extensions, Java applets and JavaScript, and VRML.

CD-ROM included

$59.99 USA, $84.95 CDN, 1-57521-096-7, 1,104 pp.   *New—Casual—Accomplished*

Web Site Construction Kit for Windows 95

Christopher Brown and Scott Zimmerman   *Internet Programming*

The *Web Site Construction Kit for Windows 95* gives you everything you need to set up, develop, and maintain a Web site with Windows 95. It teaches the ins and outs of planning, installing, configuring, and administering a Windows 95–based Web site for an organization.

- Provides a blueprint and all the tools needed to set up a complete Web site
- Teaches how to install, configure, and administer a Windows 95 server

The CD-ROM contains all the source code from the book and useful utilities. Learn how to use HTML pages, CGI scripts, image maps, and so forth.

$49.99 USA, $70.95 CDN, 1-57521-072-X, 7-5206310721-8, 560 pp.
Casual—Accomplished

Teach Yourself JavaScript in a Week

Arman Danesh   *Programming*

Teach Yourself JavaScript in a Week is the easiest way to learn how to create interactive Web pages with LiveScript, Netscape's Java-like scripting language. It is intended for non-technical people and will be equally valuable to users of Macintosh, Windows, and UNIX platforms.

■ Teaches how to design and create attention-grabbing Web pages with JavaScript

■ Shows how to add interactivity to Web pages

$39.99 USA, $56.95 CDN, 1-57521-073-8, 576 pp.
Accomplished—Expert

Designing and Implementing the Microsoft Internet Information Server

Arthur Knowles and Sanjaya Hettihewa   *Internet and Web Publishing*

This book outlines setting up and running a Microsoft Internet Information Server. Readers will learn troubleshooting, network design, security, and cross-platform integration procedures.

■ Teaches security issues and how to maintain an efficient, secure network

■ Covers Microsoft Internet Information Server

$39.99 USA, $56.95 CDN, 1-57521-168-8, 350 pp.   *Casual—Expert*

Teach Yourself CGI Programming with Perl in a Week

Eric Herrmann   *Internet Communications/Online*

This book is a step-by-step tutorial of how to create, use, and maintain Common Gateway Interfaces (CGIs). It describes effective ways of using CGI as an integral part of Web development.

■ Adds interactivity and flexibility to the information offered through your Web site

■ Includes references to major protocols, such as NCSA HTTP, CERN HTTP, and SHTTP

■ Covers Perl 4.0, 5.0, and CGI

$39.99 USA, $56.95 CDN, 1-57521-009-6, 544 pp.   *Casual—Accomplished*

Add to Your Sams.net Library Today
with the Best Books for Internet Technologies

ISBN	Quantity	Description of Item	Unit Cost	Total Cost
1-57521-039-8		Presenting Java	$25.00	
0-672-30929-7		Tricks of the Visual Basic 4 Gurus (Book/CD-ROM)	$49.99	
1-57521-073-8		Teach Yourself JavaScript in a Week (Book/CD-ROM)	$39.99	
1-57521-096-7		Teach Yourself Web Publishing with HTML 3.2 in 14 Days, Professional Reference Edition (Book/CD-ROM)	$59.99	
1-57521-168-8		Designing and Implementing the Microsoft Internet Information Server	$39.99	
1-57521-009-6		Teach Yourself CGI Programming with Perl in a Week (Book/CD-ROM)	$39.99	
1-57521-072-X		Web Site Construction Kit for Windows 95 (Book/CD-ROM)	$49.99	
1-57521-120-3		Teach Yourself Visual Basic Script in 21 Days (Book/CD-ROM)	$39.99	
		Shipping and Handling: See information below.		
		TOTAL		

Shipping and Handling: $4.00 for the first book, and $1.75 for each additional book. If you need to have it NOW, we can ship product to you in 24 hours for an additional charge of approximately $18.00, and you will receive your item overnight or in two days. Overseas shipping and handling adds $2.00. Prices subject to change. Call between 9:00 a.m. and 5:00 p.m. EST for availability and pricing information on latest editions.

201 W. 103rd Street, Indianapolis, Indiana 46290

1-800-428-5331 — Orders   1-800-835-3202 — FAX   1-800-858-7674 — Customer Service

Book ISBN 1-57521-156-4

Installation Instructions

The companion CD-ROM contains all the source code and project files developed by the authors, plus an assortment of evaluation versions of third-party products. The disc is designed to be explored using a browser program. Using the browser, you can view information concerning products and companies, and install programs with a single click of the mouse. To run the Guide to the CD-ROM, here's what to do:

Windows 95 Installation Instructions

> **Note:** If you have the AutoPlay feature of Windows 95 enabled, the CD-ROM will install automatically. If you have disabled the AutoPlay feature, please follow the instructions below.

1. Insert the CD-ROM disc into your CD-ROM drive.
2. From the Windows 95 desktop, double-click the My Computer icon.
3. Double-click the icon representing your CD-ROM drive.
4. Double-click the icon titled setup.exe to run the CD-ROM installation program.

Windows NT Installation Instructions

1. Insert the CD-ROM disc into your CD-ROM drive.
2. From File Manager or Program Manager, choose Run from the File menu.
3. Type *<drive>*\setup and press Enter, where *<drive>* corresponds to the drive letter of your CD-ROM. For example, if your CD-ROM is drive D:, type D:\SETUP and press Enter.
4. Follow the onscreen instructions in the Guide to the CD-ROM program.